# Compendium

## Volume Two

### to

## Commentary

### on

## The Book of Mormon

### Philip M. Hudson

The path described
in The Book of Mormon
that leads to the Tree of Life
is not a freeway, but a toll road.
The Savior will pay the levy that is
demanded by Justice, but until we have
offered our own sacrifice of a broken heart
and a contrite spirit, we will not comprehend
with any degree of fluency the language of
the Spirit that explains how we can make
our way to the tree, in order to harvest
its delicious fruit. (See 1 Nephi
Chapters 8 & 11).

The
Book
of Mormon
introduces us
to a ladder that
has been set up on
the earth, the top of
which leans against
the gates of heaven. As
we climb rung by rung,
we feel the presence of the
Spirit that is ever before
us, past, present, and
future.

Copyright 2024 by Philip M. Hudson.
Published 2024.
Printed in the United States of America.
All rights reserved.

No portion of this book may be reproduced,
stored in a retrieval system, or transmitted
in any form or by any means, mechanical,
electronic, photocopy, recording, scanning,
or other, except for brief quotations in
critical reviews or articles, without
the prior written permission
of the author.

ISBN 978-1-957077-63-5

Illustrations - Google Images.
This book may be ordered from
online bookstores.

Publishing Services
by BookCrafters, Parker, Colorado.
www.bookcrafters.net

As we jog along
at a measured pace
thru the pages of The Book
of Mormon, and we negotiate
the twists and turns of mortality
while enjoying the aerobic exercise of
free will, it always helps to have celestial
sign posts to guide us through the telestial
traffic jams and conceptual cul-de-sacs that
threaten to detour us from the straight and
narrow way. The expanding circles of our
opportunity, enhanced by our obedience
to gospel principles, assures each of us
that we might have direct exposure to
the perfect law of liberty. Thereby,
we abandon the tortuous route
through Idumea that is taken
by those bound for telestial
glory. Instead, we follow
the unmistakable track
that inevitably leads
to celestial surety
in a heavenly
setting.

The Book
of Mormon can
give vitality to the
Plan of Happiness. It
provides insight into the
spiritual roots that lie at the
foundation of relationships that
are themselves the products of our
interconnectivity and our
interdependence.

# Table of Contents

"Scripture consists not in what we read,
but in what we understand."
(St. Hilary).

# Introduction

Introduction..................................................................................................................1

# Questions Answered by The Book of Mormon

Fifty-Five Questions Answered in The Book of Mormon (51-55)..................................................11

- What happens when we die?
- Who will we meet at the Judgment Bar?
- Where do the righteous go after they die?
- Where do the unrighteous go after they die?
- Who were "the other sheep" referred to by Jesus in John 10:16?
- Twenty Thoughts to Ponder

Sixty Questions Answered in The Book of Mormon (56-60).................................................................33

- What happened in the Americas when Jesus was born in Bethlehem?
- What happened in America when Jesus was crucified in Jerusalem?
- Why is it necessary to be baptized?
- What is the covenant of baptism?
- Why was Jesus baptized?
- Twenty Thoughts to Ponder

Sixty-Five Questions Answered in The Book of Mormon (61-65).........................................................57

- Why do we renew our covenant of baptism?
- Do little children need to repent and be baptized?
- Why do bad things happen to good people?
- Does the Lord always protect the righteous?
- Will God ask us to extend ourselves beyond our capabilities?
- Twenty Thoughts to Ponder

Seventy Questions Answered in The Book of Mormon (66-70)............................................................79

- To Whom should we pray?
- About what should we pray?
- Why should we not put off seeking to improve ourselves?
- What happens if we persist in wicked behavior?
- How can we tell the difference between good and evil?
- Twenty Thoughts to Ponder

Seventy-Five Questions Answered in The Book of Mormon (71-75)...................................................101

- What happens when people do not believe in Satanic opposition?
- Can those who are wicked be happy?
- What happens when we are subjected to negative peer pressure?
- How can we take our stewardship responsibilities more seriously?
- How can we become missionaries with powerful testimonies of the divinity of Christ?
- Twenty Thoughts to Ponder

**Eighty Questions Answered in The Book of Mormon (76-80)**..........................................................123

- Why does the church send missionaries to Christian nations?
- What of those who are ashamed to take upon themselves the name of Jesus Christ?
- How does The Book of Mormon fulfil the prophecy of Ezekiel?
- How can we be more charitable?
- Should we seek to understand the mysteries of God?
- Twenty Thoughts to Ponder

**Eighty-Five Questions Answered in The Book of Mormon (81-85)**..................................................145

- What is the role of the prophets?
- What is a seer?
- Are there things of a religious nature we just do not yet know?
- Is immortality a free gift from God?
- What is the difference between immortality and eternal life?
- Twenty Thoughts to Ponder

**Ninety Questions Answered in The Book of Mormon (86-90)**.........................................................167

- Can God, Who is no respecter of persons, still care about us?
- Could there have been warfare on the scale described in The Book of Mormon?
- How can we become a Zion society?
- What should our relationship be to the Jews?
- Why aren't Latter-day Saint churches decorated with crosses?
- Twenty Thoughts to Ponder

**Ninety-Five Questions Answered in The Book of Mormon (91-95)**..................................................191

- Why do Latter-day Saints wear special underclothing?
- Who is the Third member of the Godhead?
- What is the gift of the Holy Ghost?
- Do Latter-day Saints believe in personal revelation?
- What is the origin of the "American Indians"?
- Twenty Thoughts to Ponder

One Hundred Questions Answered in The Book of Mormon (96-100).................................................213

- Who is responsible for raising children?
- Why is Isaiah quoted so frequently in The Book of Mormon?
- How do Latter-day Saints feel about Mary, the mother of Jesus?
- How does the Lord Jesus Christ intervene directly in our lives?
- What do we really think of Christ? Whose Son is He?
- Twenty Thoughts to Ponder

# Topical Index
## to Subjects
(Referenced by Question Number)

Topical Index to Subjects (referenced by Question Number)........................................................245

# Without
# The Book of Mormon

Without The Book of Mormon..................................................................................................251

# Observations

Observations..................................................................................................................269

# Introduction to
# The Isaiah Chapters
## 2 Nephi Chapters 12-24

Introduction to The Isaiah Chapters (2 Nephi Chapters 12-24)..................................................369

# "And it came to pass"
## In The Book of Mormon

"And it came to pass" in The Book of Mormon..................................................................377

# "And thus we see"
## In The Book of Mormon

"And thus we see" in The Book of Mormon..................................................................................383

# "Behold"
## In The Book of Mormon

"Behold" in The Book of Mormon..................................................................................405

# "Wherefore"
### and
# "Therefore"
## in The Book of Mormon

"Wherefore" and "Therefore" in The Book of Mormon..................................................................................413

# "The Appearance of Gold"

"The Appearance of Gold"..................................................................................................419

# The Use of the Name of Christ
## in The Book of Mormon

The Use of the Name of Christ in The Book of Mormon..................................................................425

# Pragmatism
## in The Book of Mormon

Pragmatism in The Book of Mormon..................................................................................................429

# Dry Humor
in The Book of Mormon

Dry Humor in The Book of Mormon..................................................................................437

# A Book of Mormon Timeline
A brief overview of the early days of the Restoration

A Book of Mormon Timeline..................................................................................443

# Commentary and Compendium Index

Commentary Volumes 1-3, and Compendium Volumes 1-7 Index..................................................................................471

If we kick
against the pricks
and remain in a state of
rebellion against the principles
and the doctrines of The Book of
Mormon, the luscious fruit of the
Tree of Life will remain just out of
reach, even if out of curiosity, we
now and again attempt to take a
bite. If we never raise our eyes to
search eternal horizons, the world
before us will appear as nothing
more than a barren desert that
is devoid of refreshing oases,
the welcoming shade of trees,
and the abundance of well-
watered gardens. When we
lack faith to nourish the
word, its living waters
will not be able to
nurture our
roots.

Book of
Mormon dogma
asks that we exhibit
forbearance, even in the
face of challenges, when
our portion seems unfair,
when our difficulties seem
unreasonable, and when
the proportions of the
problems looming
before us seem
daunting.

# Introduction

Near the end of The Book of Mormon, we are taught that the Plan allows each of us to enjoy the same access to the simplest, and yet most powerful, witness to the truth. In an inarticulate voice softer than the faintest whisper of sweet breath on the cheek, the Holy Ghost gently testifies, or bears witness, of the truth. As Moroni 10:5 teaches (in a verse that is often overlooked, as readers concentrate on the previous verse), "by the power of the Holy Ghost ye may know the truth of all things."

The Holy Ghost has revealed all that is just and true, and He continues to illuminate the principles that have guided the minds of men and women since the dawn of history. We constantly benefit from that which He reveals. In the Last Days, when the Spirit is "poured out upon all flesh, and when "young men see visions, and old men dream dreams" (Joel 2:28, see also Job 33:14-16) it is the Holy Ghost Who will provide the creative drive. The irony is that many will fail to recognize the divine source of their inspiration.

Cicero wrote: "The first law for the historian is that he shall never dare utter an untruth. The second is that he shall suppress nothing that is true. Moreover, there shall be no suspicion of partiality or of malice in his writing". The accounts in The Book of Mormon written by the prophets Nephi, Jacob, Alma, Mormon, Moroni, and others, and abridged by the prophet-historian Mormon, were true to the mandate given by Cicero. Although, as Washington Irving brooded: "It is the rule that history fades into fable; fact becomes clouded with doubt and controversy; the inscription moulders, and columns, arches, and pyramids are but heaps of sand, and their epitaphs, nothing but characters written in the dust", yet The Book of Mormon stands as a shining example of the divine model.

It "is the witness that testifies to the passing of time. It illuminates reality, vitalizes memory, provides guidance in daily life, and brings us tidings of antiquity". It is the "evidence of time, the light of truth, the life of memory, the directress of life, committed to immortality". (Cicero, "De Oratore", ii, 36). In its pages, "the centuries roll back to the ancient age of gold". (Horace, "Odes", IV, ii, 39).

In one of the beautiful simplicities of the gospel, we are taught that the Plan allows all of us to enjoy the same access to the simplest, and yet most powerful, witness to the truth. In an inarticulate voice softer than the faintest whisper of sweet breath on the cheek, the Holy Ghost gently testifies, or bears witness, of truth. As Moroni 10:5 teaches (in a verse that is often overlooked, in favor of the previous verse): "By the power of the Holy Ghost ye may know the truth of all things".

The Holy Ghost has revealed all that is true, and has illuminated every eternal principle that has guided the minds of men and women since the dawn of history. We constantly benefit from that which He reveals. In the Last Days, when the Spirit is "poured out upon all flesh, and when "young men see visions, and old men dream dreams" (Joel 2:28), it will be the Holy Ghost Who provides the creative drive. The irony is that many will fail to recognize the source of their inspiration. Job did not. He wrote: "For God speaketh once, yea twice, yet man perceiveth it not. In a dream, in a vision of the night, when deep sleep falleth upon men, in slumberings upon the bed; then he openeth the ears of men, and sealeth their instruction." (Job 33:14-16). We cannot help but think of the experience of Joseph Smith in his bedchamber, when we read Job's description of how, at certain times, Heavenly Father chooses to communicate with His children.

All who desire to have a sure personal witnesses must carefully and prayerfully read The Book of Mormon, and then ask in faith if what they have studied is true. They will then receive the testimony of the Holy Ghost to motivate them to seek out the Priesthood and to enter into sacred covenants with God. It will be as it was on the Day of Pentecost, when Peter and others were preaching to a multitude whose hearts and minds were open and receptive to the truth. The words of the Apostles carried the weight of authority, and penetrated the hearts of their listeners to the end that they asked: "Men and brethren, what shall we do? Then Peter said unto them, Repent, and be baptized every one of you in the name of Jesus Christ for the remission of sins, and ye shall receive the gift of the Holy Ghost". (Acts 2:37-38). And on that day, there were about 3,000 souls added to the kingdom of God on earth. (See Commentary Reference to 3 Nephi 15:21-24).

A similar scenario exists today. Since the Restoration of the gospel, there has been a Pentecostal outpouring of the Spirit, and those with a sincere desire to understand the will of God bring the same humble petition to the doorstep of the missionaries: "Now that we have heard your message, have put it to the test of prayerful inquiry, and have received a witness of the Spirit, what shall we do?" The response of the servants of the

It was in his play "The Tempest" that Shakespeare coined the expression: "The past is prologue." This turn of phrase was intended to imply that our past is merely a prologue, or an introduction, to the great adventure upon which we'll embark when we follow through on our plans. This original interpretation teaches us that what has come before on our journey through life doesn't matter in the grand scheme of things, because a new future lies before us that is subject to the choices we will yet make.

Our utilization of commentaries and compendia cannot replace our personal scripture study. The spiritual awakening that will surely accompany our prayerful efforts to understand the mysteries of God by undertaking an experiment upon His word cannot be achieved through another person's interpretation. Perhaps, though, my perspectives on the eternal themes that are expressed within The Book of Mormon will be helpful to you as you study and seek your own guidance. My hope for you is that you will use these volumes only to assist you as you undertake your own personal journey to Christ.

Lord is unequivocal: "You must exercise saving faith that leads to the waters of baptism and to continuing commitment, dedicated discipleship, selfless service, and sustained spirituality".

Shakespeare coined the phrase: "The past is prologue". ("The Tempest", Act 2, Scene 1, 245-254). It was intended to imply that our past is merely a prologue, or an introduction, to the great adventure upon which we will embark if we follow through on our plans. This original interpretation teaches that what has come before on our journey through life doesn't matter in the grand scheme of things, because a new future lies before us, subject to the choices we will yet make. The human condition does not change much over time, which is one reason why the Lord has revealed The Book of Mormon in the Last Days, so that we might profit from the experiences of the Nephites who are distant from us in time and yet are so like us.

Hugh Nibley observed: "Men fool themselves, when they think for a moment that they can read scripture without ever adding something to the text or omitting something from it". Therein lies the power inherent in its study. We glean insight and understanding every time we investigate the word of God. I have learned to love the scriptures, and I often think of St. Hilary, who wrote: "Scripture consists not in what we read, but in what we understand". In these Compendia, I have consistently tried to anchor to the scriptures the ideas swirling around in my head.

Utilization of commentaries and compendia does not replace personal scripture study. The spiritual awakening that accompanies prayerful efforts to understand the mysteries of God through the study of His word cannot be achieved through another person's interpretation. Perhaps, though, my own perspectives on the eternal themes expressed within The Book of Mormon will be helpful to you as you read and seek your own guidance. It is my hope that you will use these compendia only to assist you in your own personal journey to Christ.

Our challenge is to enlist the aid of the Holy Ghost as we undertake that journey. Many years ago, Dallin Oaks wrote: "Latter-day Saints know that learned or authoritative commentaries (and compendia) can help us with scriptural interpretation, but we maintain that they must be used with caution. (They) are not substitutes for the scriptures any more than a good cookbook is a substitute for food. When I refer to "commentaries", I mean everything that interprets scripture, from the comprehensive book-length commentary to the brief interpretation embodied in a lesson or an article, such as this one".

"One trouble with commentaries", he continued, "is that their authors sometimes focus on only one meaning to the exclusion of others. As a result, commentaries, if not used with great care, may illuminate the author's chosen and correct meaning but close our eyes and restrict our horizons to other possible meanings. Sometimes, those other less obvious meanings can be the ones most valuable and useful to us as we seek to obtain answers to our own questions. This is why the teaching of the Holy Ghost is a better guide to scriptural interpretation than is even the best commentary". ("Ensign", 1/1985).

Harold B. Lee taught: "We are convinced that our members are hungry for the gospel undiluted, with its abundant truths and insights. There are those who have seemed to forget that the most powerful weapons the Lord has given us against all that is evil are His own declarations – the plain and simple doctrines of salvation as found in the scriptures." (Regional Representatives Seminar, 10/1/1970).

Bruce R. McConkie explained that "revelation is necessary because ... each pronouncement in the holy

"The scriptures," including The Book of Mormon, Another Testament of Jesus Christ, aren't "the ultimate source of knowledge, but are instead what precedes the ultimate source. The ultimate source comes by revelation. We encourage everyone to make careful study of the scriptures and of prophetic teachings ... and to prayerfully seek personal revelation to know their meaning for themselves ... If we seek and accept revelation and inspiration to enlarge our understanding, we will have the mysteries of God unfolded to us by the power of the Holy Ghost."
(Dallin Oaks).

Elder Oaks concluded his own epistle to the Saints by stating a simple truth. He said we "know that true doctrine comes by revelation from God, and not by worldly wisdom." (See Moses 5:58). He was in good company, for as the Apostle Paul wrote, we are incapable of thinking any thing of ourselves; but we look to God for our wisdom. (See 1 Corinthians 3:5).

scriptures is so written as to reveal little or much, depending on the spiritual capacity of the student." ("A New Witness for The Articles of Faith", p. 71). And so, as President Oaks continued, "the scriptures are not the ultimate source of knowledge, but what precedes the ultimate source. The ultimate source comes by revelation. We encourage everyone to make careful study of the scriptures and of prophetic teachings ... and to prayerfully seek personal revelation to know their meaning for themselves ... If we seek and accept revelation and inspiration to enlarge our understanding, we will have the mysteries of God unfolded to us by the power of the Holy Ghost."

Bruce R. McConkie also said: "I sometimes think that one of the best kept secrets of the kingdom is that the scriptures open the door to the receipt of revelation." ("Doctrines of The Restoration", p. 243). And President Oaks reaffirmed: "We do not overstate the point when we say that the scriptures can be a Urim and Thummim to assist each of us to receive personal revelation."

Elder Oaks enlarged upon the perspective of the young prophet: "Joseph was, by his own admission, no writer. He felt imprisoned by what he called the 'total darkness of paper, pen, and ink". (Joseph Smith to William W. Phelps, 11/27/1832, B.Y.U. Press, 2002, p. 287). He thus considered it 'an awful responsibility to write in the name of the Lord.' (Joseph Smith Papers, 1:367).

He did not suppose that he could receive the revelations perfectly, nor did the Lord ever set that standard. Joseph and his appointed brethren edited the revelations (see D&C 70:1-4) based on (that) same premise ... namely, that he represented the voice of God as he spoke in what he characterized as his own 'crooked, broken, scattered, and imperfect language'. (Joseph Smith to William W. Phelps, 11/27/1832, quoted in "Making Sense of the Doctrine & Covenants, a Guided Tour Through Modern Revelation", Steven Harper. "Personal Writings of Joseph Smith", p. 186-187).

Elder Oaks concluded his own epistle by stating a simple truth: "Latter-day Saints know that true doctrine comes by revelation from God, and not by worldly wisdom." (See Moses 5:58). He was in good company, for the Apostle Paul wrote that we are not capable of thinking any thing of ourselves; but we look to God for our wisdom. (See 1 Corinthians 3:5).

I could not agree more heartily with these wise words of counsel. As a matter of fact, every time I proofed my compendium (and I did this many times) I found myself scribbling additional notes in the margins and thinking to myself, "Why didn't I see that before?". That is precisely what I hope will be the experience of everyone who takes the time to read my compendia. I trust the process will motivate you to search the scriptures more carefully and to be instructed by the Spirit, as you do so, that you might be led in directions that will prove to be personally illuminating.

I would expect that my older grandchildren who read this compendium will be impacted in ways that are different from my adult children or my contemporaries. I hope that my observations will touch you differently each time you read them. When I am long-gone, perhaps the considerable thought that went into its production will generate a palpable bond that will span the years separating us. Maybe, the gulf that then divides us will not be as great, and our shared energies will pave the way to an eventual joyous reunion.

From the start, our Book of Mormon study propels us in the direction of regular attendance at church meetings. When our participation is more than a custom of convenience, but instead has a foundation based on religious zeal, there is a greater incentive to make it work. In fact, a relationship with God can become the most sacred connection that exists between heaven and earth. When that rapport is represented by covenants, the penitent are more likely to weather the storms of life that inevitably arise. Shared religious experience that is animated by the Holy Ghost and consistent devotion create a sound footing upon which our connection to the Savior is anchored.

In the process of a holy anointing, the Nephites who attended the temple in Bountiful were surely blessed to come forth in the morning of the first resurrection as kings and priests, and queens and priestesses, destined thru worthiness to rule and reign in the House of Israel forever. The ordinances of the temple commemorated and celebrated lives that would have otherwise remained forever incomplete.

From the start, our Book of Mormon study propels us in the direction of regular attendance at church meetings. When our participation is more than a custom of convenience, but instead has a foundation based on religious zeal, there is a greater incentive to make it work. In fact, a relationship with God can become the most sacred connection that exists between heaven and earth. When that rapport is represented by covenants, the penitent are more likely to weather the storms of life that inevitably arise. Shared religious experience that is animated by the Holy Ghost and consistent devotion create a sound footing upon which our connection to the Savior is anchored.

In the process of a holy anointing, the Nephites who attended the temple in Bountiful were surely blessed to come forth in the morning of the first resurrection as kings and priests, and queens and priestesses, destined thru worthiness to rule and reign in the House of Israel forever. The ordinances of the temple commemorated and celebrated lives that would have otherwise remained forever incomplete.

Our spiritual growth now
and in eternity hinges largely upon
what do we do with the Book of Mormon, as
well as upon what The Book of Mormon can do for
us. Simply stated, the doctrine of Christ (see 2 Nephi
32:6) that is unfolded to our view within its covers
establishes order in the cosmos and permits us to
reach out to explore the unknown possibilities
of existence, where we will be enveloped
within the expansive Pillars of
Creation.

Every
day that we read
and study The Book
of Mormon, we are taking
our testimony temperature,
and we hope to regularly detect
its feverish pitch. It is the
scriptures that make
our blood hot to
the touch.

# Fifty-Five Questions Answered in The Book of Mormon

Alma had a clear
vision of "the state of the soul
between death and the resurrection …
The spirits of all men," he said, "whether
they be good or evil, are taken home to
that God who gave them life."
(Alma 40:11).

"And then … the
spirits of those who are righteous
are received into a state of happiness,
which is called paradise, a state of rest,
a state of peace, where they shall rest
from all their troubles and from
all care, and sorrow."
(Alma 40:12).

## What happens when we die?

Alma had a clear vision of "the state of the soul between death and the resurrection ... The spirits of all men, whether they be good or evil, are taken home to that God who gave them life." (Alma 40:11). Nevertheless, they are not immediately taken into the actual presence of God.

First, 'the spirits of those who are righteous are received into a state of happiness, which is called paradise, a state of rest, a state of peace, where they shall rest from all their troubles and from all care, and sorrow." (Alma 40:12). Paradise is not a state of perfect happiness, for that is possible only following the resurrection. As the Lord taught: "The elements are eternal, and (only) spirit and element inseparably connected, receive a fulness of joy, and when separated, man cannot receive a fulness of joy." (D&C 93:23-24).

"And ... the spirits of the wicked ... shall be cast out into outer darkness; there shall be weeping, and wailing, and gnashing of teeth, and this because of their own iniquity, being led captive by the will of the devil." (Alma 40:13). The spirit world has a second major division called outer darkness. (See Alma 40:13-24, & Matthew 8:12 & 22:13). Alma indicated that the wicked would remain in this state until their eventual resurrection. In other words, the Spirit Prison of The Unjust is a place of correction for those who have committed all but the unpardonable sin. When the penalty has been paid and Justice has been satisfied, the sinner will be released from hell, having been adequately prepared to be resurrected to a kingdom of glory. (See Psalms 16:10, 1 Peter 3:18, & D&C 76:73).

"Now this is the state of the souls of the wicked, yea, in darkness, and a state of awful, fearful looking for the fiery indignation of the wrath of God upon them; thus they remain in this state, as well as the righteous in paradise, until the time of their resurrection." (Alma 40:11-14).

In the scriptures (see D&C 76:73, 138:8 & 28, Isaiah 61:1, 1 Peter 3:19, & Moses 7:57) we learn about the Spirit Prison of The Unjust, a place that exists perpetually as a dominion of correction for those who have decided for themselves not to rely upon the merits of Christ to receive a remission of their sins. When the 'uttermost farthing' has been paid, and Justice has been satisfied, those who had died in their sins and remained unrepentant will be released from hell, inasmuch as personal payment for their transgressions will have finally adequately prepared them to be resurrected to a kingdom of glory.

"This is the state of the souls of the wicked, yea, in darkness, and a state of awful, fearful looking for the fiery indignation of the wrath of God upon them. Thus, they remain in this state, as well as the righteous in paradise, until the time of their resurrection."
(Alma 40:11-14).

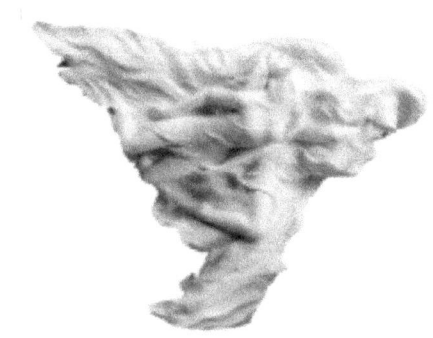

## Who will we meet at the Judgment Bar?

"And now I bid unto all, farewell. I soon go to rest in the paradise of God, until my spirit and body shall again reunite, and I am brought forth triumphant through the air, to meet you before the pleasing bar of the great Jehovah, the Eternal Judge of both quick and dead. Amen." (Moroni 10:34). Moroni bid a fond farewell to an audience that would not read his words until long after his death and following his resurrection to glory. Of that reward he was confident. Perhaps with prophetic vision, he saw his future mission, for he wrote that he would be "brought forth triumphant through the air." John the Beloved described him thus: "And I saw another angel fly in the midst of heaven, having the everlasting gospel to preach unto them that dwell on the earth, and to every nation, and kindred, and tongue, and people." (Revelation 14:6).

In his closing remarks in the Second Book of Nephi, Nephi declared: "What I seal on earth, shall be brought against you at the judgment bar, for thus hath the Lord commanded me, and I must obey." (2 Nephi 33:15). Jacob bid farewell to those who would read his words in the Last Days, as well: "Finally, I bid you farewell, until I shall meet you before the pleasing bar of God." (Jacob 6:13). When he had completed his abridgement of The Book of Ether, Moroni "bid farewell unto the Gentiles, yea, and also unto my brethren whom I love, until we shall meet before the judgment-seat of Christ." (Ether 12:38).

Millions of members of The Church of Jesus Christ of Latter-day Saints, and hundreds of millions of others, recognize Moroni's statue that stands atop many of the temples scattered throughout the world. With trumpet ready at his lips, he awaits the Second Coming of the Lord. For faithful Latter-day Saints, meeting him, Nephi, Jacob, and their Elder Brother Jesus Christ will be a wonderful reunion.

"I bid unto all, farewell. I soon go to rest in the paradise of God, until my spirit and body shall again reunite, and I am brought forth triumphant through the air, to meet you before the pleasing bar of the great Jehovah, the Eternal Judge of both quick and dead. Amen."
(Moroni 10:34).

Jacob joined Moroni in bidding a fond adieu to those who would read his words in the Last Days: "Finally, I bid you farewell, until I shall meet you before the pleasing bar of God."
(Jacob 6:13).

## Where do the righteous go after they die?

In 2 Nephi 9:13, Jacob explained that "the paradise of God" in the spirit world is the abode of the righteous. Alma taught that "the spirits of those who are righteous are received into a state of happiness, which is called paradise, a state of rest, a state of peace, where they shall rest from all their troubles and from all care, and sorrow." (Alma 40:12).

Paradise is also used in the scriptures to mean the world of spirits (see Luke 23:43, 2 Nephi 9:13, & 4 Nephi 114), the Celestial Kingdom (see 2 Corinthians 12:4 & Revelation 2:7), and the glorified millennial earth. (See the 10th Article of Faith).

At the end of The Book of Mormon, Moroni wrote: "I soon go to rest in the paradise of God, until my spirit and body shall again reunite, and I am brought forth triumphant through the air, to meet you before the pleasing bar of the great Jehovah, the Eternal Judge of both quick and dead." (Moroni 10:34). John the Revelator wrote: "He that hath an ear, let him hear what the Spirit saith … to him that overcometh will I give to eat of the tree of life (see 1 Nephi Chapter 8), which is in the midst of the paradise of God." (Revelation 2:7).

Jacob explained to the people of Nephi that "the paradise of God" in the spirit world is the abode of the righteous, (see 2 Nephi 9:13), and Alma reiterated to his son Corianton that "the spirits of those who are righteous are received into a state of happiness, which is called paradise, a state of rest, a state of peace, where they shall rest from all their troubles and from all care, and sorrow." (Alma 40:12).

The holy scriptures variously describe the "paradise" of God as 1) a world of spirits (see Luke 23:43, 2 Nephi 9:13, & 4 Nephi 114), 2) the Celestial Kingdom (see 2 Corinthians 12:4 & Revelation 2:7), and 3) as the glorified millennial earth. (See the 10th Article of Faith).

# Where do the unrighteous go after they die?

The spirits of the wicked, on the other hand, "shall be cast out into outer darkness (where0 there shall be weeping, and wailing, and gnashing of teeth, and this because of their own iniquity, being led captive by the will of the devil. Now this is the state of the souls of the wicked, yea, in darkness, and a state of awful, fearful looking for the fiery indignation of the wrath of God upon them; thus, they remain in this state, as well as the righteous in paradise, until the time of their resurrection." (Alma 42:13-14). Justice demands that they suffer the consequences of their own actions.

The unrighteous go to the Spirit Prison of the Unjust, and after necessary priesthood ordinances have been performed for them vicariously. Just as the Savior established the pattern of vicarious redemption for repentant sinners, so has the pattern of vicarious redemption been established in the temple, for the repentant dead who have been taught and accepted the gospel in the spirit world.

This is why the dead, who did not have the opportunity to join the church while in mortality, but who have been taught and who have accepted the gospel in the spirit world, are so anxious to have their family history work completed, so that their temple ordinances may be performed in their behalf. By so doing, Latter-day Saints who serve as patrons in the temple can literally become "saviours on Mount Zion" to their kindred dead. (Obadiah 1:21). In a sense, they will join ranks with the Savior, Who performed vicarious work for all of the children of God, through His Atonement.

Those in the Spirit Prison of the Unjust, however, who continue to stubbornly reject both the gospel and the power of salvation through the infinite Atonement of Jesus Christ, will have to pay for their sins themselves. They will not be redeemed from the Fall until they have personally "paid the uttermost farthing" to satisfy the demands of Justice. (Matthew 5:26).

The unrighteous will go to the Spirit Prison of the Unjust to await their day of redemption. (See 1 Peter 3:18, & D&C 76:73). That day will come when they accept the gospel, and after the necessary priesthood ordinances have been performed for them vicariously. Just as the Savior established the pattern of vicarious redemption for repentant sinners, so has that same pattern been established by the Lord's servants in the temple, for the repentant dead who have been taught and accepted the gospel in the spirit world.

Those who serve as patrons in the House of the Lord can become saviours on Mount Zion to their kindred dead. (See Obadiah 1:21). In a sense, they will join ranks with the Savior, Who, on an infinitely larger scale, performed vicarious work for all of God's children, through His Atonement.

# Who were the "other sheep" referred to by Jesus in John 10:16?

To the Nephites, the resurrected Lord said: "Ye are they of whom I said: Other sheep I have which are not of this fold; them also I must bring, and they shall hear my voice; and there shall be one fold, and one shepherd. And … behold, ye have both heard my voice, and seen me; and ye are my sheep, and ye are numbered among those whom the Father hath given me." (3 Nephi 15:17).

Christ revealed to His twelve disciples in the Americas that He had never told their brethren at Jerusalem of their existence, or that of the Ten Tribes, who had been "led away out of the land." (3 Nephi 13:15). He had only told them that He had other sheep, for He had been commanded by the Father to reveal no more. This was "because of (their) stiffneckedness and unbelief." (3 Nephi 15:18). Had the Jews been given greater insight into the status of their brethren in the New World, they would probably not have understood it anyway. As Joseph Smith said: "As far as we degenerate from God, we descend to the devil and lose knowledge, and without knowledge, we cannot be saved." ("Teachings," p. 217).

Most Christians today believe that the "other sheep" mentioned by the Savior refer to the Gentiles, who would at some subsequent day receive the gospel. But The Book of Mormon makes perfectly clear that this is not the case. The Savior explained: "And verily I say unto you, that ye are they of whom I said: Other sheep I have which are not of this fold; them also I must bring, and they shall hear my voice; and there shall be one fold, and one shepherd. And they understood me not, for they supposed it had been the Gentiles; for they understood not that the Gentiles should be converted through their preaching. And they understood me not that I said they shall hear my voice; and they understood me not that the Gentiles should not at any time hear my voice - that I should not manifest myself unto them save it were by the Holy Ghost. But behold, ye have both heard my voice, and seen me; and ye are my sheep, and ye are numbered among those whom the Father hath given me." (3 Nephi 15:21-24).

To the assembled Nephites, the resurrected Lord declared: "Ye are they of whom I said: Other sheep I have which are not of this fold; them also I must bring, and they shall hear my voice; and there shall be one fold, and one shepherd. And ... behold, ye have both heard my voice, and seen me; and ye are my sheep, and ye are numbered among those whom the Father hath given me."
(3 Nephi 15:17).

Most Christians today are quick to emphasize their own interpretation of the scriptures, claiming that the "other sheep" that were mentioned by the Lord in the Bible refers to the Gentiles who would in a subsequent day receive the gospel. (See John 10:16). However, The Book of Mormon is Another Testament of Jesus Christ, and so it naturally goes a step further to make it perfectly clear that this is not the case. The Savior explained: "And verily I say unto you, that ye are they of whom I said: Other sheep I have which are not of this fold."
(3 Nephi 15:21).

After considering these 55 questions that are answered in The Book of Mormon, take a moment to ponder any or all of these 20 thoughts:

It is
celestial
mathematics that
defines the theorems
of faith, light, and truth
that, as one body, comprise
the common and irreducible
denominators of heaven itself.
As such, they are indivisible by
anything other than themselves,
establishing God's baseline for our
acquisition of knowledge. In fact,
Joseph Smith taught: "As far as we
degenerate from God we descend to
the devil and lose knowledge, and
without (it) we cannot be saved."
Without knowledge, there can
be no faith, no light, and no
recognition of religious
truth.

Tales from the pages
of The Book of Mormon cause
our blood to run hot, reminiscent of
the microwave background radiation
that was left over after the creation of
our universe billions of years ago, as
well as from the fiery cauldron of
experience that was catalyzed in
a garden setting eastward
in Eden, that was not
so very long ago.

The Book of
Mormon teaches us
that both free will and
opposition are always before
us, and so the Spirit stands as
a sacred sentinel that beckons us
to return to the easy familiarity of
heaven's gate to find the Rest of God.
No matter that we are, for all practical
purposes, dead weight. The Spirit will
carry us until we've been revitalized
and can walk without becoming
weary, and can run, without
fainting.

Bathed in the
stunning clarity that
is provided by The Book of
Mormon, those who have been
baptized often stare in wide-eye
wonder at the beautiful simplicity
of all the colorful threads that have
been woven into a pattern of gospel
doctrine and principles that make
up the technicolor tapestry of
the Merciful Plan of our
Creator.

If
we open
our hearts to
the Holy Ghost,
and allow ourselves
to be molded through
His influence as we
study The Book of
Mormon, we can
be holy and
without
spot.

We are intertwined in
palpable connections with
Heavenly Father, Jesus Christ,
and with the Holy Ghost. They take
note if sparrows fall from trees, and on
cold winter nights, they help us to notice
the light from the explosion of supernovas
in distant galaxies. They do not play dice
with Their creations; We can be sure that
They won't leave anything to chance. In
particular, as we commune with them
during our study of The Book of
Mormon, emotions swell within
our breasts that we can be
at-one with Them.

The secret to
comprehending the hidden
treasures of knowledge that may
be found in The Book of Mormon isn't
complicated. It is simply to press on with
purpose as we feast upon the words of Christ.
Thereby, we receive the physical and spiritual
strength and nourishment that are needed to
comprehend the mysteries of the kingdom.
It is by this process that we will begin to
feel the compounding influence
of the Spirit.

The mortal
ministry and the
sacrifice of Jesus Christ
among the children of men
may be the greatest miracle of
all, but those who deny His power
that is manifested in the Atonement
will not be saved on their merits alone,
simply because they have not generated
faith with enough energy to carry their
progression onward. Only if there has
been a profound attitude adjustment
and a spiritual heart transplant, not
to mention a firm testimony of the
The Book of Mormon, will they be
capable of sustaining forward
momentum along a path
that leads to God's
Kingdom.

.

The expanding circles of opportunity that are woven into Book of Mormon scholarship leave little room for limiting beliefs. As we lift the latch and force the way, we trade the hesitant support that is embraced by those who have been trapped in mediocrity for the certain guidance that is enjoyed by celestial-bound fellow travelers.

As we grow in spiritual stature and transcendentally draw nearer to the dwelling place of God, we are exposed to the "beauty of the gate through which the heirs of that kingdom will enter, which (is) like unto circling flames of fire; Also the blazing throne of God, wherein (shall be) seated the Father and the Son." And the "beautiful streets of that kingdom, (shall exhibit) the appearance of being paved with gold." (D&C 137:2-4). Thus, is described in beautiful imagery, the inherent power of The Book of Mormon to bring us unto Christ.

Seeds
that have been planted in
fertile gospel soil will germinate
into strong plants with deep roots. (See
Alma Chapter 32). These are the covenants
we have made with God. They derive their healing
power from their association with the firm foundation
of His Holy character. In our church experience, we are like
the good seeds that have matured into a forest of trees that are
secure in numbers. When the winds of adversity blow hard,
we are unified and strengthened by our solidarity. But if
we try to stand alone, no matter how great the girth of
our trunks, no matter how securely planted are our
roots, we risk being toppled over. We become like
the solitary widow maker tree left over in
the forest after its clearing.

The redeeming
act of God, which is
expressed so powerfully
in The Book of Mormon,
only waits upon our
initiative.

We can only feel
the therapeutic energy
of The Book of Mormon after
we have warmed up our muscles
with spiritually aerobic exercise, when
we have loosened up our ligaments through
compassionate service, when we have stretched
beyond our perceived capacity and have gained
the flexibility that comes with experience, when
we have worked out the 'nots' in our physical
and spiritual muscles by pushing ourselves
to the breaking point, when our vision sees
beyond our supposed limitations, and we
have raised our sights to fix our mind's
eye on a finish line that rises up to
meet a celestial horizon. Then,
when we have finally settled
in to a comfortable pace,
we will be able to see
ourselves through
to the end.

Within the embrace of The
Book of Mormon, conformity has a
capacity to provide us with significant
sustainable support. Without consistency
that is the hallmark of the scriptures, our
lives would become meaningless. Such is
the condition of those who are confronted
by a sense of futility that accompanies
their inability to focus on the innate
upward reach of the word of God
that is found so abundantly
within the covers of that
amazing book.

The
Book of
Mormon
exhorts us
to repentance.
It will detoxify
us from the cares
of the worldly, even
as we are subjected to
the vicissitudes of life.
It allows us to return to
the hallowed halls of the
Spirit, to be re-vitalized,
as we are re-introduced to
the Magical Kingdom of
God where our dreams
can come true.

Although
we cannot save
our daylight time, we
may try to maximize it
by strangling ourselves with
what we can buy, things whose
opacity obstructs our ability to see
what is really there. In reality, we
are on Book of Mormon time. We
enjoy the Lord's time. We are on
His errand, no matter how long
it may take, or how distracted
or preoccupied we become by
trivial concerns.

If we turn our backs on The Book of Mormon, we have tacitly declined the Lord's offer to experience life abundantly. We ignore His invitation to come follow Him. We are deaf to His entreaty to search out righteousness, and to find in Him every good thing. If we live only for the moment, we will die as to the things of the Spirit.

If we do not rely upon the light-generating capacity of The Book of Mormon, we are doomed to hop around in flickering shadows that are nothing more than the caricatures of reality. The blind will stumble about in the dark until the discrepancy between their marginalized behavior and the ideals of the scriptures becomes so great that their short-lived pleasure in worldly ways will evaporate as does the morning dew in the full light of day. Wickedness never was happiness, and so, we can never find happiness as long as we persist in sin.

In words
of counsel to his
son, Alma said: "It is
as easy to give heed to the
word of Christ," our compass,
"which will point you to a straight
course to eternal bliss, as it was for our
fathers to give heed to this compass," the
Liahona, "which would point unto them a
straight course to the promised land. Do not
let us" then, "be slothful" or move slowly
"because of the easiness of the way." As
if our very lives depended on it, (as
they surely do) we must "look to
God, and live!" (Alma 37:44
& 46-47).

Through the
workings of the Holy
Ghost as we read The Book of
Mormon, we can see all the way
into heaven, with the capacity to be
transported beyond the palpable and
perceptible confines of this world as we
return in our minds' eye to our former
abode in heaven, where boundaries are
blurred, and the barricades of borders
evaporate in a flood of light. Father's
Plan was carefully crafted, that it
might create conditions wherein
we would be strengthened by
the Holy Ghost to do our
best within the cradle
and crucible of our
experience.

# Sixty Questions Answered by The Book of Mormon

"And it came to pass that the words which came unto Nephi were fulfilled, according as they had been spoken; for behold, at the going down of the sun" the day of the Lord's birth, "there was no darkness; and the people began to be astonished because there was no darkness when the night came." (3 Nephi 1:15). How appropriate that the sign of the birth of the Savior should be the dissolution of the night.

In both the Eastern and the Western Hemispheres, "it came to pass also that a new star did appear, according to the word." (3 Nephi 1:21). God had been generous not only to Nephites, but to all who had eyes to see. (See Matthew 13:16).

## What happened in the Americas when Jesus was born in Bethlehem?

"And it came to pass that the words which came unto Nephi were fulfilled, according as they had been spoken; for behold, at the going down of the sun" on the day of the Lord's birth, "there was no darkness; and the people began to be astonished because there was no darkness when the night came." (3 Nephi 1:15). The scriptures teach us that the Light of Christ is "the light which is in all things, which giveth life to all things, which is the law by which all things are governed, even the power of God, who sitteth upon his throne, who is in the bosom of eternity, who is in the midst of all things." (D&C 88:13). How appropriate that the sign of the birth of the Savior should be the dissolution of the night.

"And there were many, who had not believed the words of the prophets." (3 Nephi 1:16). However, so powerful was the sign, that many "fell to the earth and became as if they were dead, for they knew that the great plan of destruction which they had laid for those who believed in the words of the prophets had been frustrated; for the sign which had been given was already at hand." (3 Nephi 1:16). In a most dramatic way, those who had relied on their own might, and had denied God the power to influence their lives, were suddenly left without excuse, and even the strength to stand. (Se Romans 1:16). "And thus we see that the devil will not (either figuratively or literally) support his children at the last day." (Alma 30:60).

"And they began to know that the Son of God must shortly appear; yea, in fine, all the people upon the face of the whole earth from the west to the east, both in the land north and in the land south, were so exceedingly astonished that they fell to the earth. For they knew that the prophets had testified of these things for many years, and that the sign which had been given was already at hand; and they began to fear because of their iniquity and their unbelief. And it came to pass that there was no darkness in all that night, but it was as light as though it was mid-day. And it came to pass that the sun did rise in the morning again, according to its proper order; and they knew that it was the day that the Lord should be born, because of the sign which had been given. And it had come to pass, yea, all things, every whit, according to the words of the prophets." (3 Nephi 1:20).

In both the Eastern and the Western Hemispheres, "it came to pass also that a new star did appear, according to the word." (3 Nephi 1:21). The Wise Men who had traveled from afar would inquire of Herod: "Where is he that is born King of the Jews? For we have seen his star in the east and have come to worship him." (Matthew 2:2). God had been generous not only to Nephites, but to all who had eyes to see, and ears to hear. (See Matthew 13:16). He has manifested Himself not only to "those who believed after he came in the meridian of time, in the flesh, but (also to) all those from the beginning, even as many as were before he came, who believed in the words of the holy prophets, who spake as they were inspired by the gift of the Holy Ghost, who truly testified of him in all things." (D&C 20:26).

3 Nephi Chapter 8 describes
the destruction that occurred in Book
of Mormon lands. It appears to have been
one of the greatest natural disasters in the
history of the world. It was the physical
manifestation of the earth's revolt
against the crucifixion
of its Creator.

Perhaps the record of the
experience of the Nephites is as close as
any of us will come to understanding just
how overwhelming will be the spiritual darkness
that will prevail among those who are resurrected to
a kingdom without glory, which is as a "lake
which burneth with fire and brimstone,
which is the second death."
(D&C 63:17).

## What happened in the New World when Jesus was crucified in Jerusalem?

The fulfilment of the prophecy that the Savior would be crucified was recorded by the Nephites with precise accuracy. "And it came to pass in the thirty and fourth year, in the first month, on the fourth day of the month, there arose a great storm, such an one as never had been known in all the land." (3 Nephi 8:5). This scripture, as well as passages in the New Testament and in the Doctrine & Covenants, all indicate that the Savior might have been crucified the very week that He turned 33 years of age. The first month in the Hebrew calendar was in the springtime of the year, between the middle of March and the middle of April.

"And there was also a great and terrible tempest; and there was terrible thunder, insomuch that it did shake the whole earth as if it was about to divide asunder. And there were exceedingly sharp lightnings, such as never had been known in all the land." (3 Nephi 8:5-7). 3 Nephi Chapter 8 describes the destruction that occurred in Book of Mormon lands. It appears to have been one of the greatest natural disasters in the history of the world. It was the physical manifestation of the earth's revolt against the crucifixion of its Creator. In these verses, the adjectives "great and terrible" are used 7 times; "great" is used 8 times, and "terrible" is used 6 times. It must have been difficult to find words adequate to describe the massive devastation that had occurred. The "whole face of the land was changed" (3 Nephi 8:12), with such a physical contortion that "the face of the whole earth became deformed." (3 Nephi 8:17). "The thunderings, and the lightnings, and the storm, and the tempest, and the quakings of the earth … did last for about the space of three hours." (3 Nephi 8:19). It is almost impossible to conceptualize a storm of this magnitude, or an earthquake lasting for more than a just few seconds. Indeed, "it was said by some that the time was greater." (3 Nephi 8:19). To them, it must have seemed an eternity.

"And then, behold, there was darkness upon the face of the land." (3 Nephi 8:19). So overpowering was the murky blackness, so complete and total and universal, that "those who had not fallen could feel the vapor of darkness." (3 Nephi 8:20). The Spirit of Christ had been withdrawn; thus, "there could not be any light at all." (3 Nephi 8:21). The survivors of the tempest could see neither "the sun, nor the moon, nor the stars, for so great were the mists of darkness which were upon the face of the land." (3 Nephi 8:22).

Perhaps the record of the experience of the Nephites is as close as any of us will come to understanding just how overwhelming will be the spiritual darkness that will prevail among those who are resurrected to a kingdom without glory, which is as a "lake which burneth with fire and brimstone, which is the second death." (D&C 63:17). For the Sons of Perdition, existence in such a spiritual vacuum will be a living hell.

As the abridgment of Nephi's record continued, it is important to remember that this thick darkness prevailed for 3 days, after which "the darkness dispersed from off the face of the land, and the earth did cease to tremble, and the rocks did cease to rend, and the dreadful groanings did cease, and all the tumultuous noises did pass away." (3 Nephi 9:10). It must have been a very long and almost unbearable 72 hours for the survivors.

Among the Nephites, it is possible that Nephi's teachings were a re-entrenchment of ordinances that had not been recently practiced by them. If this is the case, the ministry of Nephi might be compared to the exhortations of latter-day prophets who have specifically invited less-active members of the church to follow the covenant path, and to return to the fold in full fellowship.

Baptism serves many purposes. Among them are 1) if we have matured beyond the age of accountability, it allows us to receive a remission of sins, 2) it makes it possible for us to gain admission to the church of Christ, 3) it provides us with access to personal sanctification through the Holy Ghost, even as we push through this vale of tears, and 4) it is symbolic of the gateway that leads to the Celestia Kingdom of God.

# Why is it necessary to be baptized?

"Wherefore, my beloved brethren, I know that if ye shall follow the Son, with full purpose of heart, acting no hypocrisy and no deception before God, but with real intent, repenting of your sins, witnessing unto the Father that ye are willing to take upon you the name of Christ, by baptism - yea, by following your Lord and your Savior down into the water, according to his word, behold, then shall ye receive the Holy Ghost; yea, then cometh the baptism of fire and of the Holy Ghost; and then can ye speak with the tongue of angels, and shout praises unto the Holy One of Israel." (2 Nephi 31:13, see Mosiah Chapter 18).

The Savior's example demonstrated that the entrance into the church and Kingdom is strait; that is to say, it is narrowly defined. The scriptures allow no discussion and permit no variance of opinion regarding the prescribed way. He set the pattern, and "said unto the children of men: Follow thou me." (2 Nephi 31:10). Among the Nephites, it is possible that Nephi's teachings were a retrenchment or reestablishment of ordinances that had not been recently practiced by them. If this is the case, the ministry of Nephi might be compared to the exhortations of Latter-day prophets who have specifically invited less-active members of the church to follow the covenant path, and to return to the fold in full fellowship.

To a later Nephite society, the Savior Himself taught these principles with unmistakable clarity. "And he said unto them: On this wise shall ye baptize; and there shall be no disputations among you." (3 Nephi 11:22). There followed explicit instruction to the priesthood leaders of the Nephite church regarding the manner of baptism, including the words to be used during the administration of the ordinance. It is vitally important that the doctrine of Christ be clearly understood by the members of His church. "And there shall be no disputations among you, as there have hitherto been," cautioned the Savior. "Neither shall there be disputations among you concerning the points of my doctrine." (3 Nephi 11:28).

As Nephi asked: "Wherefore, my beloved brethren, can we follow Jesus save we shall be willing to keep the commandments of the Father? And the Father said: Repent ye, repent ye, and be baptized in the name of my Beloved Son." (2 Nephi 31:10-11). Then, Nephi taught the principle of the second baptism, or receipt of the Holy Ghost. For the voice of the Son had come unto him, saying: "He that is baptized in my name, to him will the Father give the Holy Ghost." (2 Nephi 31:12).

Baptism serves many purposes. Among them, these are prominent: 1) If we have matured beyond the age of accountability, it allows us to receive a remission of sins, 2) It enables us to gain admission to the church, 3) It provides us with access to personal sanctification through the Holy Ghost, even as we push through this vale of tears, and 4) It is outwardly symbolic as the gateway to the Celestial Kingdom of God.

As he stood beside the waters of Mormon, Alma taught his flock the first principles of the gospel. He preached unto them repentance, and redemption, and faith on the Lord", offering plain counsel concerning the proper attitude of those who desire baptism. (Mosiah 18:7) When we "come into the fold o0f God" we are "called his people". (Mosiah 18:8). Our participation in the initial and introductory ordinance of baptism makes possible our further progression."

There is only one way, one fold, and one true church. Paul explained to the Ephesians that there is "one Lord, one faith, (and) one baptism". (Ephesians 4:5). If all churches were equal, then the true church would not exist anywhere. If, in education, any program were the equal of any other, then receiving any degree would be based on an indiscriminate course of study that would qualify the recipient in all fields of study. That, of course, is contrary to the natural order of things.

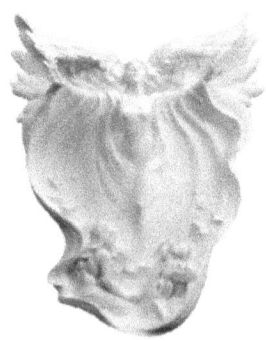

## What is the covenant of baptism?

"Behold, here are the waters of Mormon (for thus were they called) and now, as ye are desirous to come into the fold of God, and to be called his people, and are willing to bear one another's burdens, that they may be light; Yea, and are willing to mourn with those that mourn; yea, and comfort those that stand in need of comfort, and to stand as witnesses of God at all times and in all things, and in all places that ye may be in, even until death, that ye may be redeemed of God, and be numbered with those of the first resurrection, that ye may have eternal life. Now I say unto you, if this be the desire of your hearts, what have you against being baptized in the name of the Lord, as a witness before him that ye have entered into a covenant with him, that ye will serve him and keep his commandments, that he may pour out his Spirit more abundantly upon you?" (Mosiah 18:8-10).

As he stood beside the waters of Mormon, Alma taught his little flock the same first principles of the gospel. "And he did preach unto them repentance, and redemption, and faith on the Lord." (Mosiah 18:7). He offered plain counsel concerning the proper attitude of those who desire baptism. When we "come into the fold of God" we are "called his people." (Mosiah 18:8). Our participation in the initial and introductory ordinance of baptism makes possible our further progression.

There is only one way, one fold, and one true church. Paul explained to the Ephesians that there is "one Lord, one faith, (and) one baptism." (Ephesians 4:5). If all churches were equal, then the true church would not exist anywhere. If, in education, any program were the equal of any other, then receiving any degree would be based on an indiscriminate course of study that would nevertheless qualify the recipient in all fields of study. That, of course, is contrary to the natural order of things. Only by the power of the priesthood through the specific ordinances thereof, and by making sacred covenants with God, may we truly call ourselves 'Christians' in both the biblical and apostolic sense.

Alma asked those who stood beside the waters of Mormon if they were "willing to bear one another's burdens, that they may be light." We might ask ourselves, as Alma had asked these baptismal candidates in the Book of Mormon narrative: "How can we help each other as we struggle with sin?"

Ministering efforts by the members of the Lord's church can do much to alleviate suffering. It may seem to be a full-time job. But as Gordon B. Hinckley said: "The church cannot hope to save a man on Sunday, if during the week it is a complacent witness to the destruction of his soul." (C.R., 10/1977).

Alma went on to describe those who would enter into the covenant of baptism as the kind of persons who would "mourn with those that mourn; yea, and comfort those that stand in need of comfort." (Mosiah 18:9). The Lord declared: "Thou shalt live together in love, insomuch that thou shalt weep for the loss of them that die." (D&C 42:45). Grief is good ('good grief') when we mourn for those who have died in full faith and fellowship in the church, with the secure hope of eternal life in the Kingdom of God. As Joseph Fielding Smith said: "They shall never die the second death, and feel the torment of the wicked, when they come face to face with eternity." ("Church History and Modern Revelation," 1:186).

However, mourning also describes the sense of loss that is felt by those who carry with them the burden of sin, when they have not been washed clean in the waters of baptism. When we mourn together, we help our brothers and sisters overcome, through repentance, the negative consequences of sin. To the extent that we are successful, we facilitate that process of repentance, so that the joy of forgiveness may be experienced by those for whom we mourn.

We are "witnesses of God" to whomever we meet, in whatever circumstances we might find ourselves, and wherever we might be. We recognize the broad strokes with which the words of heaven's admission policy have been painted: Persons of any race, creed, color, or national origin are welcome, provided they maintain ideals and standards in harmony with those of The Church of Jesus Christ of Latter-day Saints, and meet the requirements of baptism and the ordinances of the Melchizedek Priesthood. (See 2 Nephi 26:33).

Zion comes in many different colors. It speaks Aymara, Chinese, Dutch, Fijian, Mandarin, Russian, Tongan, and dozens of other languages. It lives in over 3,500 stakes, in practically every country in the world, from Argentina to Zimbabwe. It has over 17 million members who are red, yellow, brown, black, and white. Zion wears a sarong, a grass skirt, a blue collar, a tupeno, a business suit, and a kilt. It lives in igloos, huts, fales, and high-rises. Most importantly, it shares a common testimony that Jesus is the Christ, and that His love, indeed, makes the world go around. Today, it is more important than ever to remember that there is no United States of America in heaven. The great equalizer in the sight of God is obedience by His children to His will.

It is impossible to overestimate the power inherent in the ordinance of baptism. No-one of themselves can be lifted to celestial glory. Our progression depends on the light of Christ, the guidance of the Holy Ghost, and the power of the priesthood. Religion is more than a philosophy of life; it is the generator of life itself. If we try to make it on our own, we will fail. The only way to succeed is when we yield ourselves to the power of our Father in Heaven, the Atonement of His Son Jesus Christ, and the influence of the Holy Ghost.

In Alma's day, and in our own, the vitality of its members energizes the Lord's church. It rises and falls on the tide of their personal witness of the divinity of the Savior, and of the divine authenticity of The Book of Mormon. Alvin R. Dyer warned: "We must not be caught in the bind of building a church and killing the articles of its faith or permitting form to triumph over spirit. The church and kingdom of God is built by the ardor and conviction of its members. We must be alert to the expansion of its assets at the cost of lost conviction. When buildings or institutions grow bigger and bigger, let us be fearful, lest the Spirit thins out." ("A Foundation for Education").

As members of the church bear their "witness of God at all times and in all things, and in all places," the foundation of the Kingdom of God will be planted in bedrock. The church will be as the five-foot high and eight-foot-thick wall built around our meeting houses. An Irishman who had done so around his farm, when asked why he built it so sturdily, replied that if the wind ever blew so hard that it toppled the wall, it would still be five feet thick. Baptism provides us with a foundation for life that is "eight feet thick."

Alma compared the fountain at the waters of Mormon to the attitude of the righteous who stand beside the waters of baptism, contemplating the ordinance and its associated covenants. "These currents and many more are part of the flowing fountain of the church. If we do not drink, if we die of thirst while only inches from the fountain, the fault comes down to us. For the free, full, flowing, living water is there. (Truman Madsen, "Christ & The Inner Life," p. 31).

Therefore, Alma urged his congregation to be baptized. It seems clear that the ordinance was the same then as now. Hugh Nibley felt that the baptism of Alma was the old Jewish version, in which we find historical precedent in the rites of the Dead Sea Covenanters of Qumran, and which was strictly an ordinance of purification and initiation, but was still in doctrinal harmony with the purpose of baptism in the latter days.

The Manual of Discipline from The Serek Scroll at Qumran reads: "His sin is forgiven him and in the humility of his soul he is for all the Laws of God; his flesh is cleansed shining bright in the waters of purification, even in the waters of baptism, and he shall be given a new name in due time to walk perfectly in all the ways of God." ("An Approach to The Book of Mormon," p. 149).

In just the same way that King Benjamin's people had reacted, (see Mosiah 5:1-8), Alma's baptismal candidates "clapped their hands for joy, and exclaimed: This is the desire of our hearts." (Mosiah 18:11). For many years, the spirit of these people had been stifled by the oppressive rule of a wicked king. Now, they yearned for the opportunity to find an avenue for the expression of the indescribable feelings welling up inside them. They wished to put to death the old sinful person, and to experience the rebirth of the new, spiritual self that had been lying dormant within them. Baptism was their solution to the dilemma created with the Fall of Adam. "For as in Adam all die, even so in Christ shall all be made alive." (1 Corinthians 15:22). Or, as Benjamin explained: "As in Adam, or by nature, (we) fall, even so the blood of Christ atoneth for (our) sins." (Mosiah 3:16).

As he worshipped
with his congregation beside the
waters of Mormon, Alma taught his little
flock the first principles of the gospel, just as the
missionaries do today. "And he did preach unto
them repentance, and redemption, and faith
on the Lord." (Mosiah 18:7). He offered
plain counsel to those who desired
to enter into the fold, at the
waters of baptism.

Baptism is the Lord's
solution to the dilemma that was
created by the Fall of Adam. "For as in
Adam all die, even so in Christ shall all be
made alive." (1 Corinthians 15:22). Or, as
Benjamin explained: "As in Adam, or by
nature, (we) fall, even so the blood of
Christ atoneth for (our) sins."
(Mosiah 3:16).

## Why was Jesus baptized?

"If the Lamb of God, he being holy, should have need to be baptized by water, to fulfil all righteousness, O then, how much more need have we, being unholy, to be baptized, yea, even by water! And now, I would ask of you, my beloved brethren, wherein the Lamb of God did fulfil all righteousness in being baptized by water? Know ye not that he was holy? But notwithstanding he being holy, he showeth unto the children of men that, according to the flesh he humbleth himself before the Father, and witnesseth unto the Father that he would be obedient unto him in keeping his commandments. Wherefore, after he was baptized with water the Holy Ghost descended upon him in the form of a dove. And again, it showeth unto the children of men the straitness of the path, and the narrowness of the gate, by which they should enter, he having set the example before them." (2 Nephi 31:5-9).

Fifty years before Nephi delivered the discourse recorded in Second Nephi Chapter 31, he had preached to the people about the mission of John the Baptist. (See 2 Nephi 31:4). Nephi now emphasized that the Lord would be baptized "to fulfil all righteousness," which is to obey every commandment and to perform every ordinance necessary to inherit eternal life. (2 Nephi 31:5).

The record does not make any special mention of the manner of baptism among the Nephites. It was well understood by Nephi's people that baptism had always been the standard for the Children of the Covenant. Five hundred years later, when John the Baptist went into the wilderness of Judea preaching repentance and baptism, his actions didn't arouse any curiosity among the people, as would have been the case if he were introducing some new and strange doctrine. The Jews of that day understood it as an essential gospel ordinance, and so it was. Even the Jewish Encyclopedia states: "John stood forth in the spirit of the prophets of old to preach his baptism of repentance symbolized by cleansing with water." (Volume 2, p. 499).

"The fact that baptism was practiced in ancient Israel might also help to explain why the Savior was not criticized by the orthodox Jews when He was baptized. The Pharisees were quick to (rebuke) Him whenever He did anything contrary to their law. However, not a single word of criticism concerning the baptism of Jesus Christ is found in the entire New Testament." ("Commentary on The Book of Mormon," p. 155).

Interestingly, the traditional place of the Savior's baptism in the River Jordan is today called "El Maghtas," which is an Arabic expression, meaning "the place of immersion."

As early as 914 B.C., during the prophet Elijah's ministry in Israel, there is Old Testament evidence of baptism. Can it be that "John's baptism was the counterpart of Elijah's novel rite on Mt. Carmel? We recall that when Elijah was testing the gods of Baal against the power of Jehovah, on their altar he covered the sacrifice with water, and then called down fire from heaven to consume it. (Can there be) similarity between this rite and the gospel's ordinance of baptism by water and by the Spirit? ("Christ's Eternal Gospel," p. 118).

It is obvious that baptism is an ordinance of great antiquity, and one that demands humility and obedience before God the Father. The Lamb of God was indeed baptized, for Elder Howard W. Hunter declared that he "entered into all the saving ordinances of the ... priesthood," and baptism is the gate by which we enter, in order to qualify to participate in all others. (Los Angeles Area Conference address, 1980).

After considering these 60 questions that are answered in The Book of Mormon, take a moment to ponder any or all of these 20 thoughts:

As Alice in Wonderland asked the Cheshire Cat: "Would you please tell me which way I ought to go from here?" The cat responded: "That depends a good deal on where you want to go". "I admit," responded Alice, "I don't much care where." Said the cat: "Then it doesn't matter which way you go". "Just so I go somewhere!" cried Alice. "Oh," responded the cat, "you are sure to do that, if you walk far enough."

As a Companion to our Book of Mormon study, the Spirit teaches us how to become engaged in fashioning defensive weapons in our armory of thought. With these tools, the Holy Ghost will show us how to reconfigure an arsenal of heavenly munitions with which we are already familiar. He will bring to our remembrance the firearms safety course that we completed in a premortal setting, that focused on our faith, hope, and charity, as well as on peace, joy, and strength.

The Book of
Mormon helps us to
understand ourselves. It
is when we have discovered
the answers to where we came
from and why we are here that
we will be prepared to embark,
with unbounded confidence,
upon an incredible journey
of faith into our future,
to discover where we
are going.

The Book of Mormon's teachings
will provide us with a glimpse of what
it must have been like to live with Father
during our pre-mortal existence, and next,
they explain the purpose of our life on earth.
Then, they will open up our hearts and minds
to soul-expanding eternal opportunities. If we
will conform to their overall success strategies,
we will become better friends, neighbors, and
witnesses of Jesus Christ. When we do the
math and we crunch the numbers, we'll
find that we are better prepared to
deal with the elusive equations
that define happiness.

We have
been foreordained
in heaven before the world
was to have glory added upon
our heads, on the condition of our
faithfulness to God, as we support Him
in His work by our actions. We'll be better
prepared to do so when we listen intently for
answers, as we study The Book of Mormon.
We'll open up our minds to options we had
never considered, envisioning a special
place called Kolob, signifying the
first creation, that is to say, the
closest body to the celestial,
or to the residence of
God.

With The
Book of Mormon
as our guide, we've chosen
liberty and eternal life, instead
of captivity and spiritual death. We
choose to live our lives within the context
of the gospel of Jesus Christ and His laws.
Without its structure, our unbridled freedom
could very well have led to tyranny. We're free
to choose, but we cannot choose to escape the
consequences if we do so unwisely, or if
we ally ourselves with an anarchist
who is the adversary of all that
is good and true.

Revelation may
be recognized when we
have permitted ourselves to be
mesmerized by the Holy Ghost.
The reception of its communication
from the heavens only waits upon our
initiative. So it is with the true principles
that are revealed within The Book of Mormon,
whose doctrine will never be surrendered to any
misguided, private, or uninspired interpretation
as long as those who read it maintain practiced
fluency in the pure and unadulterated
language of the Spirit.

The prophets of
The Book of Mormon
encourage us to vividly
role-play, as well as to pre-play
and re-play with animation the
lines we have been taught to deliver
on the grand stage that is the theater
of life. They give us the tools we need
as worthy understudies to the Star
of the production, Who is our Lord
and Savior Jesus Christ, Whose
name alone appears on an
illuminated marquee
in the heavens.

It is
our Father's
desire that all of
us might satisfy the
entrance requirements
for admittance into heaven.
We could not be blessed with a
greater means to do so, than that
of the Spirit, Who will confirm our
yearning to receive a sure witness of
The Book of Mormon, and Who will
certify our worthiness to enjoy
the blessings of immortality
and eternal life.

We, who
make our way
through The Book
of Mormon to enjoy
its quiet serenity and
partake of the fruit of the
tree of life, must negotiate a
treacherous path past the great
and spacious buildings that so
insidiously dominate our lives'
landscapes, enticing us to pause
and sample their pleasures, while
at the same time diverting the
focus of our attention from
our worthy goals.

The Book of Mormon stands as a witness that we may take God at His word when He declares that it is His work and glory to accomplish what we could never do on our own: to bring to pass our immortality and our eternal life.

When our Book of Mormon study wanes it may be because it is easy to be distracted by the desire to obtain what we do not need, to amass what we do not deserve, to hoard what we have not earned, and to stockpile what we cannot ultimately utilize. Each fall and winter, several million unvaccinated people worldwide succumb to the effects of an influenza virus that manifests itself in frustratingly mutated forms, but the truth is that more will die spiritually because they have been infected by avarice, and by greed, covetousness, lust, conceit, and prejudice. The prideful and stubborn "seek not the Lord to establish his righteousness, but every man walketh in his own way, after the manner of his own God." (D&C 1:16, see Isaiah 55:2).

One line in particular stands out in all of our favorite fairy tales, that reads "..... and they all lived happily ever after." It isn't written in the second act of life's Three Act Play, but in the third act. Nevertheless, during mortality, and particularly because we've been blessed with the longitudinal perspective of The Book of Mormon, we get a foretaste of the happiness that has been prepared for the Saints, that awaits each of us in that land of enchantment just beyond the veil, where our dreams will come true.

As we read The Book of Mormon with questions that have been on our minds, we find ourselves poised upon the edge of forever. We jump off into a stream of revelation, to be carried along in quickening currents that we may recognize as nothing less than our direct experience with God. It is in the scriptures where we will find divine guidance that relates to how we can take our bearings on distant mile posts, as well as on eternity.

The Book
of Mormon can
define the path to a
religious recalibration
thru repentance. It allows
us to become reinvigorated by
the refreshing breeze of celestial
air. The scriptures paint a portrait
of free-will where we may take risks.
If, in our efforts, we fail to measure up
to God's entreaties, the Savior will step
in to intervene in our behalf, by using
the bargaining chip of the Atonement,
thereby allowing the Law of Mercy to
satisfy the otherwise unalterable
and inexorable demands of its
contrary, that goes by the
name of Justice.

Since the restoration of truth
and of the guiding principles that
are illustrated throughout The Book of
Mormon, a knowledge of our origin and
destiny has become available to all of the
children of our Father in Heaven. In the
Last Days, our sons and our daughters
will prophesy, our young men shall
have visions, and our old men
will dream dreams. (See Joel
2:28 & Job 33:14-16).

The Book of
Mormon is where we
seek to shelter our spirits
and to rest our racing hearts.
We grasp the horns of sanctuary,
so that we might relieve the tensions
that always threaten to overwhelm us
were we to allow ourselves to be caught
up and remain in the fast lane of life.
In the scriptures, we quietly reflect
upon our quality of preparation
to breathe celestial air and to
live in eternal felicity
in the company of
the Gods.

The Book
of Mormon dynamo
stands ready to liberate
our energies to be creative and
it fosters creativity, that we might
experience a greater capacity. Its design
is the perfect law of liberty. The key to our
welfare in eternity has been integrated into
the scriptures. President Kimball recognized
their nurturing potential when he urged us to
lengthen our stride. Our renewed diligence
in scripture study can bless us with an
awakening sensitivity that will
put us in touch with our
divine destiny.

Without the
Book of Mormon's
longitudinal perspective,
we may remain ever learning,
while never coming to a knowledge
of the truth. We'll grasp at straws, failing
to understand that nothing will keep us out
of Zion more surely than a self-assurance that
cannot acknowledge the influence of powers that
are greater than ourselves. Nothing will kill the
influence of the Spirit faster than absolute
self-confidence that too easily mutates
into unbridled pride, selfishness,
vanity, and haughtiness.

"The Book
of Mormon and the
holy scriptures are given
of me for your instruction,
and the power of my Spirit
quickenth all things."
(D&C 33:16).

# Sixty-Five Questions Answered in The Book of Mormon

The sacred ordinance of the Sacrament that has been preserved for us in Moroni Chapters 4 & 5, prods our memories of how we felt at our baptism by water and the Spirit. It immobilizes time, and is reminiscent of a line from the motion picture "Frozen." "For the first time in forever, nothing's in my way!" Just so, nothing gets in the way of the Sacrament. It is an ordinance of sanctification, and ultimately of justification by the Spirit. (See Moses 6:60).

The prophet Moroni was determined to include the words of the sacramental prayer in his record because he knew the ordinance would raise our testimony temperature to get our juices flowing and give us a healthy whack on our status quo, when and where we need it most. It would prod us off our complacency plateaus and help us to feel complete, whole, and at peace, and it would bind up our wounds. It would complete the process of repentance and forgiveness through the Atonement, and instill within our hearts a burning desire to re-commit ourselves to the discipline of Christ and the guidance by the Holy Ghost.

## Why do we renew our covenant of baptism?

Alma the Younger said: "I have repented of my sins and have been redeemed of the Lord; behold I am born of the Spirit." (Mosiah 27:24-25). In his own life, he had given himself completely to the Savior, Who is mighty to save. Perhaps, each of us must ultimately follow the path to our own personal and individual Garden of Gethsemane, with its attendant Calvary. We need not go unassisted, and if we are prepared, "we need not fear in our hearts when we are conscious of having lived up to the principles of truth and righteousness as God has required it at our hands, according to our best knowledge and understanding." (Joseph F. Smith, "Gospel Doctrine," p. 66).

The ordinance of the Sacrament, preserved for us in Moroni Chapters 4 & 5, blesses us to remember how we felt when we were baptized with water and the Spirit. It immobilizes time, which is reminiscent of a line from the motion picture "Frozen." "For the first time in forever, nothing's in my way!" So too, nothing gets in the way of the Sacrament. There is no pomp and circumstance, no splendid celebration with ceremony and fuss, and no histrionics to detract from the simplicity of the ordinance. No outside interferences compete for our attention, and there are no distractions to obstruct our direct conduit to God's listening ear. For the first time in forever, nothing's in our way!

The Book of Mormon provides a model of how it can feel to participate in Sacrament services, to always have His Spirit to be with us. For Alma and his sons "preached the word, and the truth, according to the spirit of prophecy and revelation; and they preached after the holy order of God by which they were called." (Alma 43:2).

In Book of Mormon times, the Sacrament would have been administered to those who had entered into the waters of baptism. It would have been as an independent constant, with a powerful and influential capacity to provide a bastion of stability in the midst of turmoil. The language of the Sacrament in the ancient Americas would have been the gospel standard.

As Moroni taught: "The first fruits of repentance is baptism; and baptism cometh by faith unto the fulfilling the commandments; and the fulfilling the commandments bringeth remission of sins; and the remission of sins bringeth meekness, and lowliness of heart; and because of meekness and lowliness of heart cometh the visitation of the Holy Ghost, which Comforter filleth with hope and perfect love, which love endureth by diligence unto prayer, until the end shall come, when all the saints shall dwell with God." (Moroni 8:25-26).

The irreducible elements of the Sacrament have always defined the lowest common denominator of baptism, that breaks down the Plan of Salvation into easily digestible bite-sized principles, while positioning the solemnities of eternity in the cross hairs. After our baptism, as we partake of the emblems of the Sacrament, we take our understanding as far as our capacity allows us to go, because the ordinance is tailored to suit our individual circumstances, and yet it is collectively understood and is universally applicable. Insofar as the Sacrament is concerned, God "doeth nothing, save it be plain unto (us); and he inviteth (us) all to come unto him and partake of his goodness; and he denieth none that come unto him ... and all are alike unto God." (2 Nephi 26:33).

The Sacrament is the perfect schoolmaster to bring us to Christ. (See Galatians 3:24). In the weeks, months, and years following our baptism, we notice the stirrings of the spirit of revelation. We feel pure intelligence flowing into us, as we grow into the principle of revelation.

We've all had these revelatory experiences. Our chords of memory are touched when we enjoy the quiet reverence of the Sacrament service. Hugh B. Brown said: "Sometimes during solitude, I hear truth spoken with clarity and freshness; uncolored and untranslated it speaks from within myself in a language original but inarticulate, heard only with the soul, and I realize I brought it with me, was never taught it, nor can I efficiently teach it to another."

But as President Kimball cautioned: "Expecting the spectacular, (we) may not be fully alerted to the constant flow of revealed communication." (C.R., 4/1977). The Sacrament, that lowest common denominator that, following our baptism keeps us all on an equal footing, gives each of us an opportunity to recognize these universal feelings and to act upon them.

The Sacrament raises our testimony temperature and gets our juices flowing. It gives us a healthy "whack" right in our status quo, where we need it the most, to get us off our complacency plateaus. It makes us feel complete, whole, at peace, and it binds up our wounds. It completes the process of repentance and forgiveness through the Atonement, and instills within us a burning desire to re-commit ourselves to be disciples of Christ.

We feel as Joseph Smith did, when he exclaimed: "I can taste the principles of eternal life, and so can you. They are given to me by the revelations of Jesus Christ." (H.C. 6:304-5). Thus, Moroni urged: "I would commend you to seek this Jesus of whom the prophets and apostles have written, that the grace of God the Father, and also the Lord Jesus Christ, and the Holy Ghost, which beareth record of them, may be and abide in you forever." (Ether 12:41).

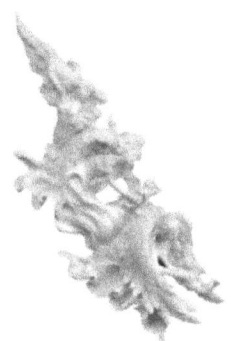

## Do little children need to repent and be baptized?

"Behold I say unto you that (parents) must repent and be baptized, and humble themselves as their little children, and they shall all be saved with their little children. And their little children need no repentance, neither baptism. Behold, baptism is unto repentance to the fulfilling the commandments unto the remission of sins. But little children are alive in Christ, even from the foundation of the world; if not so, God is a partial God, and also a changeable God, and a respecter to persons; for how many little children have died without baptism!" (Moroni 8:10-12).

The doctrine of infant baptism denies that Jesus Christ atoned for the "original sin" of Adam and refutes the concept of blessing based upon individual accountability. It demands that little children who die without baptism cannot enter heaven. But The Book of Mormon clearly teaches that the Atonement redeemed them from the Fall. They are capable of actions that are inconsistent with gospel principles, but they are not counted against them as sins. They are not culpable.

Rather, Mormon wrote: "This thing shall ye teach - repentance and baptism unto those who are accountable and capable of committing sin." (Moroni 8:10). It was an integral part of the Plan of Salvation, ordained in the Grand Councils in Heaven before the world was, that little children who died before the age of accountability would be saved in the Celestial Kingdom by the power of the Infinite Atonement.

The abominable practice
of infant baptism denies that Jesus
Christ atoned for the 'original sin' of Adam,
and refutes the concept of blessing based upon
our individual accountability. It demands that we
believe that innocent little children who have died
without baptism cannot enter heaven.

The Book of Mormon clearly
teaches that the Atonement of Jesus
Christ, which is infinite and eternal in its
depth, breadth, and scope, has redeemed little
children from the Fall. They are capable of
actions that are inconsistent with gospel
principles, but they are not counted
against them as sins. They
are not culpable.

## Why do bad things happen to good people?

In the wicked city of Ammonihah, "when Amulek saw the pains of ... women and children who were consuming in ... fire, he ... was pained; and he said unto Alma: How can we witness this awful scene? Therefore, let us stretch forth our hands, and exercise the power of God which is in us, and save them from the flames. But Alma said unto him: The Spirit constraineth me, that I must not stretch forth mine hand; for behold the Lord receiveth them up unto himself, in glory; and he doth suffer that they may do this thing, or that the people may do this thing unto them, according to the hardness of their hearts, that the judgments which he shall exercise upon them in his wrath may be just; and the blood of the innocent shall stand as a witness against them, yea, and cry mightily against them at the last day." (Alma 14:10-11).

Spencer W. Kimball taught, "If pain and sorrow and punishment immediately followed the doing of evil, no soul would repeat a misdeed. If joy and peace and rewards were instantaneously given the doer of good, there could be no evil. All would do good, and not because of the rightness of doing good. There would be no test of strength, no development of character, no growth of powers, no agency, but only satanic controls. If all the sick were healed, if all the righteous were protected, and the wicked destroyed, the whole program of the Father would be annulled and the basic principle of the gospel, agency, would be ended." ("The Teachings of Spencer W. Kimball", p.77).

Spencer W. Kimball taught: "If pain and sorrow and punishment immediately followed the doing of evil, no one would repeat a misdeed. If joy and peace and rewards were instantaneously given the doer of good," there could be no contrary from which we could learn life's valuable lessons.

Without opposition in our lives "there would be no test of strength, no development of character, no agency, no growth of powers, but only satanic controls. If all the sick were healed, if all the righteous were protected and the wicked destroyed, the whole program of the Father would be annulled, and agency, the basic principle of the gospel, would be ended."
(Spencer W. Kimball).

## Does the Lord always protect the righteous?

"The Lord suffereth the righteous to be slain that his justice and judgment may come upon the wicked; therefore ye need not suppose that the righteous are lost because they are slain; but behold, they do enter into the rest of the Lord their God." (Alma 60:13). In the depths of World War II, Harold B. Lee offered this consolation to the church: "Many of our boys who bear the priesthood and are worthy to do so will be called to that missionary service after they have departed this life." (C.R., 10/1942).

Some become martyrs, or "witnesses," slain for their testimony and that alone. The physical discomforts endured by those who refuse to renounce their testimonies of the truth do not seem to be significant to God. His focus seems to be on the preservation of the eternal life of our spirits.

Captain Moroni always viewed the glass as half-full. He told Pahoran: "The Lord suffereth the righteous to be slain that his justice and judgement may come upon the wicked; therefore, ye need not suppose that the righteous are lost because they are slain; but behold, they do enter into the rest of the Lord their God."
(Alma 60:13).

Some martyrs are slain for their testimony, and that alone. The physical discomforts endured by those who refuse to renounce their witness of truth do not seem to be significant to God. He is more focused on the development and preservation of the eternal welfare of our spirits.

# Will God ask us to extend ourselves beyond our capabilities?

Sometimes, when we are seemingly stretched beyond our capacity to endure, we are tempted to ask ourselves: Is it easier to choose wrong, and harder to choose the right? Is it easier to be wicked, and harder to be righteous? Is it easier to be sad, and harder to be happy? Is it easier to just put your life on cruise control, and harder to take the high road? Is it easier to go with the flow, and harder to swim upstream, against the current? Is it easier to walk with turkeys, and harder to soar with eagles? Is it easier to just throw in the towel and give up, and harder to continue the good fight? Is it easier to be mediocre or average, and harder to be exceptional? Is it easier to adopt the ways of the world, and harder to acknowledge that there is an autobiographical thread within each of us that leads back to Deity? Is it easier to yield to temptation, and harder to resist sin? Is rebellion an easier alternative, and obedience a harder choice? Is it easier to live in a confusing fog of conflicting values, and harder to be grounded and principled?

Is it easier to be immoral, and harder to be virtuous? Is it easier to be slothful and indolent, and harder to be upright? Is it easier to be swayed by secular humanism, and harder to be faithful? Is it easier to be carnal and worldly, and harder to be holy? Is it easier to live in wanton defiance of God's laws, and harder to pattern our lives after obedience? Is it easier to be depraved, and harder to be moral? Is the pursuit of nobility akin to a quest to find the Holy Grail? Are those who attempt to follow the teachings of the Savior only tilting with windmills?

The Book of Mormon teaches that when we resolve to choose the harder right, instead of the easier wrong, as fire in the sky, the air in the theater of life will be charged with an electricity that represents the inevitable merger of the universal encouragement of the Light of Christ, with the pointed and providential guidance provided by the Holy Ghost. When these influences streak in tandem across the heavens, their trajectories will coalesce to trace a flaming trail that sparkles over a vast cosmic ocean of thought. Over the ebb and flow of its tide, the Spirit will create an effectual bridge of understanding that is buttressed by the cohesive influence of the mighty foundation of faith. Then, the difficulty of making hard choices will melt away as the morning dew evaporates in the noonday sun.

"Yea, come unto Christ, and be perfected in him, and deny yourselves of all ungodliness; and if ye shall deny yourselves of all ungodliness, and love God with all your might, mind and strength, then is his grace sufficient for you, that by his grace ye may be perfect in Christ; and if by the grace of God ye are perfect in Christ, ye can in nowise deny the power of God. And again, if ye by the grace of God are perfect in Christ, and deny not his power, then are ye sanctified in Christ by the grace of God, through the shedding of the blood of Christ, which is in the covenant of the Father unto the remission of your sins, that ye become holy, without spot." (Moroni 10:32-33).

After considering these 65 questions that are answered in The Book of Mormon, take a moment to ponder any or all of these 20 thoughts:

At the Judgment Bar, the evidence will be presented, and our acceptance or rejection of The Book of Mormon will largely determine our reward or our punishment. There is within each of us an inherent capacity to generate faith with the impetus to do so coming from the Holy Ghost. This makes our trials, tailor-made though they may be, eminently fair. As a matter of fact, the deck has been stacked in our favor by the Light of Christ and the Holy Ghost to embrace the book as Another Testament of our Savior.

Before we commit to any significant course of action, such as when we determine to study The Book of Mormon, we make the issue a matter of ardent prayer, in order to experience the confirming witness of the Spirit. When, in our bosoms, we receive fire for the deed, we cannot fail, no matter how challenging, daunting, or problematic our holy quest might seem to be.

How often in The
Book of Mormon do we read
about cultural collapse because
a faithless society has decayed from
within? In every case, iniquity was the
companion of those who'd yield themselves
"unto the power of Satan." (3 Nephi 7:5). The
world does not seem capable of understanding
that Lucifer was a first-grade dropout and his
influence was the companion of anarchy. As
his disciples do in our day, at the Council, he
dismissed the power of the Atonement and
denied the righteous application of free
will, that would be vital if we were to
work out our salvation before God,
angels, and witnesses.

In The Book of
Mormon, we learn that
without a Redeemer, it would
not have been possible for Adam
and Eve to inherit celestial glory. In
their fallen state without repentance and
forgiveness of their sins, there would have
ben no avenue of escape. They would have
been incapable of obedience to celestial law,
and would therefore have lived forever in
their sins. God's Plan of Redemption
would have been frustrated, and
Lucifer's treachery would
have carried the day.

As we read
and study The Book
of Mormon's teachings, we
become aware of a divine design
that has been mapped out for each
one of us. "Our lives are fairy tales
waiting to be written by the finger
of God." (H.C. Anderson). The Holy
Ghost is ever conscious of the Plan.
He will bless us with the regularly
recurring reassurance of religious
recalibration that will autocorrect
with a fortuitous frequency and
with a celestial precision. He is
always waiting in the wings
to help us should we stumble,
having forgotten the lines
that we'd memorized for
the Second Act of the
Three Act Play of
God's Plan.

The Book of
Mormon has "been
translated by the gift
and power of God, for His
voice hath declared it unto us;
wherefore, we know of a surety
that the work is true." (The
Testimony of the Three
Witnesses).

It is
with faith
to see all the
way to heaven that
The Book of Mormon's
power is released. It can
penetrate the barriers that
isolate us from the sum and
substance of our existence; from
our characters that more accurately
identify us as beings of light. We've
come down to Earth from our heavenly
home, trailing clouds of glory, and as
we ascend on a ladder of faith, we are
decisively and securely reintroduced
to the potency of the Spirit. We will
see lightnings, and mountains
smoking, and we will perceive
the voices of trumpets and
hear thunderings out of
heaven, all of which
insistently speak
to our souls.

How we accept the teachings of The
Book of Mormon reveals if we possess the
spiritual and intellectual maturity to handle
knowledge with accountability. When we dare
to grapple with these interrogatives, we come
to an epiphany, as we determine to do our
best to be righteous stewards, not only
through all generations of time,
but also throughout all
of eternity.

The
Book
of Mormon
can instill within
us with the resolve to
abandon idolatry that is
always waiting to cloud our
vision. Its teachings give us the
necessary ammunition to conquer
our self-deification. We renounce the
adoration of our own creations and we
discover insights into human behavior.
The application of the principles of the
book can liberate us from our lust for
domination and power, and from
the mesmerizing influence of
the cult of the state.

The Book of
Mormon opens up
the portals to principles,
ordinances, and covenants,
that enable us to be sanctified, to
be worthy to live again in a state of
holiness in the presence of our Father in
Heaven. When we're willing to submit to
His will, we'll "continue unceasingly in
the supplicating of his grace", that we
might one day stand before him in
innocence at His Pleasing Bar.
(See Alma 7:3).

The sturdiest plants that
bear the best fruit are those with
deep roots that are anchored in lush,
nurturing soil. The scriptures invite us
to integrate ourselves into a loam that's
rich in art, courtesy, decency, example,
honor, music, and virtue. Their object is
to nurture our spirits to freely flourish
beyond the narrow confines that are
equivalent to a one-pint nursery
container. With the scriptures,
we are able to send down our
taproots into gospel soil
and anchor ourselves
to the Infinite.

Of all the
holy sanctuaries
that have been created
by the benevolent hand of
God to be safe havens from the
insanity of the world, The Book of
Mormon remains as one of the least
understood, reminding us that the
natural man will never receive the
things of the Spirit, for they are
foolishness to him. He cannot
know them, no matter how
hard he tries, for they are
spiritually discerned.
(See 1 Corinthians
2:14).

Not only
the Land of Canaan, but
also many other locations all
over the world, may be thought of as
Lands of Promise. Many groups over the
years left Jerusalem in search of such lands.
(See 1 Nephi 2:20, 5:22, 7:13, 13:14, 2 Nephi
1:9, Alma 37:45, & Ether 2:7, to name a few).
The Dead Sea Covenanters who lived at Qumran
near the shores of the Salt Sea have become the
most conspicuous in our day. But there must
have been many other righteous families
who, over the millennia, were similarly
led by the Spirit amid deteriorating
conditions in Israel to leave, and
to begin life anew in the
wilderness.

The
meager
substitutes
for the rewards
of Book of Mormon
study include wealth,
affluence, authority, style,
influence, position, fashion,
and dominion. When lumped
together, these become the holy
grail to those who engage in a
blind quest for the power and
control that are the contraries
of the sound doctrine that
is illustrated in the
scriptures.

If it's become
our heartfelt desire
to accept The Book of
Mormon as the word of God,
we cannot maintain a vacation
home in Idumea as an intermittent
refuge from our life on the strait and
narrow way. Such diversions will cause
us to lose traction and impede our forward
momentum, derail us from our footing
on gospel sod, and delay our progress
toward our determined destination
that has been envisioned by the
foreknowledge of God.

We're
sanctified
by our Book of
Mormon study. Our
"minds become single
to God, and the days will
come that (we) shall see him;
for he will unveil his face" unto
us. (D&C 88:68). We will no longer
be hobbled by limiting beliefs. "Now
we (only) see through a glass, darkly;
but then face to face; now (we) know
in part; but then (we) shall know
even as also (we are) known."
(1 Corinthinans 13:12).

Our
Redeemer
has gloried in
the possibility, and
even in the probability,
that there will come a day
in the eternities when we will
have progressed to become as He
is. (See Moses 1:39). Thus, He has
blessed us with an endowment that
is described in The Book of Mormon;
specifically, His grace, consisting of
the gifts and power by which we may
be brought to His perfection and His
stature, so we may then enjoy the
blessings that relate to those who
have conformed every aspect of
their lives to the laws of the
Celestial Kingdom. (See
3 Nephi 12:48, and
Moroni 10:32).

The
ability
of The Book
of Mormon to
order our chaotic
world, and to bless
our lives with clarity
rather than confusion;
to simply teach us how to
be fluent in the language
of the Spirit, boggles the
mind and can be life
changing.

There are some
who hope to find
joy as they wander
and play. They don't
consider a key feature of
The Book of Mormon – how
it can embolden us to ponder
and pray, and to analyze and
apply the doctrine and principles
that bring about lasting happiness.
When they've disregarded the counsel
in the scriptures, they might very well
remain in their old habit patterns that
perpetuate their vulnerability to the
enticements of the adversary that
tempt them to ignorantly reject
that which is good and true.

Wherever
and however we may
ultimately fit into the grand
scheme of the cosmos, we do know
this: God quickens life by igniting
our animation within a physical world
with which we may freely interact. He will
"lend (us His) breath, that (we) may live and
move and do according to (our) own will, and
(He will never falter in His determination to
support us) from one moment to another,"
when our burdens seem too heavy for
us to bear. (Mosiah 2:21).

# Seventy Questions Answered by The Book of Mormon

After teaching the Nephites in Bountiful how they might always have the Spirit to be with them, the Lord gave His disciples a key to successfully remembering Him. "Verily, verily," He said to them: "Ye must watch and pray always, lest ye be tempted by the devil, and ye be led away captive by him."
(3 Nephi 18:15).

To the assembled multitude, He then revealed: "For Satan desireth to have you, that he may sift you as wheat. Therefore, ye must always pray unto the Father in my name."
(3 Nephi 18:19).

## To Whom should we pray?

Immediately after teaching the Nephites how to always have the Spirit to be with them, the Lord gave His disciples the key to successfully remembering Him. "Verily, verily," He said to them: "Ye must watch and pray always, lest ye be tempted by the devil, and ye be led away captive by him." (3 Nephi 18:15). To the multitude, He then revealed: "For Satan desireth to have you, that he may sift you as wheat. Therefore, ye must always pray unto the Father in my name." (3 Nephi 18:19).

The Savior is the Standard of Righteousness. He said: "Behold I am the light; I have set an example for you." (3 Nephi 18:16). He urged the Nephites to pray as He did: "Pray in your families unto the Father, always in my name." (3 Nephi 18:21). All were welcome at their meetings, but to the members of the congregation of the faithful, the Savior said: "Ye shall pray for them unto the Father, in my name." (3 Nephi 18:23).

Christ is our Example to follow. When He said: "Let your light so shine before this people that they may see your good works and glorify your Father who is in heaven," He meant that He should be reflected in all that we do, so that when others see our good works, their thoughts will turn to Christ, to Whom belongs the credit. His most pious disciples are not worthy to even unloose the latches of His shoes. (Luke 3:16).

During His brief ministry among the Nephites, Christ gave the glory to His Father. He said: "Behold, ye see that I have prayed unto the Father, and ye all have witnessed." (3 Nephi 18:24). The Lord's Prayer, found in Matthew 6:9-13 and in 3 Nephi 13:9-13, is an example to us all, (see J.S.T. Matthew 6:14), and in chapters 4 and 5 in The Book of Moroni, and in D&C 20:77 & 79, we see that the Sacrament Prayer is addressed to the Father in the name of Jesus Christ. This is the proper form that prayer in general should take, which the Savior reiterated to the Nephites many times. (See 3 Nephi 13:6 & 9, 17:15 & 18, 18:23, 24 & 30, 19:6-8, 20-24 & 26-35, 20:1, & 27:2, 7, & 28). Moroni also reiterated: "Ye shall call on the Father in my name, in mighty prayer; and after ye have done this ye shall have power." (Moroni 2:2).

The Savior Jesus
Christ is our Standard of
Righteousness. "Behold, I am
the light (He said, and) I have
set an example for you."
(3 Nephi 18:16).

Christ gave
the glory to His Father,
saying: "Behold, ye see that I
have prayed unto the Father, and ye
all have witnessed." (3 Nephi 18:24).
Moroni also quoted the counsel of Christ:
"Ye shall call on the Father in my name,
in mighty prayer; and after ye have
done this, ye shall have power."
(Moroni 2:2).

## About what should we pray?

"Cry unto him for mercy; for he is mighty to save. Yea, humble yourselves, and continue in prayer unto him. Cry unto him when ye are in your fields, yea, over all your flocks. Cry unto him in your houses, yea, over all your household, both morning, mid-day, and evening. Yea, cry unto him against the power of your enemies. Yea, cry unto him against the devil, who is an enemy to all righteousness. Cry unto him over the crops of your fields, that ye may prosper in them. Cry over the flocks of your fields, that they may increase. But this is not all; ye must pour out your souls in your closets, and your secret places, and in your wilderness. Yea, and when you do not cry unto the Lord, let your heart be full, drawn out in prayer unto him continually for your welfare, and also for the welfare of those who are around you." (Alma 34:17-27).

Prayer is a way to exercise faith and is a powerful weapon against the devil. Joseph Fielding Smith, Jr. taught: "No man can retain the spirit of the Lord unless he prays." Thus, Paul wrote: "Pray without ceasing." (1 Thessalonians 5:17).

But Amulek cautioned that "after ye have done all these things, if ye turn away the needy, and the naked, and visit not the sick and afflicted, and impart (not) of your substance, if ye have, to those who stand in need, behold your prayer is vain and availeth you nothing, and ye are as hypocrites who do deny the faith." (Alma 34:28).

In His teachings, the Savior warned against pedestrian rhetoric in prayer, and helped His disciples to understand how to keep their prayers free of hypocrisy: "But when ye pray," he cautioned, "use not vain repetitions, as the heathen do: for they think that they shall be heard for their much speaking." (Matthew 6:7).

Something is "in vain" when it is performed without effect, or when it lacks the desired or intended result. For example, to "try in vain" is to try without success. The reason taking the name of the Lord in vain is blasphemous is because it is using His name improperly and without authority. Those who do so are imposters, invoking the name of Deity in a false, misleading, and counterfeit way. This is Satan's approach, in contrast to the righteous use in prayer of the name of God, by the meek and lowly in heart, who are guided by the Spirit.

In His sermons, the Savior warned against the use of pedestrian rhetoric in prayer, and He helped His disciples to understand how to keep themselves free of hypocrisy: "But when ye pray," he cautioned, "use not vain repetitions, as the heathen do, for they think that they shall be heard for their much speaking." (Matthew 6:7, see 3 Nephi 13:7).

Our actions are "in vain" when they are performed without effect, or when they lack the power to bring about an intended result. For example, to "try in vain" is to try without success. The reason taking the name of the Lord in vain is blasphemous is because it is using His name improperly and without authority. Those who attempt to do so are whited sepulchres. They are imposters who invoke the holy name of God in a false, misleading, and counterfeit way.

## Why should we not put off seeking to improve ourselves?

Mortality is a probationary state; it is a learning laboratory where we are given the means to improve ourselves through trial and error. The lynchpin of the Plan, the Atonement of Christ, takes into account our failure to be unswervingly obedient to eternal principles. Therefore, our improvement is inexorably tied to repentance.

"This life is the time for men to prepare to meet God; yea, behold the day of this life is the day for men to perform their labors. And now, as I said unto you before, as ye have had so many witnesses, therefore, I beseech of you that ye do not procrastinate the day of your repentance until the end; for after this day of life, which is given us to prepare for eternity, behold, if we do not improve our time while in this life, then cometh the night of darkness wherein there can be no labor performed." (Alma 34:32-33).

When we procrastinate our repentance, we unwittingly put ourselves in the hands of the adversary, so now is the time to repent. Repentance after death is possible, but gospel doctrine suggests that it is a lot easier for us to do so in mortality. This is the time when we are more pliable and susceptible. When clay is soft it can be molded, but after it has set, it is nigh unto impossible. The last group in the Spirit Prison of the Unjust will be resurrected 1,000 years after the Savior comes, perhaps because the process of repentance will be so much more difficult after this life is over. (See 1 Peter 3:18, & D&C 76:73).

When Amulek characterized life in the spirit prison as a night of darkness wherein there can be no labor performed, he was not saying that repentance is impossible there, but rather that within its cold walls, Justice is so more easily satisfied. When the bargaining chip of the Atonement of Christ is off the table, negotiation with Justice breaks down, meaningful dialogue grinds to a halt, and it is nigh into impossible to obtain mercy. It is when Justice and Mercy cannot reach an accord, that the uttermost farthing must be paid.

President Spencer W. Kimball taught: "It is true that the great principle of repentance is always available, but for the wicked and rebellious there are serious reservations to this statement. As the transgressor moves deeper and deeper in his sin, and his error is entrenched more deeply and the will to change is weakened, it becomes increasingly near hopeless, and he skids down and down until either he does not want to climb back, or he has lost the power to do so." ("The Miracle of Forgiveness," p. 117).

unless we repent, the Spirit of the Lord is withdrawn, and we remain spiritually dead, as if there had been no redemption made. But forgiveness through repentance that is tied to the Atonement is so total and complete that the prophets utilize the vivid imagery of a garment soaked in the redeeming blood of the Savior when describing the process, telling us that, in the miracle of forgiveness, our "garments should be made white through the blood of the Lamb." (Alma 31:36).

## What happens if we persist in wicked behavior?

"Do not suppose, because it has been spoken concerning restoration, that ye shall be restored from sin to happiness. Behold, I say unto you, wickedness never was happiness." (Alma 41:10). As Samuel the Lamanite told the wicked inhabitants of the land of Zarahemla: "Ye have sought all the days of your lives for that which ye could not obtain; and ye have sought for happiness in doing iniquity, which thing is contrary to the nature of that righteousness which is in our great and Eternal Head." (Helaman 13:38).

Moroni taught, "Despair cometh because of iniquity." (Moroni 10:22). Every law has both a blessing and a punishment affixed to it. When the law is obeyed, a blessing is given that results in happiness, or joy. When that law is disobeyed, punishment is meted out that results in unhappiness, or misery. Despair is the feeling of hopelessness that accompanies disobedience.

As Alma explained: "All men that are in a state of nature, or I would say, in a carnal state, are in the gall of bitterness and in the bonds of iniquity; they are without God in the world, and they have gone contrary to the nature of God; therefore, they are in a state contrary to the nature of happiness." (Alma 41:11). The Savior taught that if we lack vision, and build "upon the works of men, or upon the works of the devil, verily I say unto you they have joy in their works for a season, and by and by the end cometh, and they are hewn down and cast into the fire, from whence there is no return." (3 Nephi 27:11).

"Do not suppose," Alma taught his son Corianton, "because it has been spoken concerning restoration, that ye shall be restored from sin to happiness. Behold, I say unto you, wickedness never was happiness." (Alma 41:10). Samuel the Lamanite explained to the unrighteous inhabitants in Zarahemla: "Ye have sought all the days of your lives for that which ye could not obtain. Ye have sought for happiness in doing iniquity, which thing is contrary to the nature of that righteousness which is in our great and Eternal Head." (Helaman 13:38).

Alma explained: "All men that are in a state of nature, or I would say, in a carnal state, are in the gall of bitterness and in the bonds of iniquity. They are without God in the world, and they have gone contrary to the nature of God; therefore, they are in a state contrary to the nature of happiness." (Alma 41:11).

## How can we tell the difference between good and evil?

"It is given unto you to judge, that ye may know good from evil; and the way to judge is as plain, that ye may know with a perfect knowledge, as the daylight is from the dark night. For behold, the Spirit of Christ is given to every man, that he may know good from evil; wherefore, I show unto you the way to judge; for every thing which inviteth to do good, and to persuade to believe in Christ, is sent forth by the power and gift of Christ; wherefore ye may know with a perfect knowledge it is of God. But whatsoever thing persuadeth men to do evil, and believe not in Christ, and deny him, and serve not God, then ye may know with a perfect knowledge it is of the devil; for after this manner doth the devil work, for he persuadeth no man to do good, no, not one; neither do his angels; neither do they who subject themselves unto him." (Moroni 7:17).

Considering the wicked state of the Nephite nation at the time that Mormon was addressing the congregation in the synagogue, perhaps the Light of Christ was the sole source of their spiritual direction. "And now, my brethren, seeing that ye know the light by which ye may judge, which light is the light of Christ, see that ye do not judge wrongfully; for with that same judgment which ye judge ye shall also be judged." (Moroni 7:18).

It seems that he was speaking to those who had not entered into covenants with God or who had received the gift of the Holy Ghost. "Wherefore, I beseech of you, brethren, that ye should search diligently in the light of Christ that ye may know good from evil." (Moroni 7:19). Mormon promised: "If ye will lay hold upon every good thing, and condemn it not, ye certainly will be a child of Christ." (Moroni 7:19). There are no shades of grey for those who have received the ordinances of the Priesthood of God. Members of the church have not only the Light of Christ, but also the greater light and knowledge given by the Holy Ghost.

Moroni 2:2 confirms that if we respond to the Light of Christ, we will be led to the Holy Ghost and will receive it as an ordinance of the gospel. The Holy Ghost is only given through obedience to gospel principles. "The Holy Ghost is a personage in the Godhead, and is not that which lighteth every man that comes into the world, which is the Spirit of God which proceeds through Christ to the world, that enlightens every man that comes into the world, and that strives with the children of men until it brings them to a knowledge of the truth and the possession of the greater light and testimony of the Holy Ghost." (Joseph F. Smith).

"It is given
unto you to judge,"
Mormon explained, "that
ye may know good from evil;
and the way to judge is as plain,
that ye may know with a perfect
knowledge, as the daylight is
from the dark night."
(Moroni 7:17).

Moroni 2:2 confirms that
if we respond to the Light of
Christ, we will be guided
to the Holy Ghost.

After considering these 70 questions that are answered in The Book of Mormon, take a moment to ponder any or all of these 20 thoughts:

After carefully observing for a period time the stellar conduct of members of The Church of Jesus Christ of Latter-day Saints, the 19th Century Russian author Leo Tolstoy was moved to declare: "If only Mormonism could be true to its foundations and remain unchanged for four generations, it might well become the most powerful social influence in the world." (Reportedly in an exchange with Andrew White, President of Cornell University).

The Book of Mormon is the loom upon which we busily weave the tapestry of our lives, as we create our own coats of many colors. But central to the vitalization and execution of our efforts is detailed instruction that comes from above, in the form of personalized guidance from the Master Tailor Himself, as well as from those who serve as His seamstresses on the earth.

The Book of Mormon
unambiguously teaches us
that our Heavenly Father is the
Grand Architect of the cosmos. His
divine design establishes our familial
roots and confirms His Fatherhood, that
we might enjoy a witness that it is in Him
alone that "we live, and move, and have our
being; as certain also of (our) own poets have
said ... we are also his offspring." (Acts 17:28).
When we seek to understand ourselves from an
eternal perspective, as the sons and daughters
of God, we raise our sights to the possibility
of an expanded view of life, and we are up
and moving forward along the pathway
that leads to religious re-cognition
and personal re-discovery.

The fire
that was kindled
on Sinai burned all
the way from the earth
"unto the midst of heaven"
itself. (Deuteronomy 4:11).
Those who'd witnessed this
manifestation imagined
they could see through a
brilliant conduit into
eternity itself. So it
is, as we leaf thru
each chapter of
The Book of
Mormon.

Because
the messages of
The Book of Mormon
can only be spiritually
discerned, its mysteries will
forever be unfathomable to those
with unenlightened minds, whose
lifestyles are defined by sensual
and carnal preoccupations. Its
rituals are of no interest to
those whose only desire is
the sensual titillation
of telestial trivia.

The Book of Mormon
serves as a fitness manual for
all who are poor in spirit. Its workout
program may be rigorous, and is sacred,
but it is not a secret. If it suggests shadowy
rituals to the uninitiated, that may be because
it was translated from a foreign language that
had never been subjected to the curriculum of
the ivory towers of academia. Much of its
liturgy is inarticulate and inaudible,
and can only be heard when we
listen attentively to the
Holy Ghost.

The
Book
of Mormon
nudges us off
our complacency
plateaus as we steer
away from the trendy
cafés situated along the
broad avenues of Idumea.
We are lifted as on the wings
of eagles, beyond the detours of
our self-imposed limitations, to a
familiar highway that was created
by our Father to conduct us all the
way to heaven, where a foreordained
rendezvous with destiny awaits
each of us.

It would be naive to
expect the teachings of The
Book of Mormon to deliver us
from consequences. They provide
no protection from poor choices, show
no leniency to those who have permitted
themselves to be mesmerized by mediocre
performance, and allow no justification
for rationalization. Because they refuse
to be taught by the Spirit, those whose
only desire its theological titillation
are forbidden by the Holy Ghost to
trespass upon the sacred ground
upon which the foundations
of The Book of Mormon
have been laid.

It was thru His prophet Isaiah that the Lord declared: "I will proceed to do a marvellous work among this people, even a marvellous work and a wonder. For the wisdom of their wise men shall perish, and the understanding of their prudent men shall be hid." (Isaiah 29:4, see 2 Nephi 9:43).

If we listen exceedingly carefully as we read The Book of Mormon, we can almost hear the gentle rustling of angels' wings coming from behind a slightly-parted veil. A company of beings from the unseen world will sweep the cobwebs from our minds, and open up to our view undreamed of vistas of otherwise inaccessible experience.

The doctrine of Christ that is found in The Book of Mormon provides the mortar that holds together the bricks forming the parapets of the Celestial Kingdom. A sense of 'forever families' grounds us to mortality, while anchoring us to the Infinite, blessing us with a perspective that is eternal. Families that are bound together by covenants made with God provide a much needed longitudinal perspective in those societies where just about everything, including relationships, is increasingly disposable. But if there's been no deposit made, we can be pretty sure there will be no expectation of a return.

By making covenants with God, we can break the bands of death, and we are made free to enjoy His grace. "There is no other name given whereby salvation cometh," said Benjamin; "therefore, I would that ye should take upon you the name of Christ, all you that have entered into the covenant with God." (Mosiah 5:8).

In our busy and complex world, we habitually see through a glass darkly. This makes it very difficult to discern how to harness the energy of the elusive equations that are found within the mathematics of The Book of Mormon.

The Book of Mormon emphasizes that profound obedience and our recurring repentance liberate us from the bondage of sin, and qualify us by worthiness to enjoy the blessings of heaven. The Atonement of Jesus Christ allows us to overcome our limitations, while unleashing the powers of heaven in our behalf. It shatters the bands of death, and throws wide open the gates of the Celestial Kingdom itself.

The marvelous principles of the Plan of Salvation are stitched into nearly every page of The Book of Mormon. Without the illumination that is provided by their patterns, we would be doomed to suffer in shadows where we would experience only an indistinct flicker of reality's illusions. The disparity between the marginalized behavior of the worldly and the ideals expressed within that body of scripture are readily apparent. It has been masterfully addressed by the covenants it urges us to make as we stand before God, angels, and holy witnesses.

The direct frontal assault that is being made by the adversary on the divine principles espoused by The Book of Mormon utilizes mutated forms of honor, truth, love, goodwill, and virtue. These dreadful distortions of character are composed of bellicose behavior and hostile habits, cunning customs, recalcitrant rituals, duplicitous deviations, sneaky social conventions, insincere institutions, not to mention treacherous telestial traditions. These fiery darts can sabotage our best efforts to embrace the truth.

The virtue of The Book of Mormon is its ability to touch our hearts, to change our nature, to soften us, and to humble us, to make us as pliant clay in the hands of the Master Potter, to mold us as children, and then to comfortably envelop us within the happiness that has been prepared for the Saints of God who are the spiritual offspring of His Only Begotten Son.

We will inherit perfected bodies in the resurrection that are bonded with our spirits, never again to be separated. "The spirit and the body shall be reunited again in its perfect form; both limb and joint shall be restored to its proper frame." (Alma 11:43). Therefore, our bodies must be kept as pure and as holy as are our spirits, that the gospel may bless our lives, not only now, but also through all eternity, as has been envisioned by our Father Who is in Heaven.

By the time we
rather unexpectedly encounter
the promise that is made in Moroni
10:4, near the conclusion of The Book of
Mormon, we are prepared to act. We sense the
expansion of God's powers, as the glittering
facets of the life of the Spirit wash over us.
Quiet stirrings that penetrate to our very
core will propel us into the company of
beings from the unseen world, Who
will instill within us fire
for the deed.

The enemy of
all righteousness finally
betrays his followers because
they can only oppose the covenant
consciousness of those who've embraced
The Book of Mormon for so long before his
cunning caresses lead them into conceptual
cul-de-sacs and doctrinal dead-ends from which
all possible exits lead to uncertainty, ambiguity,
doubt, confusion, hesitancy, and a retreat that
will plunge them headlong into a perceived
freedom that, on closer inspection, is a
bottomless pit of misery.

# Seventy-Five Questions Answered in The Book of Mormon

Simply put: "Wickedness never was happiness." (Alma 41:10). When people do not believe in satanic opposition, and doggedly try to buy their way into happiness, they may be particularly vulnerable to depression and melancholy, which are the very things they seek so desperately to avoid.

As a contrary, opposition is a necessary condition of our happiness, but it can be overpowering when it lacks the tempering influence of our obedience to gospel principles. When we feverishly attempt to homogenize our mortal experiences by overzealously trying to smooth out all their rough edges, if our efforts lack the stabilizing influences of the Spirit and we ignore the guidance of the Plan, we just may inadvertently be neutralizing the very things that would have most significantly contributed to our joy.

## What happens when people do not believe in satanic opposition?

Simply put: "Wickedness never was happiness." (Alma 41:10). When people don't believe in Satanic opposition, and doggedly try to buy their way into happiness, they may be particularly vulnerable to depression and melancholy. These are the very things they seek so desperately to avoid.

Opposition is necessary to happiness, but it can be overpowering without the tempering influence of obedience to gospel principles. If we attempt to homogenize our mortal experiences by smoothing out all the rough edges without the stabilizing influence of the Spirit and of obedience to the Plan, we may inadvertently be neutralizing the very things that would have contributed most significantly to our happiness.

If we have only a one-dimensional view of life, without the eternal perspective of the Plan of Happiness, and without including a gospel-oriented perspective on the principle of opposition in all things, we might find ourselves running to and fro and never coming to a knowledge of the truth. We will come face to face with the stark reality that wickedness never was happiness. Distorted perceptions may influence us to use mind-altering drugs in a desperate attempt to recalibrate with reality. Chemicals cooked up in a meth lab will definitely change our perception, but endorphins stemming from obedience to gospel principles constitute a better choice.

Happiness can stem from want. The gospel invites us to consider that fruited orchards, vineyards laden with plump grapes, and well-watered gardens exist somewhere beyond the hills of time. If we continually glut ourselves, however, in order to experience gratification, we will eventually diminish our capacity for enjoyment. Progressively greater enhancements will be required for the same level of satisfaction. Perhaps this is why happiness cannot be found in serial relationships that focus on physical attraction that has a distorted emotional connection. As with the adulterer, greater and greater stimulation will be necessary to achieve the same level of excitement, until there is a final retreat into the hollow core of oneself, and that is a very lonely place.

Those who have only
nurtured a one-dimensional view of
life that lacks both the eternal perspective
of the Plan of Happiness and a gospel-oriented
perspective relating to the principle of opposition
in all things, might find themselves running
to and fro, but never come to a knowledge of
the truth. They will come face to face with
the stark reality that wickedness
never was happiness.

It is important to remember that our happiness can
stem from want. The gospel invites us to consider that fruited
orchards, vineyards laden with plump grapes, and well-watered gardens
exist somewhere beyond the hills of time. If we continually glut ourselves,
however, in order to experience gratification, we will eventually diminish
our capacity for enjoyment. Progressively greater enhancements will
be required for the same level of satisfaction. Perhaps this is why
happiness cannot be found in serial relationships that focus
our attention on physical attraction that has a distorted
emotional connection. As with the adulterer, greater
and greater stimulation will be necessary to
achieve the same level of anticipation and
excitement, until we beat a final and
disorganized retreat into the hollow
core of ourselves, and that can
be a very lonely place.

## Can those who are wicked be happy?

"All men that are in a state of nature, or I would say, in a carnal state, are in the gall of bitterness and in the bonds of iniquity; they are without God in the world, and they have gone contrary to the nature of God; therefore, they are in a state contrary to the nature of happiness." (Alma 41:11).

One of the greatest challenges faced by our society is the insatiable desire for pleasure, immediate gratification, and repetitive waves of greater and greater stimulation. We are frustrated by the limitations of our RAM, the horsepower of our automobiles, the capacity of our iPods, the features of our cell phones, and the speed of our micro-processors. We have only a dim recollection of operator assistance, two-lane country roads, sipping lemonade on a lazy summer afternoon while seated in a rocker on the front porch, typewriters, and erasable-bond paper.

As society demands an escalating array of telestial toys to maintain a false standard of comfort and entertainment, we are blinded to the sobering comparison to a heroin addict's progressive tolerance and destructive reliance on his own false gods of wood and stone.

In the Twenty First Century, too many of us "tend to fill space, as if what we have, what we are, is not enough. Being affluent, we strangle ourselves with what we can buy, things whose opacity obstructs our ability see what is really there." (Gretel Erlich, Under Wyoming Skies, Atlantic Magazine).

"All men that are in a state of nature, or I would say, in a carnal state, are in the gall of bitterness and in the bonds of iniquity; they are without God in the world, and they have gone contrary to the nature of God; therefore, they are in a state contrary to the nature of happiness."
(Alma 41:11).

As our society demands an escalating array of telestial toys to maintain a false standard of comfort and entertainment, we are blinded to the sobering comparison to a heroin addict's progressive tolerance of and destructive reliance upon his own false gods of wood and stone.

## What can happen when we are subjected to negative peer pressure?

"There were many of the rising generation that could not understand the words of king Benjamin, being little children at the time he spake unto his people; and they did not believe the tradition of their fathers." (Mosiah 26:1).

In the Land of Zarahemla, there were many young people who were sorely tempted, yielded to Satan's influences, and who then fell into apostasy. As Brigham Young said, "Though our children are begotten in righteousness, and brought forth in holiness, they must be tried and tempted, for they are agents before our Father, the same as you or I." It is inevitable that some will stumble as they make their way along the path leading to the Tree of Life.

The order in which their difficulties were enumerated is significant. Because of unbelief, they could not understand the word of God. This resulted in spiritual sclerosis, or a hardening of their hearts. As a result, they would not hearken to the commandment to be baptized and to join the church, or if they were already members, they would not remain on the covenant path.

They also had become cultural Lamanites. They had committed sins that required repentance, but they could not muster the faith necessary to call upon God, which is the pathway leading to forgiveness. Therefore, they were in a tailspin, spiraling downward in a sustained stall from which it became increasingly difficult to regain control.

Perhaps, they had fallen in with the wrong crowd. Benjamin warned his people: "this much I can tell you, that if ye do not watch yourselves, and your thoughts, and your words, and your deeds, and observe the commandments of God, and continue in the faith of what ye have heard concerning the coming of our Lord, even unto the end of your lives, ye must perish." (Mosiah 4:30).

In the Land of Zarahemla, there were many young people who were sorely tempted, yielded to Satan's influences, and who then fell into apostasy. As Brigham Young said: "Though our children are begotten in righteousness, and brought forth in holiness, they must be tried and tempted, for they are agents before our Father, the same as you or I." It is inevitable that some will stumble, as they make their way along the path leading to the Tree of Life.

"This much I can tell you, that if ye do not watch yourselves, and your thoughts, and your words, and your deeds, and observe the commandments of God, and continue in the faith of what ye have heard concerning the coming of our Lord, even unto the end of your lives, ye must perish."
(Mosiah 4:30).

## How can we take our stewardship responsibilities more seriously?

Moroni wrote of "great pollutions upon the face of the earth." (Mormon 8:31). He was referring, not so much to industrial or environmental pollutions, but rather to those qualities that canker our souls and corrupt the expression of the Spirit. It is interesting that Moroni would call our attention to "pollution" in a day when it is fashionable to have an "environmental awareness," but when it is also common for many to ignore even the most basic principles of decency and morality, which are conditions that are far more dangerous than our carbon footprint.

In this context, it is worth retelling the story of "reconverted Mormon, Jesse Knight, (who) as a center for the operation of his silver mines (in the late Nineteenth Century) built a town unique in the world of mining. At his own expense, and in a sense of gratitude, he built a chapel and an attractive cultural hall. He set up evening activities, lively and enlightening enough to compete with, and often to defeat, the fleshpots in a nearby place called Eureka. He established a school, hired a first-rate teacher, taxed every miner to contribute to its operation, and kept the town spotless. He sponsored lectures, concerts, town dances, basketball games, and socials. Meantime, he paid his men more than the prevailing wage, closed down the operation on the Sabbath, and fired any man who would not leave alcohol alone. His accumulated fortune ended up saving the credit of the church and substantially underwriting the beginnings of the huge enterprise now known as Brigham Young University." (Truman Madsen, "Defender of The Faith," p. 64-65).

Jesse Knight understood the concept of stewardship responsibility, and he used the principles of the gospel taught in The Book of Mormon to make a difference within the sphere of his influence.

Moroni wrote about "great pollutions upon the face of the earth" in the latter days. He was probably referring, not so much to industrial or environmental effluents, but instead to the more insidious toxic waste that cankers our souls and corrupts the expression of the Spirit. (Mormon 8:31).

When, from an eternal perspective, we understand the concept of stewardship responsibility, we will use the principles of the gospel that are explained in The Book of Mormon to make a difference within the sphere of our influence.

## How can we become powerful missionaries with testimonies of the divinity of Christ?

"Alma did rejoice exceedingly to see his brethren; and what added more to his joy, they were still his brethren in the Lord; yea, and they had waxed strong in the knowledge of the truth; for they were men of a sound understanding and they had searched the scriptures diligently, that they might know the word of God. But this is not all; they had given themselves to much prayer, and fasting; therefore, they had the spirit of prophecy, and the spirit of revelation, and when they taught, they taught with power and authority of God." (Alma 17:2-3).

It must have seemed altogether remarkable to Alma that his highest and best hopes for the welfare of his brethren were now confirmed. As he learned the details of their experiences during the fourteen long years of their mission to the Lamanites in the Land of Nephi, he must have recognized and appreciated the unchangeable formula for success.

The scriptures had become their message and were the tools of their trade. Their confidence was directly related to their knowledge of God's word, and they had endured and conquered every obstacle that had been thrown in their path. "God help all honest men and women," said Marion G. Romney, "to be born again and come to be of sound understanding and to know the word of God and maintain the spirit thereof by study, fasting, prayer, and work, that we may be blessed with His power and authority!" (C.R., 10/1941).

"Who shall ascend into the hill of the Lord?" asked David. "Or who shall stand in his holy place? He that hath clean hands, and a pure heart; who hath not lifted up his soul unto vanity, nor sworn deceitfully. He shall receive the blessing from the Lord, and righteousness from the God of his salvation." (Psalms 24:3-5).

It must have given the prophet-historian Mormon a great deal of satisfaction to make a report concerning the missionary success of the Sons of Mosiah among the Lamanites in the Land of Nephi: "Now these sons of Mosiah were with Alma at the time the angel first appeared unto him; therefore, Alma did rejoice exceedingly to see his brethren; and what added more to his joy, they were still his brethren in the Lord; yea, and they had waxed strong in the knowledge of the truth; for they were men of a sound understanding and they had searched the scriptures diligently, that they might know the word of God. But this is not all; they had given themselves to much prayer, and fasting; therefore, they had the spirit of prophecy, and the spirit of revelation, and when they taught, they taught with the power and authority of God."
(Alma 17:2-3).

It must have seemed altogether remarkable to Alma that his highest and best hopes for the welfare of his brethren were now confirmed. As he learned the details of their experiences during the fourteen long years of their mission to the Lamanites in the Land of Nephi, he must have recognized and appreciated God's unchangeable formula for success.

After considering these 75 questions that are answered in The Book of Mormon, take a moment to ponder any or all of these 20 thoughts:

"The Book of Mormon will change your life. It will fortify you against the evils of our day and will bring a spirituality into your life that no other book can. It will be the most important book you will read in preparation for life."
(Ezra Taft Benson).

The Book of Mormon will test the mettle of our convictions. Through our repentance, we'll put our money where our mouth is, but we have no proof until we act on the basis of trust. Then, comes the confirmation of the reality, as feelings of self-confidence grow and purposeful action replaces tentative overtures. In sum, we let go, and we let our Father guide us as He promised to do before we left our heavenly home.

Our sphere of wisdom expands when we're under the influence of the Spirit as we study The Book of Mormon. But so, too, will the perimeters of darkness. The more we know, the more we'll need to learn. It should do no violence to our faith if we realize that, with a greater understanding of truth, we will surely have additional questions that we'll wish to ponder, even those matters that relate to mysteries of the kingdom.

"Thou shalt be brought down, and shall speak out of the ground, and thy speech shall be low out of the dust, and thy voice shall be as one that hath a familiar spirit, out of the ground, and they speech shall whisper out of the dust." (Isaiah 29:4, see 2 Nephi 26:16).

Mighty testimonies from The Book of Mormon reintroduce us to the power of the Atonement, that can save us from our natural state of carnality, sensuality, and devilish inclinations. It activates the Law of Mercy, which mitigates for those who conform to its requirements the effects of the first Law, which demands justice. It lifts us to a state of holiness, spirituality, angelic innocence, and happiness, and prepares us to feel comfortable in the celestial precincts where we will find ourselves one more time in the presence of angels who are softly singing heavenly lullabies that communicate only love. The Holy Ghost will be there as well, to welcome us home; to personally re-introduce Himself, and to bear His witness to the Father of that which He has both seen and heard during our sojourn on the earth.

If we are ever to obtain our exaltation and eternal life, we need to do more than simply acknowledge that Jesus Christ is Lord. The Book of Mormon makes it abundantly clear that the critical point of conversion, beyond which lie encircling flames in the Celestial Kingdom of God, rests in making the conscious decision to not only accept Jesus Christ as a Great Teacher and our Master, but also to accept the responsibility to be obedient by covenant to each and every one of His pointedly specific commandments.

The Book of
Mormon extends to
each of us an invitation
to consider the possibility
that we might one day be like
our Savior. We believe that His
grace consists of the gifts and
power by which we might be
brought to His perfection
and stature, so that we
may enjoy what He
has and is.

The Book of Mormon
puts a finishing touch on
mortality as it introduces us
to a larger view of life. It smooths
out the rough edges that are created
as we bump, grind, and lurch along
the rocky road of experience. It puts in
perspective our trials and tribulations,
while addressing questions we had never
before thought to ask. Our troubled spirits
are calmed by it's quiet influence, that we
might more easily comprehend the rolling
thunder heralding the close proximity of
the mysteries of God's kingdom. The
injunction to "be still and know
that I am God" takes on new
meaning. (Psalms
46:10).

Within the
pages of The Book
of Mormon, our Father
in Heaven encourages in
earnest our preparations for
immortality. It is there that our
eyes are really opened, our vision
is perfected, and we are taught how
to raise our sight so that it rests above
the artificial horizon of mortality. It is
there that we steal our first fleeting look
at the wonders of eternity, and where we
realize that it is in heavenly precincts
where our future really lies.

While it certainly
teaches basic economic,
social, behavioral, political,
and earth sciences, The Book of
Mormon does this in creative ways
that are alien to the understanding of
spiritual Babylon. To paraphrase King
Benjamin, the book is where we go to open
our ears to hear, our hearts to understand,
and our minds to feel the all-encompassing
love of God, so that the wonders of eternity
might be unfolded to our view and spread
out in a breathtaking panorama
of cosmic proportion.

Sacred covenants are the binding contracts that we make with God, and so they are received through revelation. No individual who has studied The Book of Mormon enters into such covenants except on the basis of direct revelation from Deity. It follows that the only ones who can legitimately make a covenant are those who humble themselves to participate in sacred ordinances that are designed to ratify these promises in a revelatory way, and to bring us back into His presence, and that of His Son, and of the Holy Ghost.

If we foolishly think to seek "all the days of (our) lives for that which (we) cannot obtain, and ... have sought for happiness in doing iniquity, which thing is contrary to the nature of that righteousness which is in our great and Eternal Head," we must face the consequences. (Helaman 13:38). It is then, under the most difficult circumstances imaginable, that the uttermost farthing must be paid to satisfy the demands of Justice, so the required reformation of character might finally take place.

The Book
of Mormon
confirms that all
who chose the Plan
of our Father in Heaven
when it was explained to
them in their pre-mortal life
now follow in the footsteps of
Adam and Eve. In mortality,
we all have opportunities to
make similar choices. We
have freedom to exercise
our moral agency in
ways that couldn't
be duplicated
elsewhere.

Our efforts to describe
our Heavenly Father utilize
abstractions, for thoughts cannot
be shaped, nor words formed, that could
accurately characterize His glory. We use
figures of speech because we would otherwise
find ourselves at a complete loss for words when
seeking even a basic understanding of profound
metaphysical realities. Thus, we can only gain
a testimony of The Book of Mormon if, in an
attitude of heartfelt prayer, we've invited the
Spirit to lift the latch and force the way.
This is one of those cases where there
is nowhere to turn but to heaven
for the help we need. (See 1
Corinthinans 13:11).

Those who have gained a testimony of the divine origin of The Book of Mormon will accept Jesus Christ, enter the fold thru the covenant of baptism, and receive the Holy Ghost. They will make a conscious determination to serve God while enduring to the end of their days in righteousness.

The blessings of The Book of Mormon are within reach of each of us, no matter our cultural, social, political, economic, or religious circumstances. The principles that testify of their universal accessibility are supported by other scriptures, and are buttressed by the affirmations that are found in the parable of the Prodigal Son, that our Heavenly Father is no respecter of persons. (See Luke 15).

The Book of Mormon is the whole enchilada and the complete package. It describes the depth, breadth, majesty, and capacity of our Heavenly Father to encircle all of His children within His warm embrace. As the poet wrote, so does The Book of Mormon affirm: "He scribed a circle that drew me out. Heretic, rebel, a thing to flout! But love and I had the wit to win. We scribed a circle that drew him in."

Those who rely more on their economic security than upon spiritual preparedness are more inclined in times of crisis to grasp at straws instead of rededicating themselves to the proven principles that are taught in The Book of Mormon. Those who put their trust in idea gods have no-where to look for help when hot winds of change melt the triple scoop cones of their misplaced faith in the flavor of the day.

As we devour
The Book of Mormon, we
will be caught up in a rapture
where we can almost hear legions
of angels confirming that the earth
was designed from before its foundation
to be a machine for the making of gods. We
are strangers from a realm of light, who have
forgotten all, the memory of our former life, and
the purpose of our call. And so we need to listen
to the Spirit, to learn who we really are, and
why we're here on earth. As we do so, the
stage will be set for the heaven-sent
reawakening of magical
memories.

Our faith in the divine
Plan of our Father in Heaven is
confirmed by our acceptance of The
Book of Mormon as holy scripture. It is
there where we learn how to return to His
kingdom after we have grown up unto
the Lord, have spiritually matured,
and have recognized that the
basis of our hope lies in
His Atonement.

# Eighty Questions Answered by The Book of Mormon

"Many of the Gentiles shall say: A Bible! A Bible! We have got a Bible, and there cannot be any more Bible." (2 Nephi 29:3). In 1974, President Spencer W. Kimball wrote: "I am positive that the blessings of the Lord will attend every country which opens its gates to the gospel of Christ. Their blessings will flow in education, and culture, and faith, and love. There will come prosperity to the nations, comfort and luxuries to the people, joy and peace to all recipients, and eternal life to those who will accept and magnify" its teachings.

In the half-century since President Kimball made that prophetic statement, significant changes have taken place in the world, as the gospel is being taken to nearly every nation, kindred, tongue, and people. The stone cut out of the mountain is rolling over the earth, and it cannot be stopped, although Satan is trying his best to do so. Heavenly Father always keeps His promises, while the Adversary was a liar from the beginning.

## Why does the Church send missionaries to Christian nations?

"Many of the Gentiles shall say: A Bible! A Bible! We have got a Bible, and there cannot be any more Bible." (2 Nephi 29:3). In 1974, President Spencer W. Kimball wrote: "I am positive that the blessings of the Lord will attend every country which opens its gates to the gospel of Christ. Their blessings will flow in education, and culture, and faith, and love. There will come prosperity to the nations, comfort and luxuries to the people, joy and peace to all recipients, and eternal life to those who will accept and magnify it." ("When The World Will Be Converted," Ensign, 10/1974).

In the half century since President Kimball made this prophetic statement, significant changes have taken place in the world, as the gospel is being taken to virtually every nation, kindred, tongue, and people. The stone cut out of the mountain is rolling over the whole earth, and it cannot be stopped. Heavenly Father always keeps His promises.

It will be as it was on the Day of Pentecost, when Peter and the other apostles were preaching to a multitude whose hearts and minds were open and receptive to the truth. Their words carried the weight of authority and penetrated the hearts of their listeners, prompting them to ask Peter: "Men and brethren, what shall we do? Then Peter said unto them, Repent, and be baptized every one of you in the name of Jesus Christ for the remission of sins, and ye shall receive the gift of the Holy Ghost." (Acts 2:37-38). On that day, there were about 3,000 souls added to the kingdom of God on earth.

A similar situation exists today. Since the Restoration of the gospel, there has been a Pentecostal outpouring of the Spirit, and those with a sincere desire to understand the will of God bring to the missionaries the same humble petition: "Now that we have heard your message, and have successfully put it to the test of prayerful inquiry, what shall we do?" The appropriate response is a demonstration of faith that leads to the waters of baptism, continuing commitment, dedicated discipleship, selfless service, and sustained spirituality.

The time is at hand when it will be as it was on the Day of Pentecost, when Peter and the other apostles were preaching to a multitude whose hearts and minds were open and receptive to truth. Their words carried the weight of authority and penetrated the hearts of their listeners, prompting them to ask Peter: "Men and brethren, what shall we do? Then Peter said unto them, Repent, and be baptized every one of you in the name of Jesus Christ for the remission of sins, and ye shall receive the gift of the Holy Ghost." (Acts 2:37-38). On that day, there were about 3,000 souls added to the kingdom of God on earth.

The same scenario exists today. Since the Restoration of the gospel, there has been a Pentecostal outpouring of the Spirit, and those with a sincere desire to understand the will of God bring to the missionaries the same humble petition: "Now that we have heard your message, and have successfully put it to the test of prayerful inquiry, what shall we do?" The appropriate response illustrates a demonstration of faith that will lead to the waters of baptism, and to continuing commitment, dedicated discipleship, selfless service, and sustained spirituality.

### What of those who are ashamed to take upon themselves the name of Jesus Christ?

Moroni asked that very question: "Why are ye ashamed to take upon you the name of Christ?" (Mormon 8:38). He knew that there is no room for summer soldiers or sunshine patriots in the missionary army of God. Only as our own testimonies reach the same intensity as Moroni's faith, will our conversion enable us to understand the penetrating nature of his question. B.H. Roberts taught that if you feel a thing, you can express it. If you can't, you do not feel it strongly enough. "Once, in a sermon delivered in Logan, Utah, he described Christ and the raising of Lazarus. So vivid were his images, and so moving his presence, that the audience was carried with him. When, in a loud voice, he repeated the Master's words, 'Lazarus, come forth!', the entire congregation involuntarily came to its feet." (Truman Madsen, "Defender of The Faith," p. 355). From The Book of Mormon, we can almost hear Moroni imploring each of us to come to our feet in defense of our witness of the Savior.

Moroni asked a similar question: "Why are ye ashamed to take upon you the name of Christ?" (Mormon 8:38). He knew that there is no room for summer soldiers or sunshine patriots in the missionary army of God.

From The Book of Mormon, we can almost hear Moroni imploring each of us to leap to our feet in defense of our witness of the Savior.

### How does The Book of Mormon fulfil the prophecy of Ezekiel?

Because of The Book of Mormon, we have a Second Witness of Christ, we learn to rely on Him not only as our protector but also as the generator of life itself, we have a standard by which we can judge the Bible, we have a weapon more powerful than military might, we have clear definitions of authority, the essential ordinance of baptism is re-defined, the army of God is equipped with superior firepower as it teaches the nations, from a unique perspective the missionaries confidently and strategically preach the gospel, and we can draw upon the life experiences of others and learn life-lessons from their similar challenges.

The words of Christ were to be made known in The Book of Mormon, as well as in the Bible," and they were to be "established in one." (1 Nephi 13:41). As Ezekiel wrote: "Take thee one stick, and write upon it, For Judah, and for the children of Israel his companions: then take another stick, and write upon it, For Joseph, the stick of Ephraim, and for all the house of Israel his companions. And join them one to another into one stick; and they shall become one in thine hand." (Ezekiel 37:16-17).

Without The Book of Mormon, we would lack a Second Testament and perhaps the best witness of Jesus Christ. "For behold, (The Book of Mormon) is written for the intent that ye may believe (the Bible); and if ye believe (the Bible) ye will believe (The Book of Mormon) also; and if ye believe (The Book of Mormon) ye will know concerning your fathers, and also the marvelous works which were wrought by the power of God among them." (Mormon 7:9).

"And now, I would commend you to seek this Jesus of whom the prophets and apostles have written, that the grace of God the Father, and also the Lord Jesus Christ, and the Holy Ghost, which beareth record of them, may be and abide in you forever." (Moroni speaking in Ether 12:41).

It is because of The Book of Mormon that we have a
most powerful Second Witness of Jesus Christ. We learn to rely
upon Him not only as our protector but also as the generator of life
itself; we have a standard by which we can judge the Bible; we have a
weapon more powerful than military might; we have clear definitions
of authority; the essential ordinance of baptism is re-defined; the
army of God is equipped with superior firepower as it teaches
the nations; missionaries confidently and strategically
preach the gospel from its unique perspective, and
its readers draw upon the life experiences of
others to learn life-lessons from their
similar challenges.

The words
of Jesus Christ are made
known in The Book of Mormon,
as well as in the Bible," and in these
two volumes they have been "established in
one." (1 Nephi 13:41). As Ezekiel wrote: "Take
thee one stick, and write upon it, for Judah, and
for the children of Israel his companions: then take
another stick, and write upon it, for Joseph, the stick of
Ephraim, and for all the house of Israel his companions.
And join them one to another into one stick; and
they shall become one in thine hand."
(Ezekiel 37:16-17).

## How can we be more charitable?

Charity is built upon the foundation of faith and hope, and is the supreme characteristic of the disciples of Christ. Mormon taught "if a man be meek and lowly in heart, and confess by the power of the Holy Ghost that Jesus is the Christ," with a sure hope born of faith, "he must needs have charity." (Moroni 7:44).

"Charity suffereth long (or is the quality of patience from the perspective of God toward people and circumstances), and is kind (or is characterized by sensitivity toward others, and is empathic), and envieth not (or is less concerned with telestial trinkets and more focused on celestial sureties), and is not puffed up, (or is humble), seeketh not her own (or is selfless), is not easily provoked (but reflects poise under provocation), thinketh no evil (or has no secret agenda to follow), and rejoiceth not in iniquity (but is repulsed by sin), but rejoiceth in the truth, beareth all things, believeth all things, hopeth all things, endureth all things (or is drawn toward the light, and is continually open to that which is good)." (Moroni 7:45).

Without these qualities, we are nothing, because our progression stops. "If ye have not charity, ye are nothing, for charity never faileth. Wherefore, cleave unto charity, which is the greatest of all (the spiritual gifts), for all things must fail (without it)." (Moroni 7:46). It is one of the greatest of all the qualities of God Himself, Who is the Possessor of all spiritual gifts.

"Charity is the pure love of Christ, and it endureth forever, and whoso is found possessed of it at the last day, it shall be well with him." (Moroni 7:47). Charity can motivate us to Christian service, but it also prepares us to be like God, so that we will feel comfortable in His Presence. As such, it is a gift of the Spirit that is bestowed upon the faithful by the grace of God.

"Wherefore, my beloved brethren," urged Mormon, "pray unto the Father with all the energy of heart, that ye may be filled with this love, which he hath bestowed upon all who are true followers of his Son, Jesus Christ; that ye may become the sons of God; that when he shall appear we shall be like him, for we shall see him as he is; that we may have this hope; that we may be purified even as he is pure. Amen." (Moroni 7:48).

Charity is built
upon the foundation of faith and
hope, and is the supreme characteristic of
the disciples of Christ. Mormon taught: "If a
man be meek and lowly in heart, and confess
by the power of the Holy Ghost that Jesus is
the Christ," with a sure hope born of faith,
"he must needs have charity."
(Moroni 7:44).

"Charity is the pure
love of Christ, and it endureth forever,
and whoso is found possessed of it at the last
day, it shall be well with him." (Moroni 7:47).
Charity motivates us to Christian service, but
it also elevates our discipleship by preparing
us to be like the Savior, so that one day we
will feel comfortable in His Presence.
It is a gift of the Spirit that is
bestowed upon the faithful
by the grace of
God.

## Should we seek to understand the mysteries of the kingdom?

Benjamin bore his testimony to his sons, and taught them the value of the Plates of Brass, explaining that were it not for them, the Nephites would not have known "the mysteries of God" which are the saving principles of the gospel of Jesus Christ. (Mosiah 2:3).

They are referred to as mysteries since they are unavailable to the natural man because they must be revealed by God on condition of faith and obedience. Mysteries are designed to lead those who see with the eye of faith to eternal life.

When we approach a gospel discussion in faith, the mysteries of God may be unfolded to our view. Joseph Smith described his own experience in these words: "Our minds being now enlightened, we began to have the scriptures laid open to our understandings, and the true meaning and intention of their more mysterious passages revealed unto us in a manner which we never could attain to previously, nor ever before had thought of." (After his baptism, May 15, 1829. J.S.H. 1:74).

To understand spiritual things, we must have discernment or guidance from the Holy Ghost. The Spirit teaches all of the children of God, and when we are confirmed as members of the church, we receive the special gift of the Holy Ghost by ordinance. One of His purposes is to guide the faithful from the covenant waters of baptism, along the strait and narrow path leading to the other ordinances of the priesthood that are necessary for us to obtain eternal life. This is one reason why members of the church are given the Holy Ghost in an initial priesthood ordinance.

And then, "he that will not harden his heart, to him is given the greater portion of the word, until it is given unto him to know the mysteries of God, until he know them in full." (Alma 12:10). We may all understand the mysteries of God.

Those who harden their hearts to the truth, however, "to them is given the lesser portion of the word, until they know nothing concerning his mysteries, and then they are taken captive by the devil, and led by his will down to destruction. Now this is what is meant by the chains of hell." (Alma 12:11).

The terrible thing about hardening our hearts is that understanding of "the word" is withheld, which leaves us vulnerable to the devil's influence. The scriptures identify the consequences of sin in very plain language. Its effect on those who have been taught the principles of the gospel in plainness is that the guidance of the Spirit is withdrawn, and they are left alone to grope in darkness. Guilt causes them to shrink from church activity, and in the absence of the Spirit, they have no claim on blessings, prosperity, or preservation.

Tragically, feeling uncomfortable in proximity to spiritual experiences, they then typically withdraw to lifestyles devoid of such associations. Thus, begins a downward spiral that gains momentum as sinful practices, more easily committed, become entrenched. Even worse, those "that doeth this, the same cometh out in open rebellion against God." (Mosiah 2:37).

Still, there are certain points of doctrine that simply are not clear, even to the faithful. To his son, Alma once declared: "Now these mysteries are not yet fully made known unto me; therefore, I shall forbear". (Alma 37:11). He felt that it was always better to keep one's opinion to oneself, rather than to speculate without the foundation of fact or specific revelation. Sometimes, it is better to remain silent and be thought a fool, rather than to speak and remove all doubt.

Joseph Smith once declared to an assembly of the Saints: "I could explain a hundred-fold more than I ever have of the glories of the kingdoms manifested to me in vision, were I permitted, and were the people prepared to receive them". (Joseph Smith, Jr., H.C., 5:402). The fact remains that we have not been given the revelation that certain questions, and these need to remain on our "spiritual shelves" until, in the due time of the Lord they are revealed to us either individually or institutionally.

After considering these 80 questions that are answered in The Book of Mormon, take a moment to ponder any or all of these 20 thoughts:

We are as "children coming down as gentle rain thru darkened skies, with glory trailing from our feet as we go, and endless promise in our eyes. Strangers from a realm of light, who have forgotten all ... the memory of our former lives and the purpose of our call." With The Book of Mormon, we can learn why we're here, and who we really are. (Adapted from "Saturday's Warrior", lyrics by Doug Stewart).

In The Book of Mormon, we encounter the shining examples of prophets, seers, and revelators. They speak prophetically as they teach the body of known truth. They are seers, who see with spiritual eyes and publish hidden truth, and they are revelators each time they bring to the attention of the people new truth that has never before been made known to the children of men, or that has been lost through apostasy.

When designing His Plan, God knew that, with only nine months to put the final touches on our pre-natal preparations, we would transition from the eternal world where we had enjoyed the warmth of hearth and home in heaven, to the bleak atmosphere of the lone and dreary world here on earth. When we did so, He knew that there would be an immediate disconnect that would be both brutal and unrelenting in its intensity. It is that disengagement that makes it imperative that we find our way to the teachings that are found within the pages of The Book of Mormon.

It is not enough only to have received The Book of Mormon. If we casually coast to a standstill before we have found our way to the feet of our Savior Jesus Christ, we are at risk of toppling over. We need forward momentum to maintain our equilibrium, or the heavenly balance, that was taught to us when we were only toddlers in heaven, and pedaled shiny new tricycles to and from our celestial classrooms.

The
spiritual
sixth sense
that blesses us
with a witness of
the truthfulness of
The Book of Mormon
may just be the lowest
common denominator in
a theory of everything. The
influence of the Holy Ghost is
a grand unifying phenomenon,
and although it is self-evident and
exists without question, it defies any
rational explanation on a chalkboard,
let alone convoluted interpretation
within the algorithms of obtuse
mathematical equations.

You
must study
each principle in
The Book of Mormon
"out in your own mind;
then you must ask me if it
be right, and if it is right, I will
cause that your bosom shall burn
within you; therefore, you shall
feel that it is right."
(D&C 9:8).

We wrestle for our
blessing and yearn to
immerse ourselves in the
gospel, that we might learn
to govern ourselves by the laws
of the Celestial Kingdom even as
we dwell upon the earth, that our
hearts might burn within us as
the Spirit speaks to us. It will
unfold the doctrine of The
Book of Mormon to our
heads as well as to
our hearts.

The vibrant
embroidery of the
narrative that may be
discovered on nearly every
page of The Book of Mormon
allows us to aim high. With its
perspective, we can discard the
poor lenses of the body, with
its myopic view of life, and
instead raise our sights
to the rolling vistas
of eternity.

The Prophet Joseph Smith stated: "There are but a very few beings in the world who understand rightly the nature of God, and if they do not understand the character of God they do not comprehend themselves." One of the purposes of The Book of Mormon is to help us to discover the qualities and character traits of our Father, that we find are consistent with His divine nature.

As we read and study about the administration of ordinances that are illustrated in The Book of Mormon, (such as in Mosiah 18 and Moroni 2-6), we are taught about the temporal and spiritual principles of government that relate to both time and eternity.

The
priesthood
is gladdened by
the magic of the grace
of God as it administers
the ordinances of salvation,
sanctification, justification, and
exaltation. These allow us to receive
the blessings of the gospel by binding
us to Him through covenants of action.
The Book of Mormon helps us to enjoy
a wider perspective relating to our
place in the cosmos, and gives
us a greater understanding
of the Plan of Salvation,
and of the nature of
our Father.

To optimally
function, the Plan
requires that we take
God's labor of love and
somehow ease onto a world
stage that is lit only by fire.
The Book of Mormon amplifies
our desire to create a comfortable
connection with the Holy Ghost,
as well as a relationship with
the cosmos, that bridges the
gulf that exists between
heaven and earth.

It's precisely because of the ever-present threat stemming from our behavioral instability that we've been blessed to enjoy The Book of Mormon. It can reorient us in the direction of righteousness, and recalibrate our moral compass to safely guide us home to the happiness that has been prepared for the Saints.

Obedience to the admonitions that are found in The Book of Mormon gives us the opportunity to catch a glimpse of heaven. "Abundance is multiplied unto (us) through the manifestations of the Spirit" that are so intensely felt that they are nearly overwhelming as we labor to achieve our righteous objectives. (D&C 70:13). These will remain in focus because the spiritual guideposts of The Book of Mormon provide an orientation that is gyroscopically centered on eternity. They bless us with a proven perspective in a world overflowing with voices that are in competition for our attention.

In the lives of every individual whose behavior is not harmonious with the Plan, there will come a time when a readjustment must obliterate a façade of hypocrisy. As painful as the process of reformation may be, it is necessary to allow for the cultivation of a more nurturing lifestyle that is only possible when we embrace the special promises that are made by the prophets of The Book of Mormon.

The Book of Mormon has created a technicolor backdrop for the worldwide tapestry that is being woven by the army of God that has been commissioned to seek out and find the elect. Once that has been accomplished, it tasks its soldiers to seamlessly stitch those who have come up out of the waters of baptism into the fold of the Good Shepherd.
(See Ephesians 2:19).

Keeping
the covenants we
make beside the waters
of baptism, as described in
Mosiah Chapter Eighteen, puts
us all beyond the influence of the
adversary, and it endows us with the
priesthood and spiritual power that is
necessary to overcome evil, until we
have completed our work on the
earth, and have received
our exaltation.

When we attempt to
subvert the Plan by turning
our backs on The Book of Mormon,
our futile and destabilizing efforts to
obtain benefits that we don't merit, as
well as to retain blessings we don't
deserve, will reward us with a
pyrrhic victory, at best.

Book of
Mormon study
helps us to break
away from limiting
beliefs. As we brush up
against the stars, we are
awakened to a new vision
that is, at first, blinding, but
as our eyes adjust to the light,
we might be surprised to see,
not just the world as it
really is, but the
eternities, as
well.

With The Book of Mormon,
our Heavenly Father has provided
a way for us to return to the secret garden
of our childhood, that we might fully mature.
As Wordsworth wrote: "Heaven lies about us in our
infancy. Shades of the prison house begin to close
upon the growing boy, but he beholds the light and
whence it flows. He sees it in his joy. The youth,
who daily farther from the (garden) must travel,
still is nature's priest, and by the vision
splendid, is on his way attended. At
length the man perceives it die
away, and fade into the
light of common
day."

# Eighty-Five Questions Answered in The Book of Mormon

Jacob's passionate declaration of belief illustrates how the Nephite prophets felt about their divine commission to preserve their records. (See Jacob 4:4-6). At the same time, it demonstrates the power of The Book of Mormon to stand with the Bible as a Messianic text.

All of God's holy prophets who ministered among the children of men before the Nephites burst upon the world stage taught the same basic principles of the gospel as did Lehi, Nephi, and Jacob, and the record keepers who followed in their footsteps. If they seem to repeat themselves, it is because their message is essentially unchanging, and they receive their inspiration from the same Source.

## What is the role of the prophets?

"For this intent have we written these things, that they may know that we knew of Christ, and we had a hope of his glory many hundred years before his coming; and not only we ourselves had a hope of his glory, but also all the holy prophets which were before us. Behold, they believed in Christ and worshipped the Father in his name, and also we worship the Father in his name. And for this intent we keep the law of Moses, it pointing our souls to him; and for this cause it is sanctified unto us for righteousness, even as it was accounted unto Abraham in the wilderness to be obedient unto the commands of God in offering up his son Isaac, which is a similitude of God and his Only Begotten Son. Wherefore, we search the prophets, and we have many revelations and the spirit of prophecy; and having all these witnesses we obtain a hope, and our faith becometh unshaken, insomuch that we truly can command in the name of Jesus and the very trees obey us, or the mountains, or the waves of the sea." (Jacob 4:4-6).

Jacob's dramatic declaration of belief explains the divine commission of the prophets to keep the Nephite record and demonstrates the inherent power of The Book of Mormon as a Second Witness of Jesus Christ to stands with the Bible as a Messianic text.

In the Holy Land, the Jewish scribes and Pharisees determined to eradicate every reference to Jesus Christ from the scriptures, for every prophet of the Old Testament had a sure testimony of His divinity. But the writings of the prophets of The Book of Mormon suffered no such diminutions, so the Spirit in that text remains unrestrained to bear a powerful witness.

Evidently, all the holy prophets before the Nephites taught the same basic principles of the gospel as did Lehi, Nephi, and Jacob, and the record-keepers who followed in their footsteps. If they seem to repeat themselves, it is because their message is essentially unchanging, and they receive their inspiration from the same Source.

We recall the captain of a ship who was seen to carefully examine a certain drawer at the desk in his cabin, shortly before the commencement of each voyage. This elicited much curiosity on the part of the officers and crew, but they were never so bold as to inquire as to the significance of his habit.

One day, the captain reached the age of retirement, and he was piped ashore for the last time. As soon as he was gone, the crew rushed to his former quarters and pulled open the drawer. There, taped to a 3 x 5 card on the bottom of the drawer was this message: "Starboard is right, port is left." The point is that we should all stick to the basics and emphasize fundamental principles. Prophets tend to do exactly that.

So did Jacob, as he encouraged his people to worship God the Father. Today, we need to listen to the prophets more than ever, because without their gentle correction, we sometimes get caught up in the mechanics of the Law and forget to Whom it points. We get caught up in the thick of thin things. The prophets help us to remain converted to the gospel of Jesus Christs, rather than to the church. They give us the tools we need to avoid getting tangled up in the machinery of the church without making contact with the Savior. Prophets help us to 'hear Him.' Without prophetic guidance, life can become a treadmill. Gospel ordinances, administered by the prophets or by those under their direction, can and should create a springboard that helps all of God's children to reach greater spiritual heights.

## What is a seer?

"Ammon said that a seer is a revelator and a prophet also; and a gift which is greater can no man have, except he should possess the power of God, which no man can." (Mosiah 8:16).

"A seer is one who may see God, who may talk with God, who may receive personal instruction from God. Our prophet is a seer and a revelator. There must be someone to whom the people can turn and trust, who can speak for God. God must have someone on earth who can point the way and teach true doctrine. God has given us a living seer and prophet (who) reveals personal testimony that Jesus is in very deed the Risen Savior, the Living God." (Theodore Burton). A seer is an interpreter and clarifier of eternal truth; one who walks in the Lord's light with open eyes. (See D&C 21:1). A seer is literally a 'see-er,' one who has the right to use the Urim and Thummim, to reveal truth that has been hidden from the world.

By seers "shall all things be revealed." (Mosiah 8:17). A seer can see the storm clouds before they appear on the horizon. Helen Keller once remarked, "There is one tragedy in life worse than to be born without sight, and that is to be born with sight, but without vision." A loving God has "provided a means that (seers), through faith, might work mighty miracles; therefore (they) becometh a great benefit to (their) fellow beings." (Mosiah 8:18).

"Ammon said that a seer is a revelator and a prophet also; and a gift which is greater can no man have, except he should possess the power of God, which no man can." (Mosiah 8:16).

By seers "shall all things be revealed." (Mosiah 8:17). A seer, such as Mosiah in The Book of Mormon, can see the storm clouds before they appear on the horizon.

## Are there things of a religious nature we just do not yet know?

Alma, the Chief Judge and titular head of the church in Zarahemla, was always ready to acknowledge that there were certain points of doctrine that were not clear to him. To his son Helaman, who peppered him with penetrating questions, he once declared: "Now these mysteries are not yet fully made known unto me; therefore, I shall forbear." (Alma 37:11).

Although the mysteries of the kingdom are the saving principles and ordinances of the gospel, and are readily available to the faithful, Alma felt that it was always better to keep his opinion to himself, rather than to speculate without the foundation of fact or specific revelation. Sometimes it is better to remain silent and be thought a fool, rather than to speak and remove all doubt. He emphasized, "There are many mysteries which are kept, that no one knoweth them, save God himself." (Alma 40:3). But he reassured his son Helaman that when God withholds understanding from His children, it is "for a wise purpose," and that there is no intent to mislead, deceive, or dodge the question. We can always be confident that "his paths are straight." (Alma 37:12).

We should not be impatient to gain an intellectual or even a spiritual mastery of that which is apparently beyond our comprehension, or which is unnecessary for us to have at our current stage of development.

Alma, the Chief Judge and titular head of the church in Zarahemla, was always ready to acknowledge that there were certain points of doctrine that were not clear to him. To his son Helaman, who peppered him with penetrating questions, he once declared: "Now these mysteries are not yet fully made known unto me; therefore, I shall forbear."
(Alma 37:11).

We shouldn't be impatient in our quest to gain an intellectual or even a spiritual mastery of that which is apparently beyond our comprehension, or which is unnecessary for us to have at our current stage of development.

## Is immortality a free gift from God?

Because of the resurrection of Christ, we will all pass from physical death to immortality, which is the condition of the body when reunited eternally with the spirit. (2 Nephi 9:15). This will come as a free gift to all who have ever lived on the earth. When we pass from spiritual death, we will have the opportunity to meet God at the Judgment Bar. Thus, the resurrection automatically and totally overcomes physical and spiritual death, which are effects of the Fall. At least briefly, all will come back into the presence of God, to be judged. Those who have refused to repent will be banished from His presence, for they could not long endure His glory. But for the righteous, the place of judgment will be "the pleasing bar of the great Jehovah." (Moroni 10:34).

Those who have not been cleansed in the blood of the Lamb, in the sense that they have not responded to His invitation to accept His grace, and rely on His merits and the power of His Atonement through the first principles and ordinances of the gospel, are described as being "filthy." (2 Nephi 9:16). They deny the power of the Atonement to pay the penalty for their sins. Therefore, the Law of Mercy is of no effect for them. They must submit themselves, instead, to the Law of Justice, as if there had been no Atonement made, and the torment that must necessarily follow has been symbolically described "as a lake of fire and brimstone, whose flame ascendeth up forever and ever and has no end." (2 Nephi 9:16).

Because of the resurrection
of our Lord and Savior Jesus Christ
following His mortal ministry, we will
all pass from physical death to immortality,
which is a term that describes the condition of
our bodies when they are eternally reunited
with our spirits. (2 Nephi 9:15). This will
come as a free gift to all those who
have ever lived on the earth.
(See 2 Nephi 31:20).

The
resurrection
will automatically
overcome physical and
spiritual death, that are the
unalterable effects of the Fall.
At least briefly, all the children
of our Heavenly Father will come
back into His presence, to be
judged of Him.

# What is the difference between immortality and eternal life?

In the scriptures, immortality is differentiated from eternal life. (See Matthew 19:16, 25:46, Luke 10:25, John 3:15 & 36, 4:36, 5:39, 6:47, 54, & 68, 10:28, 17:3, Acts 13:48, Romans 2:7, 5:21, 6:23, 1 Timothy 6:12, 1 John 5:11, Titus 1:2, 2 Nephi 2:27, 9:39, 31:18, 33:4, Enos 1:27, Jacob 6:11, Mosiah 26:20, Alma 11:45, 12:20, 40:2, 41:4, 3 Nephi 28:36, 3 Nephi 9:13, & Moroni 7:41, to name a few).

"O how great the plan of our God! For on the other hand, the paradise of God must deliver up the spirits of the righteous, and the grave deliver up the body of the righteous; and the spirit and the body is restored to itself again, and all men become incorruptible, and immortal, and they are living souls, having a perfect knowledge like unto us in the flesh, save it be that our knowledge shall be perfect." (2 Nephi 9:13).

In order to enjoy the paradise of God, we "must press forward with a steadfastness in Christ, having a perfect brightness of hope, and a love of God and of all men. Wherefore, if (we) shall press forward, feasting upon the word of Christ, and endure to the end, behold, thus saith the Father: (We) shall have eternal life." (2 Nephi 31:20).

"I would that ye should be steadfast and immovable, always abounding in good works, that Christ, the Lord God Omnipotent, may seal you his, that you may be brought to heaven, that ye may have everlasting salvation and eternal life, through the wisdom, and power, and justice, and mercy of him who created all things, in heaven and in earth, who is God above all. Amen." (Mosiah 5:15).

Because of the resurrection of Christ, we will all pass from physical death to immortality, which is the condition that is reflected in our bodies when they are reunited eternally with our spirits. This will come as a free gift to all who have ever lived on the earth.

However, eternal life is different from immortality. Christ urged His disciples to be perfect, even as His Father in Heaven is perfect. (Matthew 5:48). God knows all things, "being from everlasting to everlasting." (D&C 132:20). He is eternal, which spans the time from uncreate intelligence, through our spiritual development as His children, on into mortality, and finally to our reunion with Him in the resurrection. He is absolutely perfect, and the stylus of faith, hope, and charity circumscribes His attributes. Of all those after whom we might model our behavior, our Father chose His Son Jesus Christ, Who is in every sense One with Him. Thus, Mormon taught: "In Christ there should come every good thing." (Moroni 7:22).

All things of any worth are connected to the Savior. (Moroni 7:24). Quite simply, when He is the focus of our lives, His power to bless us with eternal life is unleashed. When our priorities are ordered and our lives are Christ-centered, we are quickened by the Spirit. The Lord has blessed us with His gospel in the Dispensation of the Fulness of Times to clarify the principles of perfection that are emulated by His example and validated by the Spirit. Without His protective influence, we are vulnerable to the lethal storms initiated by the Destroyer that are sweeping the face of the earth and whose suffocating winds would suck the very life-sustaining marrow from our bones.

After considering these 85 questions that are answered in The Book of Mormon, take a moment to ponder any or all of these 20 thoughts:

"Because that I
have spoken one word,
ye need not suppose that
I cannot speak another; for
my work is not yet finished ..
Wherefore, because that ye have a
Bible ye need not suppose that
it contains all my words;
neither need ye suppose
that I have not caused
more to be written."
(2 Nephi 29:9).

The
Book
of Mormon
links the riches
of eternity with the
resources of the earth.
But those who disregard
the former because they are
obsessed with the latter, will be
doomed to live out their lives in
scarcity of their basic spiritual
needs. They will live beneath
the poverty level, without
even being aware
of it.

How fitting it is, when our testimonies of The Book of Mormon consist of expressions that relate to the guidance we receive from the Spirit, that is beyond our limited understanding, and that helps us as we face our challenges, as we make important decisions, and as we grapple with the momentous questions relating to our place in the cosmos.

In moments of deep reflection as we read The Book of Mormon, and as we soak up the doctrine of Christ, we'll discover that we are the begotten spirit children of Heavenly Parents, and that we lived with Them in pre-mortal felicity long before we began our sojourn on earth. We all have flashes of déjà vu, when awakening memories confirm we are strangers who've wandered from the familiar precincts of a more exalted sphere.

The Book of Mormon will caress our spirits with the inexplicable images of religious recognition that will remind us that we are of a noble lineage. The Holy Ghost lights our way with the torch of truth; a beacon to guide us safely home. It makes no difference how far or wide its net may be cast, science will remain powerless to explain the flickering shadows of eternity that dance around us. The forgotten features of immortality will once again be illuminated by the steady light of the Spirit, for all to see.

As significant cast members in life's Three Act Play, we can better understand our roles if we have engaged others in the scenes we play. We need to be on familiar terms with those who participate in the drama, and share the stage with them as we rehearse. Through our study of The Book of Mormon, we can better face the challenges that are related to mastering the assignments that are attached to each of our individual parts.

When we've read
The Book of Mormon,
we come to an epiphany:
that we had beforehand been
living in only one dimly lighted
corner of reality that had, in turn,
provided us with a very narrow
perspective that had been
frozen in time.

In an episode
of "Star Trek," Q
told Captain Picard:
"You just don't get it, do
you, Jean Luc? The trial never
ends. We wanted to see if you had
the ability to expand your mind and
your horizons. And for one brief moment
you did. For that one fraction of a second,
you were open to options that you had never
considered. That is the exploration that awaits
you. Not mapping stars and studying nebula,
but instead charting the unknown possibilities
of existence." We don't have to be crew members
on Galaxy Class Starships to do that. We just
need to get our hands on a copy of The Book
of Mormon, and then let the Spirit be our
Guide as we embark upon a wild ride,
not to the far reaches of the galaxy,
but through its pages.

The Book of
Mormon helps us
discern the truths that
fueled Hamlet's euphoria:
"What a piece of work is man!
How noble in reason, how infinite
in faculty, in form and moving how
express and admirable, in action how
like an angel, in apprehension how
like a god - the beauty of the
world, the paragon of
animals!"

The Book of
Mormon is where we
turn for triage, when
we have been wounded by
the adversary's fiery darts.
It is our safe haven, where we
can firmly grasp the horns of
sanctuary and where our spirits
can be restored. Within its pages,
while we haven't as yet encroached
upon its sacred precincts, we can
still learn all about the order of
heaven, and how to honor the
sacred covenants that will
qualify us to live there
in a coming day.

Our eyes
become single
to the glory of God
when we catch the vision
of Book of Mormon study.
Over time, we will be converted
to its power, and our bodies will
be filled with light. There will be
no darkness in us, and we will
come to realize that it's withinq3
the realm of possibility to
comprehend all things.
(See D&C 88:67).

During our
study of The Book
of Mormon, we will surely
interact with members of the
church who grapple with their own
custom-tailored challenges, but who
through the grace of God have managed
to make the transition from hesitancy to
conviction, from instability to commitment,
from timidity to confidence, from indecision
to resolution, from doubts to certainty, from
struggle to celebration, and from vacillation
to purpose. In short, we will join the joyful
throngs who have made the transition
from spiritual itinerancy to
moral discipline.

With its
breathtaking reconciliation
of the Law of Justice with the Law
of Mercy, the doctrine of Atonement
within The Book of Mormon permits the
worst of us to work out our salvation with
fear and trembling before the Lord, as we
earn the privilege, as prodigal sons and
daughters of a Father Who loves us, to
rejoin His household of faith in full
fellowship, with all the privileges
one might hope for, subject to
the reformation of errant
behavior and flawed
character.

Within The Book
of Mormon, the fulness
of the gospel reassures us that
when the process of securing our
celestial legacy has been completed,
there will be no breaches in the shield
wall of our family history, there will be
no names missing from the book of life
that has been carefully compiled by the
angels in heaven, and there will be no
empty seats around the table, when
we all sit down together to enjoy
a reunion at family dinner
in our heavenly home.

It's been said
that time is a fire in
which we burn. This may
be true, in the sense that it is
by fire and the Holy Ghost that
time becomes an element we use
to work out our salvation with
fear and trembling before
the Lord, as we read The
Book of Mormon.

Possibly, the most
significant difference that
accounts for the superiority of the
principles of God's Plan of Salvation
that is revealed in The Book of Mormon
is the process whereby the gospel of Jesus
Christ is internalized by His disciples. The
wonder of our transformation begins with
sanctification by the Spirit at the waters
of baptism, and it only ends when we
have participated in the ordinances
of exaltation that are carried out
before holy altars in the
House of the Lord.

We read The
Book of Mormon
because our Lord of
Whom it testifies has
already accomplished
His exaltation, while we
clearly have yet to do so.
The pledges we make with
our Heavenly Father are as
stamps on our passports to
perfection. The promises in
Moroni 10:4-5 invite us to
clear customs with nothing
to declare but our testimony
of Jesus Christ. Emerging
into the light of day, there
will then be revealed before
us the rolling vista of an
undiscovered country-at
one and the same time
our destination and
our destiny.

After we have read and re-read The
Book of Mormon again and again, we
realize that the passage of time and growing
old with one of our favorite books of scripture is
simply a feature of mortality designed by God
as a brilliant mechanism that would afford us
the opportunity to gauge the approach of our
reunion with Him in the eternal world,
that will outlast time and will
endure throughout all
eternity.

In The Book
of Mormon, we learn
"how to give and not count
the cost, to fight and not heed
the wounds, to toil and not seek
for rest, and to labor and not ask
for reward, save that of knowing
that we do God's will."
(Loyola).

Nephi clearly
taught that, in the Last
Days, Satan would once again
raise the spectre of rebellion, and he
will "rage in the hearts of men, and stir
them up to anger against that which is good."
(2 Nephi 28:20). As the process of Restoration has
unfolded, he's fought a desperate battle to prevent the
receipt, translation, publication, and distribution of
The Book of Mormon. Having failed in those efforts,
he now struggles to substitute the sophistry of men
for the simplicity of the message. But that fraud is
all form and no substance, because it contributes
nothing to the welfare of Zion. Its driving force
seems to be a brazen craving for personal gain,
with a duplicitous message that is propelled
by a perceived power that is nothing more
substantive than the fleeting adoration
of an irrational world that, in its blind
fanaticism, has completely lost sight
of its objectives. His only option, it
would seem, is to hysterically
redouble his efforts in the
absence of a Plan.

# Ninety Questions Answered by The Book of Mormon

We can be sure that the Lord will do "nothing save it be plain unto the children of men; and he inviteth them all to come unto him and partake of his goodness; and he denieth none that come unto him, black and white, bond and free, male and female; and he remembereth the heathen; and all are alike unto God, both Jew and Gentile."
(2 Nephi 26:33).

Joseph Fielding Smith taught that "every soul coming into this world came here with the promise that through obedience he or she would receive the blessings of salvation. No one has been foreordained to sin, or to perform a mission of evil."

## Can God, Who is no respecter of persons, still care about us?

The Lord "doeth nothing, save it be plain unto the children of men; and he inviteth them all to come unto him and partake of his goodness; and he denieth none that come unto him, black and white, bond and free, male and female; and he remembereth the heathen; and all are alike unto God, both Jew and Gentile." (2 Nephi 26:33).

Joseph Fielding Smith taught that: "Every soul coming into this world came here with the promise that through obedience he or she would receive the blessings of salvation. No one was foreordained to sin, or to perform a mission of evil." ("Doctrines of Salvation," 1:61).

"The Lord God worketh
not in darkness (and) doeth not anything
save it be for the benefit of the world; for he loveth
the world, even that he layeth down his own life that he
may draw all men unto him, Wherefore, he commandeth
none that they shall not partake of his salvation." (2
Nephi 26:23-24). "For God so loved the world, that
he gave his only begotten Son, that whosoever
believeth in him should not perish,
but have everlasting life."
(John 3:16).

We are blessed to be able to live
out our days of probation in the light of life
that illuminates priesthood actions, ordinances,
covenants, and prayers. These exercises strengthen our
spiritual muscles and increase our capacity to stay spiritually
aerobically fit, but they have meaning and purpose only because of
God's grace, which blesses us to inhale deeply of a celestial ether that
defies explanation and begs description. We are saved by grace,
no matter what else we might have or do. Grace is a sine
qua non, an essential condition for salvation, and
the Saints, in particular, are blessed to
be its beneficiaries.

## Could there have been warfare on the scale described in The Book of Mormon?

Mormon recorded: "And it came to pass that my men were hewn down, yea, even my ten thousand who were with me, and I fell wounded in the midst; and they passed by me that they did not put an end to my life. And when they had gone through and hewn down all my people save it were twenty and four of us, (among whom was my son Moroni) and we having survived the dead of our people, did behold on the morrow, when the Lamanites had returned unto their camps, from the top of the hill Cumorah, the ten thousand of my people who were hewn down, being led in the front by me. And we also beheld the ten thousand of my people who were led by my son Moroni. And behold, the ten thousand of Gidgiddonah had fallen, and he also in the midst. And Lamah had fallen with his ten thousand; and Gilgal had fallen with his ten thousand; and Limhah had fallen with his ten thousand; and Jeneum had fallen with his ten thousand; and Cumenihah, and Moronihah, and Antionum, and Shiblom, and Shem, and Josh, had fallen with their ten thousand each." (Mormon 6:14).

When the final battle at Cumorah was over, Mormon recorded that of all the Nephites present at the commencement of the battle, all "save it were those twenty and four who were with me, and also a few who had escaped into the south countries, and a few who had deserted over unto the Lamanites, had fallen." (Mormon 6:15). "And their flesh, and bones, and blood lay upon the face of the earth, being left by the hands of those who slew them to molder upon the land, and to crumble and to return to their mother earth." (Mormon 6:15).

Among the few survivors was his son Moroni, who had witnessed the final destruction of his people from the top of the hill Cumorah. The scriptures clearly teach that there were Nephite survivors after this last great battle, but they were no longer identified as Nephites. Some escaped into the south countries. Some had dissented from the Nephites and had switched their allegiance to the Lamanites. Many likely had never gathered at Cumorah in the first place, because of the great confusion in the Land of Zarahemla during this period of anarchy. The Doctrine & Covenants teaches that in the Last Days, many of the descendants of these Nephites will be identified. (D&C 3:17-20, & 10:48). But, as far as Mormon was concerned, the thousand-year history of the Nephite people was over. His people "had fallen, and their flesh, and bones, and blood lay upon the face of the earth, being left by the hands of those who slew them." (Mormon 6:15). Is this plausible? The central Mexican chronicler, Ixtlilxochitl, reported of the Tultecas around A.D. 1,060 that in a three-year war, 5,600,000 were slain on both sides. Even allowing him considerable room for exaggeration, we are left with little doubt that the battle at Cumorah was within the realm of the plausible in Meso-American terms.

"The ten thousand of my people ... were hewn down, being led in the front by me. And we also beheld the ten thousand of my people who were led by my son Moroni. And behold, the ten thousand of Gidgiddonah had fallen, and he also in the midst. And Lamah had fallen with his ten thousand; and Gilgal had fallen with his ten thousand; and Limhah had fallen with his ten thousand; and Jeneum had fallen with his ten thousand; and Cumenihah, and Moronihah, and Antionum, and Shiblom, and Shem, and Josh, had fallen with their ten thousand each." (130,000 in total). (Mormon 6:14).

The Central American Mexican chronicler, Ixtlilxochitl, reported of the Tultecas around 1,060 A.D. that in a three-year war, over five million were slain on both sides. Even allowing him considerable room for exaggeration, we are left with little doubt that the battle at Cumorah was within the realm of the plausible in Meso-American terms.

## How can we become a Zion society?

"Therefore, the redeemed of the Lord shall return, and come with singing unto Zion; and everlasting joy and holiness shall be upon their heads; and they shall obtain gladness and joy; sorrow and mourning shall flee away." (2 Nephi 8:11).

The Lord's promise is before the Latter-day Saints as both a challenge and an opportunity: "And righteousness and truth will I cause to sweep the earth as with a flood, to gather out mine own elect from the four quarters of the earth, unto a place which I shall prepare; an holy city, that my people may gird up their loins, and be looking forth for the time of my coming, for there shall be my tabernacle, and it shall be called Zion, a New Jerusalem. And the Lord said unto Enoch, Then shalt thou and all thy city meet them there; and we will receive them into our bosom; and they shall see us, and we will fall upon their necks, and they shall fall upon our necks, and we will kiss each other; And there shall be mine abode, and it shall be Zion, which shall come forth out of all the creations which I have made; and for the space of a thousand years shall the earth rest." (J.S.T. Genesis 7:70-72).

Ultimately, it will be a great day for those who wait upon the Lord, but terrible for those whose vessels lack the oil of gladness (See Joel 2:31). In the meantime, the Saints would first build the City of Joseph on the banks of the Mississippi River, and would then make the desert blossom as the rose in the midst of the Rocky Mountains. There, they would finally be established. The prophecy of Isaiah would be fulfilled, wherein he had declared: "And it shall come to pass in the last days, that the mountain of the Lord's house shall be established in the top of the mountains, and shall be exalted above the hills; and all nations shall flow unto it. And many people shall go and say, Come ye, and let us go up to the mountain of the Lord, to the house of the God of Jacob; and he will teach us of his ways, and we will walk in his paths; for out of Zion shall go forth the law, and the word of the Lord from Jerusalem." (Isaiah 2:2-3). And "they shall not hurt nor destroy in all my holy mountain: for the earth shall be full of the knowledge of the Lord, as the waters cover the sea. And in that day, there shall be a root of Jesse, which shall stand for an ensign of the people." (Isaiah 11:9-10).

We live in the midst of a raging war that subjects us to violence, crime, and danger every day. We seek shelter from a bombardment of evil, all too often feeling frustrated and helpless. In school, at work, and sometimes in our own homes, we face challenges that test the limits of our strength to endure. But Nephi said that we "must press forward with a steadfastness in Christ, having a perfect brightness of hope, and a love of God and of all men." (2 Nephi 31:20). What a great thought! If we remain strong and unfaltering, we can all stand fast in holy places, enjoying the safety and security of Zion.

In January 1831, the Lord explained: For this cause, "that ye might escape the power of the enemy, and be gathered unto me a righteous people, without spot and blameless, I gave unto you the commandment that ye should go to the Ohio." (D&C 38:30). This was the answer to those who wondered why they should move 300 miles further west, in the dead of winter. There, the Lord would seek to establish a standard of equality within the membership of the church through the implementation of the Law of Consecration. But if the church would not respond to the call to gather to Zion, it would ultimately lose its individual and collective freedom, even as it clamored for its personal rights.

The prophet Ether had seen in vision, "the Jerusalem from whence Lehi should come, (and that) after it should be destroyed it should be built up again, a holy city unto the Lord; wherefore, it could not be a new Jerusalem for it had been in a time of old." (Ether 13:5). He also saw that "a New Jerusalem should be built up upon this land" of America. (Ether 13:6). Here, the remnant of the house of Joseph would "build up a holy city unto the Lord, like unto the Jerusalem of old." (Ether 13:8).

In this millennial New Jerusalem, there will reside only those "whose garments are white through the blood of the Lamb; and they are they who are numbered among the remnant of the seed of Joseph, who were of the house of Israel. And then also cometh the Jerusalem of old; and the inhabitants thereof, blessed are they, for they have (also) been washed in the blood of the Lamb; and they are they who were scattered and gathered in from the four quarters of the earth, and from the north countries, and are partakers of the fulfilling of the covenant which God made with their father, Abraham." (Ether 13:10-11).

For the early Latter-day Saints, Zion was the quintessential Celestial City of God, far removed from the mud and overcast skies, the hardship and persecution, and the sickness and death so familiar to them in their telestial surroundings. Joseph F. Smith said: "If we would carry out that which the Lord revealed, it would only be a matter of a very short time until this people would be in the same condition as were the people of the City of Enoch." (C.R., 4/1921). "And it came to pass (in Enoch's day) that he built a city that was called the city of Holiness, even Zion." (J.S.T. Genesis 7:25). "And Enoch and all his people walked with God, and he dwelt in the midst of Zion; and it came to pass that Zion was not, for God received it up into his own bosom; and from thence went forth the saying, Zion is Fled." (Moses 7:69).

Life has no coherence without the spiritual symmetry of the gospel, and so, the characteristics of a Zion society are simply the results of a spiritual transformation in the lives of the people that comes about as men and women live the Celestial Law of the Lord.

John Altgeld wrote that "Two forces are operating, two voices are calling - one coming out from the swamps of selfishness and force, where success means death; and the other from the hilltops of justice and progress, where even failure brings glory. Two lights are seen on your horizon - one, the last fading marsh light of power, and the other the slowly rising sun of human brotherhood. Two ways lie open for you - one leading to an ever lower and lower plane, where are heard the cries of despair and the curses of the poor, where manhood shrivels and possessions rot down the possessor; and the other leading to the highlands of the morning, where are heard the glad shouts of humanity, and where honest effort is rewarded with immortality."

Jesus Christ walks the broad, sun-kissed boulevards of Zion because its inhabitants have long-since crossed over Jordan to get there, while those who make their homes in the dark alleyways and dead-end streets of Babylon City have resigned themselves to nothing more than an overnight stay in a second-class hotel. But the City of God, although it is a five-star all-inclusive property, is not a vacation destination catering to the hedonistically self-indulgent. When we commit to make the trip, the Lord expects our undeviating dedication and the sacrifice of every worldly desire. The ticket that is offered is one-way, is non-cancelable, and is non-refundable, although we may redeem it for future travel, should our immediate plans change. Our seat assignments are not fixed, and there are unlimited upgrades to first-class, based on worthiness.

Zion is an island in the stream, and is our only safe haven on stormy seas. It is a shelter and provides security for those who refuse to capitulate to the crumbling values of the world, which are fragmenting into unrecognizable forms. The honest in heart appreciate that Zion is driven by the consummate compilation of affirmative actions.

The gathering of the Saints to the Stakes of Zion is "for a defense, and for a refuge from the storm, and from wrath when it shall be poured out without mixture upon the whole earth." (D&C 115:6). President Ezra Taft Benson taught that our church ecclesiastical units called the stakes of Zion have "at least four purposes. One is to unify and perfect the members who live within their boundaries, by extending to them church programs, ordinances, and instruction. Secondly, the members of stakes are to be models, or standards, of righteousness for the world. Third, stakes are to be a defense from the world. They do this as members unify under their local priesthood leaders and consecrate themselves to do their duty and keep their covenants. Fourth, stakes are a refuge from the storm that is to be poured out over the earth." ("Ensign," 1/1991, p. 2-5).

"The redeemed of the Lord shall return, and come with singing unto Zion; and everlasting joy and holiness shall be upon their heads; and they shall obtain gladness and joy; sorrow and mourning shall flee away." (2 Nephi 8:11). The Lord's promise is before the Latter-day Saints as both a challenge and an opportunity.

President Ezra Taft Benson taught that our church ecclesiastical units called the stakes of Zion have "at least four purposes. One is to unify and perfect the members who live within their boundaries, by extending to them the church programs, ordinances, and instructions. Secondly, the members of stakes are the models, or standards, of righteousness for the world. Third, stakes are to be a defense from the world. They do this as members unify under their local priesthood leaders and consecrate themselves to do their duty and keep their covenants. Fourth, stakes are a refuge from the storm that is to be poured out over the earth."

## What should our relationship be to the Jews?

Long ago, it was prophesied that Israel would become a "hiss and a by-word (that would) be hated among all nations." (1 Nephi 19:14). Nevertheless, the Lord would remember His covenant people. Mormon wrote: "Ye need not any longer hiss, nor spurn, nor make game of the Jews, nor any of the remnant of the house of Israel; for behold, the Lord remembereth his covenant unto them, and he will do unto them according to that which he hath sworn." (3 Nephi 29:8).

Those in the Last Days are cautioned against prejudicial behavior of any kind that is directed toward either the Jews or the remnant of Lehi. In General Conference assembled, President Heber J. Grant issued a prophetic warning to the world, concerning the conscious persecution of Israel, the Lord's Covenant People. He declared: "By the authority of the Holy Priesthood of God, that has again been restored to the earth, and by the ministration, under the direction of the Prophet of God, Apostles of the Lord Jesus Christ have been to the Holy Land and have dedicated that country for the return of the Jews; and we believe that in the due time of the Lord they shall be in the favor of God again. Let no Latter-day Saint be guilty of taking any part in any crusade against these people." (10/1921). Significantly, President Grant delivered this address just a decade before the institutional destruction of the Jews as a people was conceived as a Final Solution, by the National Socialist Party (Nazi) in Germany.

Mormon wrote to those living in the Last Days: "Ye need not any longer hiss, nor spurn, nor make game of the Jews, nor any of the remnant of the house of Israel; for behold, the Lord remembereth his covenant unto them, and he will do unto them according to that which he hath sworn."
(3 Nephi 29:8).

Heber J. Grant declared: "By the authority of the Holy Priesthood of God, that has again been restored to the earth, and by the ministration, under the direction of the Prophet of God, Apostles of the Lord Jesus Christ have been to the Holy Land and have dedicated that country for the return of the Jews; and we believe that in the due time of the Lord they shall be in the favor of God again. Let no Latter-day Saint be guilty of taking any part in any crusade against these people."
(10/1921).

## Why aren't Latter-day Saint churches decorated with crosses?

The Lord has revealed to His prophets the significance of the cross. Paul used the "cross of Christ" to impress upon the minds of his listeners the doctrine of the Atonement. Latter-day Saints see the symbolism of the cross in the ordinance of the Sacrament, where we take upon ourselves the name of Christ, and promise to always remember Him and to keep His commandments. As Alma counseled in The Book of Mormon: "Cross yourself in all these things; for except ye do this ye can in nowise inherit the kingdom of God. Oh, remember, and take it upon you, and cross yourself in these things." (Alma 39:9).

Nephi saw in vision that Jesus would be "lifted up upon the cross and slain for the sins of the world." (1 Nephi 11:33). The Savior Himself taught the Nephites: "My Father sent me that I might be lifted up upon the cross; and after that I had been lifted up upon the cross, that I might draw all men unto me, that as I have been lifted up by men even so should men be lifted up by the Father, to stand before me, to be judged of their works, whether they be good or whether they be evil." (3 Nephi 27:14).

Joseph Smith taught that the Saints have "endured the crosses of the world." (J.S.T. Matthew 16:25). "For a man to take up his cross," taught the Savior, "is to deny himself all ungodliness, and every worldly lust, and keep my commandments." (J.S.T. Matthew 16:26).

Our hope is founded on the Atonement and Resurrection of the Savior of the world. When our relationship with Him is secured, we are prepared to suffer His cross, or bear the cross of service, consecration, devotion, and obedience. When Latter-day Saints wear the cross around their necks, it reminds them of these things, although, as a rule, they have never dwelt upon such talismans.

While Latter-day Saints have never questioned the sincerity of other Christians for wearing the cross as a symbol of their discipleship, or have felt that they were doing so inappropriately, it is a custom that has never caught on with Latter-day Saints. Joseph Fielding Smith, Jr. taught: "The motive for such a custom by those who are of other churches is a most sincere and sacred gesture. To them, the cross carried the impression of sacrifice and suffering endured by the Son of God. We may be sure that if our Lord had been killed with a dagger or with a sword, it would have been very strange indeed if religious people of this day would have graced such a weapon by wearing it. A humble, contrite spirit and sincere prayer of gratitude is, we feel, a better means of worship and acknowledgement of our love for the great blessings we receive through our Savior's voluntary sacrifice." ("Doctrines of Salvation," 4:17-18).

The Lord has revealed to
His Book of Mormon prophets the
significance of the cross. Paul used the
"cross of Christ" to impress upon the minds
of his listeners the doctrine of the Atonement.
Latter-day Saints see the symbolism of the cross
in the ordinance of the Sacrament, where we take
upon ourselves the name of Christ, and promise
to always remember Him and to keep
His commandments. (See
3 Nephi 27:14).

Our hope is founded upon
the Atonement of the Savior of the
world. When our relationship with Him is
secured, we are prepared to suffer His cross, or to
bear the cross of service, consecration, devotion,
and obedience. When Latter day Saints wear a
cross around their necks, it reminds them of
these things, although, as a rule, they have
never inordinately dwelt upon
such talismans.

After considering these 90 questions that are answered in The Book of Mormon, take a moment to ponder any or all of these 20 thoughts:

"I command all men, both in the east and in the west, and in the north, and in the south, and in the islands of the sea, that they shall write the words which I speak unto them; for out of the books which shall be written I will judge the world, every man according to their works, according to that which is written."
(2 Nephi 29:10-11).

The Book of Mormon charges our vision, to enjoy an infinite perspective, wherein we experience the pulsing stream of instinct, insight, intuition, inspiration, and revelation, whose current can be monitored all the way back to its source in heaven. To that end, we're all encouraged to give ourselves completely and without reservation, so that we might enjoy an atmosphere of harmony with God, and synchronization with eternity. We tirelessly conduct our exploration, and hope to rediscover, but never to claim for ourselves, or for exploitation, the inherent power that is of God.

"He has translated the book, even that part which I have commanded him, and as your Lord and your God liveth, it is true."
(D&C 17:6).

When the Holy Ghost helps us to focus our attention on The Book of Mormon, to our delight, we will discover for ourselves the unlimited energy source of the cosmos. We will "discard the poor lenses of our bodies, and peer thru the telescope of truth into the infinite reaches of immortality." (Helen Keller). On the other hand, if we haven't nurtured our faith in the Great and Eternal Plan of Redemption, if we've relegated our faculties to telestial mechanisms of inquiry, and our engines stall for lack of celestial power, we may find ourselves caught up in a flat spin and downward spiral from which there may be no hope of recovery.

We think of
the Sons of Mosiah
when we read: "I sought
my soul, but my soul I could
not see. I sought my God but my
God eluded me. I sought my brother,
and I found all three." (William Blake).
We see in The Book of Mormon that the Lord
will send His ablest missionaries to His most
wicked children. He arms them with unwavering
faith, a sure knowledge of gospel principles, firm
and abiding testimonies of the doctrines of the
kingdom, of the Plan of Salvation, and of
the Lord Jesus Christ, a solid spiritual
endorsement by file leaders, and
the fervent prayers of the
faithful.

The
Book of
Mormon can
ground us, not
on the telestial turf
that has become soiled
by the blemishes of sin,
but on the broad celestial
boulevards that have been
paved with shiny bricks of
24 carat gold whose glitter
helps us find our way back
to the everlasting burnings
that describe the dwelling
place of our Father in
Heaven.

In between
the sights and
sounds, rides and
attractions, and thrills
and spills of our earthly
theme-park experience, The
Book of Mormon teaches us to
use spiritual hygiene practices to
remove the grit and the grime that
accumulate as a function of living,
but that always threaten to foul our
inner workings and curtail our
progress on the pathway that
leads to perfection.

The Book
of Mormon gives
us a measure of hope
that we will continue to
be able to utilize the tools
the Savior provides to make
the vital distinction between
knowledge and wisdom, and
to apply them to make correct
choices that are based on the
intelligent application of
the former, in order to
come into intimate
contact with the
latter.

If we
fail to keep our
eyes figuratively
fixed upon the statue
of the Angel Moroni that
stands atop so many of our
temples, we will be at risk of
succumbing to the pessimistic
observation that not only has
knowledge outpaced truth,
but that truth is having
a hard time holding
its own.

The
Book of Mormon
teaches that our mortal
experiences are backlighted
by the Light of Christ and the
luminosity provided by the Holy
Ghost. God has left the porch light
burning, so that its golden filament
might help us to trace our way back
home, even if it may seem for a
moment that we have lost our
orientation toward the
glow of heaven.

Far too often,
we are simply "strangers
from a realm of light, who have
forgotten all. And so, we must learn
why we're here, and who we really are."
(Doug Stewart). A testimony of the divine
origin of The Book of Mormon awakens
within us the memory of our former
home and the purpose of our call,
setting the stage for eternal
optimism.

As The Book of Mormon
teaches us that each member of
our family can become a physical
and a spiritual reminder of our Father
in Heaven, we become legitimate heirs,
thru faithfulness, of all that He is. Our
families provide the context we need, so
that we may work to become more like
Him. Families furnish the threads,
and the Plan of God is the fabric
upon which has been stitched
every word to the Primary
song: "I am a child of
God," by Naomi
Randall.

If we have foolishly built our fortresses of faith upon the shifting sands of secular humanism, if we don't have The Book of Mormon to which we can turn, where will our sanctuary be when the wind blows and the rain beats down? To what safe harbor will we flee when the ocean of life is in turmoil? When we are tossed about as flotsam and jetsam, never coming to a knowledge of the truth, to what source will we look for the stability we so desperately seek, or for the answers to life's questions that continually vex our spirits?

If we approach our study of The Book of Mormon with skepticism or doubt, or if we disdain its legitimacy before examining its merits, we have submitted to blind guides and we disallow God's power to transform our lives. We refuse His very grace as we turn our backs on the habitation of the Lord, dismissing the sacrifice of His Son and esteeming as a thing of naught His suffering. We close our hearts and our minds to soul expanding opportunities, as we are snared by Satan, and are securely bound by his strong chains.

As we read and pray
about The Book of Mormon,
and we gain a testimony of its
divine origin, the Spirit will quietly
confirm that "happiness is the object and
design of our existence, and will be the end
thereof, if we pursue the path that leads to
it, (consisting of) virtue, uprightness,
faithfulness, holiness, and keeping
the commandments of God."
(Joseph Smith).

As we study
The Book of Mormon with
silent lifting minds and quiet
words that are softly spoken,
we will draw nearer to the
untrespassed sanctity
of heaven, put out our
hands, and touch,
as it were, the
face of
God.

If we are so fortunate as to internalize gospel principles, so that the conduct of our lives is in harmony with the laws of the Celestial Kingdom, we will be at liberty to enjoy heavenly gifts. The itinerary of our journey will inevitably include a serious study of The Book of Mormon, leading to a powerful testimony of its divine origin.

Our study of The Book of Mormon helps us to realize that our mortal experience is only a tiny fraction of a much larger reality, and that as long as we believe our perspective to be unique, it is faulty. The veil helps us to appreciate the reality that mortality is not our natural dimension. We discover why we are never entirely comfortable in our temporal circumstances, and why we sometimes feel so like strangers and pilgrims on the earth. Our experiences with scripture study help us to comprehend our innate thrust always toward the future, and always beyond the horizon of our sight.

Even
with latter
day revelation
and instruction
within The Book of
Mormon, we still only
dimly perceive our noble
heritage, and we sometimes
find it hard to accept the fact
that we mingled among the
Gods before our mortal
births.

The
Savior Jesus
Christ has extended to
every one of us a personal
request to follow Him on a soul
expanding journey as He escorts
us thru The Book of Mormon. That
summons is prefaced by the action
verb "to come." As we undertake our
pursuit of greater understanding,
we are propelled in every direction
beyond an event horizon, to a
larger view of life that is
multidimensional and
incomprehensible.

# One Hundred Questions Answered by The Book of Mormon

"Wherefore, we shall have a perfect knowledge of all our guilt, and our uncleanness, and our nakedness; the righteous shall have a perfect knowledge of their enjoyment, and their righteousness, being clothed with purity, yea, even with the robe of righteousness." (2 Nephi 9:14, see 1 Nephi 12:10, Alma 5:21 & Ether 12:38).

When each of us stands before the pleasing bar of God, as we surely will, the evidence will be presented, and our previous conformity to or rejection of eternal law will determine our reward or punishment. However, due to the influence of the Light of Christ and the Holy Ghost, our innate capacity to have generated active saving faith in the divine origin of the doctrine of The Book of Mormon will make our experience there more than just a roll of the dice. We will then understand that our lives had not been a zero-sum game. In fact, the cards had been marked and the deck had been stacked in our favor. Life had not been a game of chance, but rather one of skill and adventure, for knowledge is power, rendering the Judgment a win-win for both God and man. (See Jacob 6:13 and Moroni 10:34).

## Why do Latter-day Saints wear special underclothing?

"Wherefore, we shall have a perfect knowledge of all our guilt, and our uncleanness, and our nakedness; the righteous shall have a perfect knowledge of their enjoyment, and their righteousness, being clothed with purity, yea, even with the robe of righteousness." (2 Nephi 9:14, see 1 Nephi 12:10, Alma 5:21 & Ether 12:38).

"The garment represents sacred covenants. It fosters modesty and becomes a shield and protection to the wearer. It is a visual and tactile reminder of (covenants made in the temple). For many church members, the garment has formed a barrier of protection when the wearer has been faced with temptation. Among other things, it symbolizes our deep respect for the laws of God." (Boyd K. Packer, "The Holy Temple", p. 18-20).

Elder Packer related how one of the brethren had been "invited to speak to the faculty and staff of the Navy Chaplains Training School in Newport, Rhode Island. The audience included a number of high-ranking naval chaplains from the Catholic, Protestant and Jewish faiths. In the question-and-answer period, one of the chaplains asked, "Can you tell us something about the special underwear that some Mormon servicemen wear?" "Why do you do that? Isn't it strange? Doesn't that present a problem?"

To the chaplain who made the inquiry, he responded with a question: "Which church do you represent?" In response, he named one of the Protestant churches. He said, "In civilian life and also when conducting meetings in the military service you wear clerical clothing, do you not?" The chaplain said that he did. He continued: "I would suppose that that has some importance to you, that in a sense, it sets you apart from the rest of your congregation. It is your uniform, as it were, of the ministry.

Also, I suppose it may have a much more important function. It reminds you of who you are and what your obligations and covenants are. It is a continual reminder that you are a member of the clergy, that you regard yourself as a servant of the Lord, and that you are responsible to live in such a way as to be worthy of your ordination."

He then told them: "You should be able to understand at least one of the reasons why Latter-day Saints have a deep spiritual commitment concerning the garment. A major difference between your churches and ours is that we do not have a professional clergy, as you do. The congregations are all presided over by local leaders. They are men called from all walks of life. Yet, they are ordained to the priesthood. They hold offices in the priesthood. They are set apart to presiding positions as presidents, counselors, and leaders in various categories. The women, too, share in that responsibility and in those obligations. The man who heads our congregation on Sunday as the bishop may go to work on Monday as a postal clerk, as an office worker, a farmer, a doctor; or he may be an air force pilot or a naval officer. By our standard, he is as much an ordained minister as you are by your standard. He is recognized as such by most governments. We draw something of the same benefits from this special clothing as you would draw from your clerical vestments. The difference is that we wear ours under our clothing instead of outside, for we are employed in various occupations in addition to our service in the church. These sacred things we do not wish to parade before the world." (Boyd K. Packer, "Preparing to Enter the Holy Temple," p. 20-21).

## Who is the Third Member of the Godhead?

Moroni taught that "in the mouth of three witnesses shall these things be established … in the which shall be shown forth the power of God and also his word, of which the Father, and the Son, and the Holy Ghost bear record." (Ether 5:4).

Nephi had written that he "was desirous also that (he) might see, and hear, and know of these things, by the power of the Holy Ghost, which is the gift of God unto all those who diligently seek him." (1 Nephi 10:17). He knew that without the gift of the Holy Ghost, the world would have a real problem, because in their efforts to clarify their consideration of Christ, even earnest seekers of truth would only be multiplying mirrors and studying angles without increasing the light. What is really needed is a source of light that does more than replace the darkness; it must also illuminate principles that, heretofore, have been only dimly perceived.

In their attempts to increase the light by playing the angles, the world is sporadically able to see a bit more clearly, but still, many basic principles must remain obscured. If the number of available lumens of energy has not been increased, individuals are doing little more than spinning their wheels, like hamsters in a cage. What is really needed is more light! Heavenly Father has orchestrated the Restoration in order to address the problem of gloominess in the world. Hence, the Savior appeared to Joseph Smith in the Sacred Grove as "the light which shineth in darkness." (D&C 11:11).

The Restoration that followed has set in motion a number of protocols that have been designed to dramatically increase the amount of available light. These measures generously provide more than enough to go around. The Holy Ghost coherently knits together foundation principles, doctrines, ordinances, and covenants, and stitches them into an understandable pattern, so that the power of the word and the witness of truth may be conveyed without the need for external warrant. There is no need for an external power pack. In this way, "the Lord God prepareth the way that the residue of men may have faith in Christ, that the Holy Ghost may have place in their hearts, according to the power thereof." (Moroni 7:32).

Moroni clearly taught that "in the mouth of three witnesses shall these things be established … in the which shall be shown forth the power of God and also his word, of which the Father, and the Son, and the Holy Ghost bear record." (Ether 5:4).

The Holy Ghost coherently knits together foundation principles, doctrines, ordinances, and covenants pertaining to the gospel, and then stitches them into an understandable pattern, so the power of the word and the witness of truth may be conveyed without the need for external warrant.

# What is the gift of the Holy Ghost?

"I know that if ye shall follow the Son, with full purpose of heart, acting no hypocrisy and no deception before God, but with real intent, repenting of your sins, witnessing unto the Father that ye are willing to take upon you the name of Christ, by baptism - yea, by following your Lord and your Savior down into the water, according to his word, behold, then shall ye receive the Holy Ghost; yea, then cometh the baptism of fire and of the Holy Ghost." (2 Nephi 31:13).

All that is true comes to us from the Holy Ghost. He has revealed every eternal principle that has guided the human family since the dawn of history. The children of God constantly benefit from that which is revealed by the Holy Ghost. In the Last Days, when the Spirit is "poured out upon all flesh, and when "young men see visions, and old men dream dreams," (Joel 2:28), it will be because the Holy Ghost has provided the creative drive, but the irony of the situation will be that many will fail to recognize the source of their inspiration.

Chapters 2-5 of The Book of Moroni consist of Moroni's appendices to the text that carefully document essential basic ordinances of the gospel. The fact that these were recorded at all attests to the necessity of a formal church organization among a righteous people, even though in The Book of Mormon very little is written about such a body.

"These ordinances are not empty, passive rituals; rather, they bind us to receive the promises and blessings of the gospel by means of a covenant of action between ourselves and the Lord." (Robert L. Millett, "Doctrinal Commentary on The Book of Mormon," 4:319). Having experienced the drama found within the pages of The Book of Mormon in the accounts of Nephi, Jacob, Benjamin, Mosiah, Abinadi, Alma, and of all its other historical figures, it is appropriate that in the final chapters of the text we are introduced to a few of the ordinances that bridge the gulf between earth and heaven. These ordinances also attest to the nature of God, and confirm that His church is founded on unchanging principles and that the requirements for obtaining salvation are unchanging and are the same for all.

It is appropriate that Moroni first illustrated the manner of bestowal of the Holy Ghost. Its receipt is basic to the administration of all priesthood ordinances, and to the operation of the church. Mormon had recorded how the Lord had "touched with his hand the disciples whom he had chosen, one by one, even until he had touched them all, and spake unto them as he touched them. And the multitude heard not the words which he spake, therefore they did not bear record; but the disciples bare record that he gave them power to give the Holy Ghost. And I will show unto you hereafter that this record is true." (3 Nephi 18:36-37). In this chapter, the promised explanation is given. Here, we receive "the words of Christ, which he spake unto his disciples, the twelve whom he had chosen, as he laid his hands upon them." (Moroni 2:1).

After Jesus had laid his hands upon the Twelve, "there came a cloud" that is symbolic of the presence of the Lord, that "overshadowed the multitude that they could not see Jesus." (3 Nephi 18:38, see Exodus 19:9). Within that cloud, Jesus had called each by name and taught them: "Ye shall call on the Father in my name, in mighty prayer; and after ye have done this, ye shall have power." (Moroni 2:2). The power to confer the Holy Ghost has to be earned and then retained through continuing personal righteousness. Joseph Smith taught the same principle, when he wrote: "Many are called but few are chosen," and it is critical to "learn this one lesson - that the rights of the priesthood are inseparably connected with the powers of heaven, and that the powers of heaven cannot be controlled nor handled only upon the principles of righteousness." (D&C 121:34-36).

The Savior verified that the manner in which he had instructed the Twelve to confer the Holy Ghost was procedurally correct, when He said: "For thus do mine apostles." (Moroni 2:2). This is the only instance in The Book of Mormon where the term "apostle" is used in such a context that it could refer to the Nephite Twelve and to an office within the Melchizedek Priesthood. Clearly, they held the Melchizedek Priesthood, for it is by this authority that this ordinance of the gospel is administered.

## Do Latter-day Saints believe in personal revelation?

"And while I was thus struggling in the spirit," wrote Enos, "behold, the voice of the Lord came into my mind." (Enos 1:10). When this voice comes, wrote Truman Madsen, "as a flow of pure intelligence attended by a burning in the center self, it is of God. Our search for external warrant is really the confirmation and application of what is already, and more certainly, known." ("Eternal Man," p. 73).

It almost sounds too simple. Keep the commandments and listen to the whisperings of the Spirit. The heavens are open, and God speaks to us. But there is no revelation where there is no listening ear, and there is a performance cost associated with discipleship. The Church of Jesus Christ of Latter-day Saints emphasizes that we may literally find God, and that when we do, it will be an experience of indescribable joy. The story of the struggle of Enos to find God, that is recounted in The Book of Mormon, is of great religious significance, as it stirs our hearts with renewed confidence in His grace, His mercy, His personal concern, and in His unconditional love for each of us.

Jacob explained that "no man knoweth of (God's) ways, save it be revealed unto him." (Jacob 4:8). This verse echoes the teaching of President John Taylor, who said: "No matter what ability and talent we may possess, all must come under this rule if they wish to know the Father and the Son. If knowledge of them is not obtained through revelation it cannot be obtained at all." ("The Gospel Kingdom," p. 112). Revelation is the expression of the light and knowledge we receive of God. This principle is so basic that it almost requires no definition, because it speaks to our souls.

Religion in Joseph Smith's day had become magical, when the power by which churches operated was transferred from God to those who professed to be His earthly representatives, but who were only competing for market share. Priesthood had acquired the status of an office that mechanically bestowed power and grace, without regard for the spiritual or moral qualifications of its possessor. The Bible itself had become a magical book in the eyes of many, conveying power and knowledge without the aid of revelation. Moroni saw that there would be many in the Last Days who had "transfigured the holy word of God," or who had changed the appearance and substance of the scriptures. (Mormon 8:33).

Revelation demands that we give our undivided loyalty and attention to the Head of the church, Who is Jesus Christ. J. Reuben Clark, Jr. observed that we need "a listening ear by the people and a determination to live as God has commanded." (C.R., 10/1948). Without personal revelation, our ability to do that is severely compromised.

## What is the origin of the "American Indians?"

The Book of Mormon "was written by many ancient prophets by the spirit of prophecy and revelation. Their words, written on gold plates, were quoted and abridged by a prophet-historian named Mormon. The record gives an account of two great civilizations. One came from Jerusalem in 600 B.C., and afterward separated into two nations, known as the Nephites and the Lamanites. The other came much earlier, when the Lord confounded the tongues at the Tower of Babel. This group is known as the Jaredites." (1978 "Introduction to The Book of Mormon").

That Introduction invited misunderstanding, because Lamanites were therein identified as the "principal" ancestors of the American Indians. Past LDS church leaders, particularly church President Spencer W. Kimball, made statements that were consistent with the wording of that Introduction. A new Introduction, written in 2006 and a part of The Book of Mormon since that time, reads much the same, with one significant difference, that the Lamanites "are among the ancestors of the American Indians."

Current archaeological, anthropological, and genetic research casts some doubt upon previously suggested locations about where the civilizations flourished, whose histories are recorded in The Book of Mormon. Certainly, there are many Native Americans today who could trace their lineage to peoples who co-inhabited, with the Nephites and Lamanites, the Americas two thousand years ago.

There is also a reference to white and dark skin in the text of The Book of Mormon that should be read in the context of the symbolism of spiritual darkness versus purity. "Revile no more against (the Lamanites) because of the darkness of their skins;" cautioned Jacob, "neither shall ye revile against them because of their filthiness; but ye shall remember your own filthiness, and remember that their filthiness came because of their fathers. (Jacob 3:9). Perhaps a gentler, and more charitable, translation would read: "Revile no more against the Lamanites because of their spiritual darkness; neither shall ye revile against them because of their filthiness."

In just the same metaphorical way, Nephi had written of the Lamanites in the Last Days: "And then shall they rejoice ... and their scales of darkness shall begin to fall from their eyes; and ... they shall be a pure and a delightsome people." (2 Nephi 30:6). Or: "Their scales of spiritual darkness shall begin to fall from their eyes." Before the 1978 revision of the English language Book of Mormon, this verse was rendered "white" as opposed to "pure," with the intention of illustrating the concept of spiritual blackness.

In any event, disregarding the possibility that spiritual symbolism is at play here, The Book of Mormon seems to teach that the skin of the Lamanites was darker than that of the Nephites. Nephi wrote: "That they might not be enticing unto my people the Lord God did cause a skin of blackness to come upon them." (2 Nephi 5:21). Then, when the Lamanites entered into the Lord's covenants, the curse was taken from them, and "their skin became white like unto the Nephites." (3 Nephi 2:15).

One of the signs of the times in the Last Days is that the gospel will be preached to the remnant of the seed of Lehi, who are commonly identified as "Lamanites." Some Native American peoples may have "Lamanite" blood, but certainly not all do. As Hugh Nibley wrote: "The Book of Mormon is not a history of the Lost Ten Tribes. It is not a history of the Indians. It does not describe or designate any known ancient people, civilization, or individual in the Western Hemisphere, nor does it designate any recognized place, city, or territory in the New World. Even Cumorah receives only limited recognition and (then) only by Latter-day Saints." ("Since Cumorah," p. 161).

It may be that there are influences of many cultures among the peoples of the New World. For example, there is the interesting account of a supposedly Phoenician inscription found at Parahyba, Brazil, in the 1960s, which reads: "We are the Sons of Canaan from Sidon, the city of the king. Commerce has cast us on this distant shore, a land of mountains. We embarked from Ezion-Geber into the Red Sea and voyaged with ten ships. We were at sea together for two years around the land belonging to Ham, but we were separated by a storm, and we were no longer with our companions. So, we have come here, twelve men and three women on a shore which I, the Admiral, control. But auspiciously may the exalted Gods and Goddesses favor us." (See: "History Mystery: Ancients in America).

Whoever the latter-day remnants of the seed of Lehi are, the scriptures teach us the important lesson that they will be taught the gospel, "and they shall be restored to the knowledge of Jesus Christ, which was had among their fathers." (2 Nephi 30:5). In October 1960 General Conference, President Spencer W. Kimball confirmed: "The day of the Lamanites is here!" Of one thing we can be sure. As the curtain rises in the Last Days, and the children of Israel find themselves on center stage, the signs of the times will be revealed, unfolding a drama of all-encompassing proportion.

After considering these 95 questions that are answered in The Book of Mormon, take a moment to ponder any or all of these 20 thoughts:

The benevolent blindness
that is illustrated by the behavior
of Book of Mormon prophets was not
a liability. It was not spiritual myopia.
Instead, it was a catalyst, triggering acuity
that extended out to eternal perspective. It was
proof that they understood the grace of God,
and it allowed them to see things their eyes
could never behold. Benevolent blindness
permitted them to see as they were seen, to
be leaders of vision who had received the
knowledge of God, and who had beheld
His face. Benevolent blindness may
just have been the one sense that
unerringly guided them
Home.

Each
time we follow
up on the righteous
impressions we receive as
we read The Book of Mormon,
it's as if we've re-established our
connection with God's perfect faith.
As we did in a pre-mortal classroom
setting that is now a distant memory,
we are once again blessed to kneel at
His feet, as it were, to bask in the
ethereal light of His awesome
omniscience.

The enthusiastically ignorant try to drag the communication that waits to be dispensed from heaven down to their own level, until it's inaudible to their ears, much like their myopic view of life is to their eyes. The world ridicules revelation and disparages its delivery. Thus, their feeble attempts to explain the Book of Mormon, that exploded on the scene in March of 1830, ring hollow, especially when they're compared to the thunder, the lightning, and the voice that came forth from a burning bush on Sinai.

If we neglect our opportunities to expand our faith to make the connections that can only be realized when we maintain an eternal perspective, we neutralize the magical capability of the word of God to raise our testimony temperature, get our juices flowing, and stir our souls. The Book of Mormon is like a human growth hormone for our spirits that jump-starts our development on the pathway that leads to perfection.

From before
the foundation of the
world, the doctrine of Christ
as it is explained in The Book
of Mormon was custom-tailored to
eventually place each of us on trial,
to have our day in court. At the Bar of
Justice, when we kneel before His feet on
the Day of Reckoning, a Righteous Judge
will do no more than weigh the facts, and
our previous acceptance or rejection of the
gospel, together with the Atonement, will
determine our reward or our punishment.
The legal proceedings have already been
docketed to follow on the heels of our
mortal experience, and we might be
comforted to know that the Holy
Ghost will be there to see that
they will be carried out
with impartiality.

During
the Millennium,
those who remain on the
earth will not be focused on a
competition for scarce resources.
The Book of Mormon's descriptions
of millennial conditions paint a vivid
portrait where righteousness prevails and
where "the earth is full of the knowledge
of the Lord, as the waters cover the
sea." (2 Nephi 21:9).

To have the
unlimited freedom
to choose for ourselves
in an atmosphere that is so
full of dangerous deceptions,
enticing entrapments, soothing
seductions, and perilous pathways,
entails great risk. In our lives, if we
follow the teachings of the prophets in
The Book of Mormon, we will encounter
principles that will protect us, keeping us
untainted from the blood and sins of this
generation, and giving us the capacity to
flee from spiritual Babylon without
looking over our shoulders and
risk being turned into
pillars of salt.

To maintain the
momentum generated
by their introduction to The
Book of Mormon, and in order to
make it enduring, new members of
the church need to have sustaining
spiritual experiences. As Gordon B.
Hinckley said, every member of
the church, and especially new
members, needs a friend, a
responsibility, and the
nurturing influence
of the good word
of God.

The account of the Creation that was written by Moses provided only generalities that relate to the Fall of Adam and Eve and to the Atonement of Christ. That doctrine is more fully explained in The Book of Mormon. We must have a clear understanding, in order to generate the faith necessary to be clean from the blood and sins of this generation, to live life in abundance, and to become heirs of salvation and exaltation.

Following the Flood, the ancients built ziggurats that were massive towers that had been purposely constructed to reach all the way to heaven itself. The Tower of Babel is an example of these exaggerated temple steeples. However, their designers and builders, and those who flocked to behold those architectural marvels, missed the point. Instead of creating physical structures composed of nothing but brick and mortar, they could have more profitably spent their time by using the principles taught in The Book of Mormon, and more particularly in The Book of Ether (see Ether 1:5) to build enduring relationships with each other, and with God.

Near the temple in Bountiful, Jesus Christ validated the reality of higher dimensions from the unseen world. (See 3 Nephi Chapters 9-11). The Pearl of Great Price reinforces the teachings of the temple and confirms that from a superior vantage point in time and space, the Gods organized the heavens and the earth, divided the light from the darkness, created the waters and the earth, and placed all manner of vegetation thereon. Finally, they watched over all their creations until they obeyed. (See Abraham 4:1-18).

In the Word, we learn that we came into this world to die, but at the same time, thanks to the further light and knowledge we receive from the revelatory nature of The Book of Mormon, we know about the Plan of Mercy, that takes away the sting of death.

In a way, it is fortunate that a veil was dawn across our minds to keep us insulated from the realm of the Gods, to ground us on the solid and familiar bedrock of past, present, and future. For now, at least, the arrow of time moves in only one forward direction. This handy frame of reference permits us to live in an orderly fashion within a timeline woven in to the tapestry of The Book of Mormon.

Our witness of the divine authenticity of The Book of Mormon, Another Testament of Jesus Christ, requires our profoundly personal spiritual comprehension that is built on the foundation of the connections that are continually being made with our Heavenly Father, so that when we find ourselves about to be caught up into the third heaven, we will be ready to take that leap of faith right into the depths of eternity.

The Mountain of the Lord's House that is visualized in scripture is an allegorical, figurative representation of the refuge for Zion in the Last Days, when it "shall be established in the tops of the mountains." (2 Nephi 12:2). Whether it is a high place of God, a place of revelation, or perhaps the temple itself, Latter-day Saints are prone to restrict the application of this phrase to one area, that of the intermountain west, and specifically to the Valley of the Great Salt Lake. But this interpretation may be too narrow. Those who love the temple simply believe it to be the invisible summit of their imagination where cool air exists, and where the one God lives.

It was the Savior Who created the earth upon which we stand as a learning laboratory, and as a telestial testing center. It would be a citadel of higher education, and a home where we would be blessed to have all of the tools that could conceivably be necessary to validate our faith in Christ. In particular, we have been given The Book of Mormon, to see if we might be proven worthy of God's trust.

It is
in The Book
of Mormon that
we see beyond our
mortal horizons. We
even have a name for
such a state, calling it
"the depths of eternity".
Our covenants bless us to
"inherit thrones, kingdoms,
principalities, powers, (and)
dominions, (of) all heights
and depths." (D&C 132:19).
The question remains: In
what direction will these
'heights and depths'
take us?

We are not
ashamed to "declare
his doing among the people."
Without embarrassment, it's easy
"to make mention that His name is
exalted." (2 Nephi 22:4). We join with
our fellow Saints who have chosen to
"stand as witnesses of God at all
times and in all things, and
in all places ... even unto
death." (Mosiah
18:9).

When we immerse ourselves in The Book of Mormon, the Spirit will open the eyes of our understanding to undreamed of vistas of otherwise inaccessible experience. It is there that we begin to comprehend the scope of Moroni's promise that it is "by the power of the Holy Ghost that (we) may know the truth of all things." (Moroni 10:5).

The ordinances in The Book of Moroni stand in sharp contrast to the short-lived pleasure in worldly ways that always evaporates as morning dew in the full light of day. It is only unswerving obedience to our covenants that will mitigate the disastrous consequences that would surely prevail, if the spectre of rebellion were given license to determine our actions.

# One Hundred Questions Answered by The Book of Mormon

"Ye shall remember your children, how that ye have grieved their hearts because of the example that ye have set before them." (Jacob 3:10). The sobering truth is that parents are responsible for raising their children in light and truth.

"We talk of Christ, we rejoice in Christ, we preach of Christ, we prophesy of Christ, and we write according to our prophecies, that our children may know to what source they may look for a remission of their sins." (2 Nephi 25:26).

## Who is responsible for raising children?

"Ye shall remember your children, how that ye have grieved their hearts because of the example that ye have set before them." (Jacob 3:10). The sobering truth is that parents are responsible for bringing up their children in light and truth, and that if they fail to do so, the sins of the children will be upon the heads of the parents. In the latter days, the Lord declared: "Inasmuch as parents have children in Zion, or in any of her stakes which are organized, that teach them not to understand the doctrine of repentance, faith in Christ the Son of the living God, and of baptism and the gift of the Holy Ghost by the laying on of the hands, when eight years old, the sin be upon the heads of the parents. And they shall also teach their children to pray, and to walk uprightly before the Lord." (D&C 68:25 & 28).

"We talk of Christ, we rejoice in Christ, we preach of Christ, we prophesy of Christ, and we write according to our prophecies, that our children may know to what source they may look for a remission of their sins." (2 Nephi 25:26, see Mosiah 4:15, & Alma 39:16).

Before Fiorello La Guardia became mayor of
New York City, he was a magistrate. One day, there
appeared before him a man accused of stealing a loaf of
bread. Upon questioning, the accused explained that he'd
committed the crime to feed his family, for they were
starving. Whereupon, La Guardia dismissed the
case, and sentenced everyone present in the
courtroom to pay a fine for living in a
city where a man had to steal
to feed his family.

How refreshing that Heavenly Father
organized the world in such a way
that life begins with babies, who,
with untinctured innocence,
teach the world about
unconditional
love.

# Why is Isaiah quoted so frequently in The Book of Mormon?

"And now, behold, I say unto you," taught the resurrected Lord to the Nephites, "that ye ought to search these things. Yea, a commandment I give unto you that ye search these things diligently; for great are the words of Isaiah." (3 Nephi 23:1).

Nephi declared: "My soul delighteth in the words of Isaiah, for I came out from Jerusalem, and mine eyes hath beheld the things of the Jews, and I know that the Jews do understand the things of the prophets, and there is none other people that understand the things which were spoken unto the Jews like unto them, save it be that they are taught after the manner of the things of the Jews." (2 Nephi 25:5).

Readers of The Book of Mormon will repeatedly encounter direct references to Isaiah in the text. As a matter of fact, 32% of The Book of Isaiah is quoted verbatim in The Book of Mormon, while 3% is paraphrased. The New Testament follows the pattern established earlier in The Book of Mormon, for in that text there are more quotations attributable to Isaiah than to all other Old Testament prophets combined. It is little wonder then, that The Book of Mormon, which not only reflects Old World religious philosophy, but which also is a Latter-day Testament of Jesus Christ, should rely so heavily on this prophet.

Nephi delighted in the words of Isaiah because they proved the truth of Christ's coming and that, save He should come, we must perish. (See 2 Nephi 11). The writings of Isaiah that are recorded in 2 Nephi chapters 12-24 are illustrations of Nephi's faith in his prophecies. Isaiah was what we call a "Messianic Prophet." His mission was principally to point us toward the Savior, His teachings, and to salvation, which only come through obedience to the principles of the gospel.

During the ministry of Isaiah, the Ten Tribes were taken captive; they later fled to the north and were lost to history. But they carried with them the words of Isaiah, as did Lehi during his journey to the Promised Land. The Jews also retained his words, and today, Covenant Israel, or the church, has them. His is a very diversified audience.

Nephi knew that, in the Last Days, the words of Isaiah would be a pearl of great price, and to those who would suppose that they are not, he said "I (will) speak particularly, and confine the words unto mine own people; for I know that they shall be of great worth unto them in the last days; for in that day shall they understand them; wherefore, for their good have I written them." (2 Nephi 25:8).

It is most interesting that Nephi considered the writings of Isaiah, who had lived just over a century earlier, to be holy scripture. Clearly, Nephi understood that whatsoever the prophets "shall speak when moved upon by the Holy Ghost shall be scripture, shall be the will of the Lord, shall be the mind of the Lord, shall be the word of the Lord, shall be the voice of the Lord, and the power of God unto salvation." (D&C 68:4).

Today, the responsibility has shifted to the shoulders of the members of the Lord's church to carefully study and benefit from the prophecies of Isaiah, for he spoke dualistically to our generation as well as to his own people. His language might be veiled in symbolism and shadows of meaning with which we are only superficially familiar; nevertheless, we have been commanded by the Savior Himself to "seek ye out of the best books words of wisdom; seek learning, even by study and also by faith." (D&C 88:118). We must "live by every word that proceedeth forth from the mouth of God." (D&C 84:44).

It is significant that Nephi recognized Isaiah's witness of the Lord Jesus Christ to be pre-eminent among the testimonies of the prophets. It should be no surprise that the Savior declared to the Nephite Saints that Isaiah's words were great. His mission, after all, was to persuade the children of God to believe in Christ. This is why the prophets all seem to sound alike. They all draw upon the same eternal truths to prove their points. Theirs is not vain repetition, but rather is theatrical encore.

"The prophets do have much the same message, and the now recognized practice of the prophets of giving out the words of their predecessors as their own (actually) receives its first clear statement and justification in The Book of Mormon." (Hugh Nibley, "Since Cumorah," p. 40-41).

# How do Latter-day Saints feel about Mary, the mother of Jesus?

Alma taught that the Savior "shall be born of Mary, at Jerusalem, which is the land of our forefathers, she being a virgin, a precious and chosen vessel, who shall be overshadowed and conceive by the power of the Holy Ghost, and bring forth a son, yea, even the Son of God." (Alma 7:10).

This verse has been a source of confusion for some members of the church as they have read The Book of Mormon, and also has been identified by enemies of the church as an error in the text. This is not because of Nephi's reference to Mary, but because he wrote that Jesus would be born "at Jerusalem." In some early editions of The Book of Mormon, the rendering is "in Jerusalem." But that would be technically incorrect. In any event, the term, "the land of Jerusalem," occurs forty-two times in the text of the current edition of The Book of Mormon, and so we might ask ourselves: "What does this common expression mean?"

The answer is quite simple. Bethlehem, just six miles from Jerusalem, is within that area designated by the Ancients themselves as "the land of Jerusalem." When the Book of Mormon text states that Jesus was born of Mary "at Jerusalem," or "in the land of Jerusalem," there is no conflict as long as one understands the ancient context. "Such a neat test of authenticity is not often found in ancient documents," wrote Hugh Nibley. "Therefore, what at first appears as a textual error in The Book of Mormon, instead powerfully supports its claim of authenticity." ("An Approach to The Book of Mormon," p. 82).

Nephi taught that the Lord Himself would give a sign: "Behold, a virgin shall conceive, and shall bear a son, and shall call his name Immanuel." (2 Nephi 17:14). "For unto us a child is born, unto us a son is given, and the government shall be upon his shoulder: and his name shall be called Wonderful, Counsellor, the mighty God, the everlasting Father, the Prince of Peace." (Isaiah 9:6).

Alma taught that the Savior would "be born of Mary, at Jerusalem, which is the land of our forefathers, she being a virgin, a precious and chosen vessel, who shall be overshadowed and conceive by the power of the Holy Ghost, and bring forth a son, yea, even the Son of God." (Alma 7:10).

The Lord Himself would give a sign: "Behold, a virgin shall conceive, and shall bear a son, and shall call his name Immanuel." (2 Nephi 17:14). "For unto us a child is born, unto us a son is given, and the government shall be upon his shoulder, and his name shall be called Wonderful, Counsellor, the mighty God, the everlasting Father, the Prince of Peace." (Isaiah 9:6).

## How does the Lord Jesus Christ intervene directly in our lives?

"We search the prophets, and we have many revelations and the spirit of prophecy; and having all these witnesses, we obtain a hope, and our faith becometh unshaken, insomuch that we truly can command in the name of Jesus and the very trees obey us, or the mountains, or the waves of the sea." (Jacob 4:6).

Jacob was not overzealously distracted by these marvelous manifestations of spiritual and priesthood power. He knew the source from whence they came. He wrote: "Nevertheless, the Lord God showeth us our weakness that we may know that it is by his grace, and his great condescensions unto the children of men, that we have power to do these things." (Jacob 4:7).

Jacob was awed by the incomprehensible ability of God to lift him to sublime heights. "Great and marvelous are the works of the Lord." he wrote. "How unsearchable are the depths of the mysteries of him; and it is impossible that man should find out all his ways." (Jacob 4:8).

"There is no doctrine, ritual, principle, ordinance, law, performance, church, belief, program, angel, or prophet that can save us in the absence of the personal intervention in our lives of the Lord and Savior Jesus Christ. This is the teaching of the Book of Mormon, as well as of the Bible." (Stephen Robinson, "Are Mormons Christians?" p. 106).

Jacob was in awe of
the incomprehensible power of
God to lift him to sublime heights,
and into the rarified atmosphere of the
Spirit. "Great and marvelous are the works
of the Lord," he enthusiastically wrote. "How
unsearchable are the depths of the mysteries
of him, and it is impossible that man
should find out all his ways."
(Jacob 4:8).

"There is no performance, ritual,
principle, law, doctrine, ordinance, church,
belief, program, angel, or prophet that can save us
in the absence of the personal intervention in our
lives of the Lord and Savior Jesus Christ. This
is the teaching, not only of the Book of
Mormon, but also of the Bible."
(Stephen Robinson).

## What do we really think of Christ? Whose Son is He?

When "the Pharisees were gathered together, Jesus asked them, Saying, What think ye of Christ? Whose son is he?" Sadly, their sluggish response, "The Son of David," was tendered with little feeling or emotion. (Matthew 22:41-42). Although it was technically correct, it lacked spiritual horsepower. Its dearth of traction was obvious, its inability to generate spontaneity was palpable, its lack of energy to engage enthusiasm was noticeable, its incapacity to spark vitality was evident, and its failure to candidly acknowledge the powerful relationship that can exist between ourselves and God was clear.

And yet, with adequate preparation, thinking about Christ could have generated the energy to lift them heavenward on a groundswell of emotion. Their example should be motivation enough for us to elevate the level of our worship to something more dynamic than the simple mechanical observance of a multiplicity of ceremonial rules, and to help us to avoid the pit into which the Pharisees fell. Thinking about the Savior should be more than a repetitive exercise to be performed only by the numbers. As the daily antidote to our tendency toward pride, selfishness, and self-reliance, our study of The Book of Mormon, Another Testament of Jesus Christ, should help us to catalyze feeling, capture emotion, contour attitude, crystallize thought, congeal passion, compartmentalize action, and convey sentiments that lead to our spiritual revitalization.

Since those were, perhaps, among the most important and penetrating questions that could have been asked of anyone, at any time in history, or at any place on earth, we can be sure that the Pharisees were not the Savior's only intended respondents. He cast a much wider net. The Master, Who expounded all scripture in one, demands that you and I answer, as well, that we might also have the opportunity to squirm under the microscope of His scrutiny. The Book of Mormon catalyzes the intensity of that exercise.

It matters little whether we identify with the Pharisees or the Sadducees, with Buddha, Confucius, Guru Nanak, Zoroaster, or with gods of wood and stone. We may concur with the monotheism of Islam or the Bahá'í, the pantheistic theology of Hinduism, Shintoism, or Taoism, with secular humanism or irreligion, with Catholicism or Eastern Orthodoxy, with fundamentalists, evangelicals, or Protestants, or with the existential nihilism of the postmodern world. Paul observed of the Athenians, who were not so very different from us, that they were inclined to bow down before unknown gods, whom, therefore, they ignorantly worshipped. It is in the hope that this volume will help you to stand independently in your witness of the true and living God, that I have declared Him to you. (See Acts 17:23, & 1 Thessalonians 1:9).

You may be a trusting Timothy or a doubting Thomas, a spiritual giant or a philosophical naturalist, of a ready wit or resoundingly dull, earnestly enlightened or frivolously facetious, casually indifferent or energetically enthusiastic, a dedicated disciple or a distracted detractor, a true believer, an agnostic, or an atheist. In a moment of despair, you may have thrown up defensive dross designed to disregard, deflect, discourage, or disparage the question: "What think ye of Christ?" If you have wandered into disbelief, you may have deferred or deterred your response to the question: "Whose son is he?" If that day has already come, or if it looms large on your horizon, you can be sure that your stammering apologies will be unceremoniously swept aside when your true feelings and your innermost motivations are finally revealed.

In every case, no matter that you are a defender of the faith or an ambassador of the adversary, all of heaven will hold its collective breath as time stands still and your fate hangs in the air as a dandelion seed caught in the doldrums of a hot summer afternoon. How you answer these questions will define you or destroy you, for your response will delineate your dreams, as it describes your destiny and determines how, where, and with whom you will spend eternity. I hope this volume will have helped you to prepare for that great and dreadful day when you will be asked to stand and give your sworn deposition before God, angels, and witnesses, to be counted among the sheep or the goats, on His right hand or His left hand.

To ensure that your answers might be animated with energy, to have no regrets, and to avoid the fate of the Pharisees, you have been given the Light of Christ. It proceeds from His throne as a powerful influence for good that is intended to groom you to receive the Holy Ghost. It is a gift that miraculously multiplies even as it divides within a universe populated with individuals whose actions are governed by free will. It is given, the Lord revealed, "that every man may act in doctrine and principle pertaining to futurity, according to the moral agency which I have given unto him." (D&C 101:78, see D&C 93:31).

It has been benevolently bestowed upon all of us by One Whom we can be sure "denieth none that come unto him, black and white, bond and free, male and female; and he remembereth the heathen; and all are alike unto (him), both Jew and Gentile." (2 Nephi 26:33). The Light of Christ stimulates our soul-sweat as it works on our conscience, our sense of duty, and our scruples. It provides a shield of protection against the corrosive spatter of perspiration cast off by the destroyer, who is insidiously and persistently working overtime to damage our doctrinal defenses, dull our spiritual sensitivities, diminish our charitable capacity, deplete our bountiful reservoirs of sympathy, and destroy our devotions, even as we labor with an equal but opposite intensity to ennoble our work on the earth.

The Light of Christ exerts a nurturing influence, as well. Although we must daily travel farther from the East, we are nevertheless oriented toward the radiant glow emanating from that distant horizon. It provides us with the regularly recurring reassurance of a religious recalibration that autocorrects with fortuitous frequency and celestial precision. It envelops us in an intuitive appreciation of where we came from, why we are here, and where we are going. As in a heavenly language that is rhythmical, melodious, soothing to our ears, and calming to our souls, when we hear the Spirit quietly whisper: "You're a stranger here," we are comforted by the realization that we have "wandered from a more exalted sphere." (Eliza R. Snow).

The Light of Christ examines what It means to be anxiously engaged, inspires us to plumb the depths of our commitment to the Savior, sensitizes us to the nobility of His work, expands upon the visions of immortality, and makes us more acutely aware of His glory, as it brings eternal life into sharp focus.

In a way, thinking about the Savior can be likened to a primer on midwifery, because one of the purposes of the Light of Christ is to facilitate the arduous process of our spiritual rebirth, by contributing to our preparation to answer with conviction the questions that were first posed to the Pharisees so long ago: "What think ye of Christ?" and "Whose son is he?" When we feel the urge to push His agenda, the Light of Christ can be our labor coach, providing us with just the right amount of encouragement to successfully deliver our witness of the Savior without being overbearing.

One exciting element of the manifestation of the Light of Christ is the constant stream of inspiration and revelation that cascades down from above. This ensures that all may walk along illuminated pathways, and that no individual or institution may legitimately claim or have a monopoly on divine guidance. It exerts a leveling influence that is the great equalizer, giving each of us the same privileges to use our faculties of mind, intellect, and spirit to our best advantage, that we might discern between truth and error, no matter upon what spiritual plateau we might be currently relaxing, or what spiritual wall we may be climbing on the ladder of faith. It permits us to listen with sensitivity and to be receptive to the cries of the downtrodden and oppressed, to see with a lucidity that allows us to be responsive to our environment, and to be benevolently blind to the shortcomings of others.

The Light of Christ provides us with a nurturing influence that makes it easier to have lips that have learned to articulate only positive expressions of speech and never speak guile, shoulders that have developed the strength to bear the burdens of those who have been battered and bruised by the vicissitudes of life and who may be faltering under the heavy weight of sorrow or sin, backs that have become sturdy enough to brace us against the fierce winds of adversity and the subtle wiles of the adversary, hearts that have become the receptacles of pure and virtuous principles upon which we may draw in times of need, bowels that are moved to compassion for those who are struggling with misfortune, hands that have become accustomed to lifting those who are in need of support, and feet that have been conditioned to speedily carry us, as ministering angels, to those who are imprisoned by poor choices, bad habits, or unfortunate circumstances.

Even now, heavenly messengers are nursemaids to the nations of the earth, and use the power of the Light of Christ as a resource to reach out and caress those who are poor in spirit. Men and women of all persuasions feel that angels are watching over them. Witness countless newlyweds who are certain that their match was made in heaven, before the world was. Others sense that they have been assisted by acts of providence, are the beneficiaries of divine intervention, have been touched by angels, are moved to compassion, or have been otherwise blessed to "walk in the light of the Lord." (Isaiah 2:5).

Guidance in the form of spiritual promptings and impressions are more common that many would suspect. Powerful intuitive communicators strongly influence nearly all of us to move in the direction of our dreams, toward a greater appreciation of the majesty and power of our Creator. Truly, He "is no respecter of persons" Who causes the sun to shine on the wicked, as well as on the just. (Acts 10:34). Therefore, we must venture forth out of the shadows, even beyond the direction we receive from the Light of Christ and the ministration of angels, if we want to begin to appreciate the special familiarity that the Lord enjoys with those whom He has characterized as "the children of light." (John 12:36). The more we think about Christ, and the more we use The Book of Mormon as our primer, the easier it is to craft with words the sensations that naturally flow to each of us as a result of the stirrings of those feelings of intimacy.

As we think about Christ, we realize how heavily we have borrowed from the towering examples of those who, over the years, have been our mystical mentors, our sensible chaperones, our spiritual guides, our surrogate saviors, as well as our compassionate critics. They are our avatars, who have shown us the way, strengthened our testimonies, taught us humility, been there to steady and nurture us, applied the Balm of Gilead and bound up our wounds, provided both tangible and immaterial support, emboldened us with words of encouragement, and cheered us on with wise counsel. When think of this multitude of angels thinly disguised as our family, friends, and peers, we remember the words of Sir Isaac Newton, who, when pressed to reveal the great secret behind his accomplishments, simply replied: "I stood on the shoulders of giants."

If we are fortunate, we are privileged to do so, as well. We count the Book of Mormon prophets among our mentors, chaperones, guides, and even surrogate saviors. As we think about the Son of God, we draw upon the faith, testimony, and spiritual insight of the General Authorities and lay members of The Church of Jesus Christ of Latter-day Saints, as well as numerous playwrights and poets, philosophers and humanitarians, authors, journalists, essayists, classicists, religious scholars of all persuasions, statesmen, sages, mystics, stoics, and the composers and lyricists with whom we are familiar. Our friends and family are often more influential than they could ever imagine. We are fortunate if we have been blessed with such wonderful traveling companions during our journey of faith. Such gurus and guides have touched our lives with a profound influence that has helped us to shape the tender feelings that we clothe in words, as we think about how The Book of Mormon can be Another Testament of Jesus Christ.

In the end, however, we sometimes need to ask for the pardon of our traveling companions when they are confronted by the literal and figurative blemishes, the idiosyncratic foibles, and the objective and subjective imperfections that too often subtly work their way into our character, if we are not vigilant.

Whenever we stray from the foundation teachings of The Book of Mormon, when we take poetic license with principles, or add needless ecclesiastical embroidery to its gospel truths, we beseech the indulgence, and the forgiveness, of our peers. If our passion clouds our vision or overpowers our zealous intentions, if the syntax of our speech seems tortuous, too bland, or too spicy, if our feelings are understated or if we have been given over to hyperbole, or even if we appear to drift over the line separating true doctrine from baseless speculation, we beg for the forbearance of our contemporaries, that they might take a step back and allow our expressions to simmer for a while before returning to sample anew their flavor. We can only hope and pray that the reduction sauce of time may enhance the palatability of our perspective.

In any case, as the congealed distillate of our life experiences, our thoughts and feelings relating to the Savior stand revealed as our innocent attempts to yoke our emotions to language. We find ourselves paraphrasing the teachings of The Book of Mormon, for gospel principles stand as independent witnesses and need no external warrant. As we share with others the words of the prophets, we hope that they will find them refreshing, and will use them as food for thought.

We dream that we might feel the gentle caress of the touch of the Master Potter, as He turns our lives with the hand of time. We want Him to mold us and shape us as the Artisan of our destinies. "As the clay is in the potter's hand, so are ye in mine hand," said the Lord to His prophet. (Jeremiah 18:6). As Isaiah declared: "O Lord, thou art our father; we are the clay, and thou our potter; and we all are the work of thy hand." (Isaiah 64:8). We hope and pray that as The Book of Mormon turns our thoughts to the Savior, we may remain pliable and impressionable to the things of the Spirit.

All of us need to learn to utilize the divinely designed accouterments of the matchless and multi-talented Carpenter of Nazareth, Who will help us to construct the stages upon which will be enacted the drama of our lives. We can imagine that our efforts will be validated by appreciative applause from the audience, and an occasional bouquet of red roses thrown at our feet. But it will be even more satisfying to remain as His poor understudies, and to give our best efforts to supporting roles in off-Broadway performances that count for more than mere entertainment.

His Plan does not require that we be the stars of the show. Our path of progress to perfection is a process, and not a point. We do not need top billing to fulfill our dreams. We do not seek to garner a People's Choice Award. Rather than becoming the objects of attention of an adoring paparazzi, we foresee ourselves being enveloped instead in dazzling clouds of divinely directed diamond dust that glitters with thousands of points of light, and we dream of becoming the participants in daily dramas that far surpass the pomp and circumstance of any "American Idol" production.

As we study The Book of Mormon, ours will be performances exhibiting displays of celestial energy worthy of notice from above. As fire in the sky, the air in the theater of life will be charged with an electricity that represents the inevitable merger of the universal encouragement of the Light of Christ with the pointed and providential guidance provided by the Holy Ghost. When these influences streak in tandem across the heavens, their trajectories will coalesce to trace a flaming trail that sparkles over a vast cosmic ocean of thought. Over the ebb and flow of its tide, the Spirit will create an effectual bridge of understanding that is buttressed by the cohesive influence of the mighty foundation of faith.

Our innermost longings to apprehend these visions of the eternal world are epitomized in our triumphant realization of dreams fulfilled. Our emotions are painted by words that depict our progression toward distant mileposts along the well-marked paths that lie before us. Our quest for the Holy Grail is defined as much by the obstacles we have encountered, as it is by the hurdles we have yet to face. We are molded by personal victories and by our commemoration of the achievement of our goals, but we are also refined by our frustrated plans, and shaped by our preparations to address challenges that lie just around the next bend in the road. On all these points, The Book of Mormon is encouraging and supportive.

In the learning laboratory of life, experience is the active ingredient in a fertile matrix carefully created by God as He meticulously prepares the personalized petri dishes that are best suited to our individual circumstances. This rich culture medium becomes just the agar we need in order to nurture our metamorphosis, as we are transformed, not by maturation but by generation, into the full stature of our spirits. The infusion of a heavenly element readies us to receive with equanimity whatever might come during an incubation process that was designed to be just as challenging as it would be rewarding.

All this leads back to our basic objective, which is to keep the Savior in our thoughts by studying The Book of Mormon, that we might encourage a daily atmosphere of reflection, maintain an eternal perspective, initiate positive change, and harmonize our behavior with His charitable example. Our determination to do so comes, in part, thanks to Moroni, whose words stir our souls as a voice whispering from out of the dust. On one occasion, he wrote: "I speak unto you as if ye were present, and yet ye are not. But behold, Jesus Christ hath shown you unto me, and I know your doing." (Mormon 8:35).

Because we will one day be asked to give accountability reports to the Savior, we try to heed King Benjamin's ancient but apropos warning to watch ourselves judiciously, to be the meticulous guardians of our thoughts, the scrupulous custodians of our words, and the prudent caretakers of our deeds, to fastidiously observe the commandments of God, and to continue evenly in the faith. (See Mosiah 4:30). As we hesitantly inch our way through mortality, this admonition invigorates us with renewed energy, and instills in us the desire to redouble our efforts to know the Savior better.

We persist, because the simple questions: "What think ye of Christ?" and "Whose son is he?" should make a difference to each of us. These inquiries demand that we dig deeply within ourselves before we tender our responses, because it is all too easy to superficially retreat into colorless and insipid verbiage as the easy way out. If we casually and carelessly steer a course away from Him with offhand, dismissive, and inconsiderate remarks, until He is conveniently out of sight and far from our minds, we can realistically expect in return no more than a stupor of thought.

Any fleeting, albeit faux, feelings of liberation from the constraints of conscience will soon give way to an inner emptiness that cannot be satisfied with the poor imitations of the settled conviction in our minds of the peace that surpasses understanding, that could have been ours. If, in our knee-jerk reactions to the healthy opposition that stimulates our growth, we kick against the pricks, we will surely further estrange ourselves from the Spirit, until we are left with neither root nor branch. We will be tossed to and fro by every wind of doctrine, as flotsam and jetsam on the sea of life. We will suffer the same fate as so many of the protagonists in The Book of Mormon.

None of us would choose to perish because of our willful neglect of the things that matter most, or to lead marginalized lives because we had intentionally become spiritually depleted on a personal or an institutional level. We persevere because we do not want to die of spiritual starvation, doctrinal dehydration, or intellectual inhibition, while only inches away from the living bread that would have satisfied our hunger, or from the healing fountains of truth that could have slaked our thirst.

Instead, we elect to think about our Savior in positive and meaningful ways that lead us to green pastures and still waters. We use The Book of Mormon as our guidebook and roadmap on the highways and byways of life. The process draws us into the warmth of His embrace, where we are permitted to enjoy an intimacy that allows us to pause for a moment to feel the touch of His garment, before His strident call to action reawakens within us a sense of our duty that quickens the pace of the inexorable journey back to our beginnings.

Precious few "self-help" books address the issues of self-denial, meekness, and charity, or ask that we surrender to the greater good our desire for self-actualization, self-renewal, self-determination, self-fulfillment, or self-aggrandizement. Not often are we taught to concentrate our efforts on the quality of self-control that honors God's design, rather than some twisted temporal theory of emotional or spiritual well-being that lacks an upward thrust. But that is exactly what The Book of Mormon asks us to do, and what we must do. We must "let go and let God."

Only through the discipline of a life-long study of The Book of Mormon will we catch a religious fever that elevates our testimony temperature enough to get our juices flowing with an appreciation of Who the Savior really is. Only then, will we experience the earth shaking and mind-bending theophany that we are His spiritual offspring, and will we recognize the potential of our position. The precious emanation of familiar and soothing oscillations of energy resonating from within the limitless reserves that are selflessly shared with us by the Holy Ghost will carry us along on rolling waves of the spirit toward a more sure witness of the Savior's divinity. That is why we must study The Book of Mormon, and keep Him in our thoughts.

This pulsing arpeggio ignites our souls with passion, and may have been the catalyzing influence that was missing from the pedantic model of righteous behavior that was adopted, almost by default, by the Pharisees. We want our preparation for the performance of our lives to include fast scale runs through more than half a dozen octaves on all 88 of the glistening black and white ivory keys of experience. As we rehearse in our minds our witness that Christ is our Savior, we want to be accompanied by a celestial symphony that has been scored for every conceivable instrument. We want to expand our repertoire to include, not only inspiring artistic compositions representing every epoch of musical literature, but also our own original and signature harmonic inventions.

But most of all, in the orchestration of life that is so beautifully displayed in The Book of Mormon, we want the Senior Recital that showcases our command of pitch, rhythm, dynamics, timbre, and texture, to be worthy of the Savior's approbation. Along the way, we want to find our way back to the Source of our inspiration, that we might one day enjoy master classes as we sit at the feet of the Maestro Who first created musicality by matching movement and form to the melody and mood of His celestial creations.

We want to become reacquainted with our perfect fit. Then, when we have finally completed our dissertation on life, we hope that our composition may be recognized as our magnum opus. After we have successfully defended our thesis, we would like to be able to express our thanks at the exercises that not only celebrate our lives, but that also observe and honor our commencement. We hope to gratefully acknowledge our devotion to, and our complete and total reliance upon, the One who became our doctoral advisor, who was none other than "the Christ, the son of the Living God." (Matthew 16:16).

The Book of Mormon can instill within each of us a yearning to consecrate our lives to Him. It can empower us to throw ourselves upon an altar of faith that is of our own construction, but whose foundation is buttressed by a supernal display of divine direction. It can bless us with us an unwavering confidence that drives us relentlessly forward so that we might one day squarely and unflinchingly meet His penetrating gaze with clear eyes, that His power to save might thereby be unleashed in our behalf, that it might flow over our wounds as a healing balm.

When we look around at those who have made the study of The Book of Mormon a life-long project, we want to find ourselves among those who have been Born Again, who are "called the children of Christ, his sons, and his daughters." (Mosiah 5:7). We want to experience the thrill of being spiritually begotten of Him, and of having our hearts changed through faith on His name. We want Him to be ever before us so that, without distraction, our thoughts might turn to Him, that we might feel His energy building within us until it lifts us to the zenith of experience where the lines distinguishing mortality from eternity blur, and we find ourselves consumed in a fire of everlasting burnings.

We want the teachings of The Book of Mormon to empower us to resoundingly declare that we have been born of God, and have received His image in our countenances; that we have experienced a mighty change in our hearts. (See Alma 5:14 & 26). Only then, through saving faith, will we be prepared to respond to the questions that loom before us: "What think ye of Christ?" and "Whose son is he?"

As we ponder our relationship with the Savior, our proper prior preparation will prevent performance, as it relates to Book of Mormon scholarship. It will nudge us off our complacency plateaus, away from the trendy cafés situated along the broad avenues of Idumea, and transport us as on the wings of eagles beyond the boundaries of our self-imposed limitations, right to the edge of eternity, where "forever" will finally stand revealed before us.

At that moment, as the power fueling our study charges our spiritual batteries and energizes our sight with infinite perspective, there will be created a pulsing stream of inspiration whose flow has no temporal or spatial boundary. We will be swept up by quickening currents into the direct experience of a holy communion with God. Although the heavens will always be higher than the earth, His thoughts will somehow have become our thoughts, and His ways our ways. (See Isaiah 55:8-9). We will be caught up in His work and His glory, and finally understand that "the universe is a machine for the making of gods." (Henri Bergson).

After considering these 100 questions that are answered in The Book of Mormon, take a moment to ponder any or all of these 20 thoughts:

"The best education is to be perpetually thrilled by life."
(Edward Everett Hale).

The Book of Mormon helps to reacquaint us with Heavenly Father's Plan as we put finishing touches on our dissertations on life. As we near perfection, our expositions will be esteemed by God for what they've become: each one of them a true magnum opus reflecting His divine design. By soliciting the Holy Spirit to release us from captivity, we are permitted to see things as they really are, and to enjoy lucidity that comes more from our hearts than from our heads. Thus, we are reminded of the peaceful setting back in our heavenly home, and of God's promises that so gently massaged our spirits there.

The
world
exerts an
ever-present
negative energy,
while the promptings
that quietly influence
us to prayerfully examine
The Book of Mormon are our
most effective countermeasures.
Our Redeemer's only stipulations
are that we confess when we have in
any way yielded to the temptations
that lie before us, and that when we
do so, we immediately initiate the
safety protocol of repentance that
is required by the Atonement,
to steer us back to the strait
and narrow way, and to
our focus on heaven.

"For behold, and lo, the
Lord is God, and the Spirit
beareth record, and the record
(of The Book of Mormon) is true,
and the truth abideth forever and
ever. Amen." (D&C 1:39).

In The Book of Mormon, every time that we encounter the doctrine of the Atonement of our Savior Jesus Christ, our sinews will resonate with recognition. It is in this way that we have all been blessed with the innate capacity to hearken to the voice of the Spirit, even to the Light of Christ, that guides us to the warm embrace of our Father, Who will reach out to us from heaven and draw us to His bosom.

Speaking to us from eternity, the Savior promised: I will go before your face (and) will be on your right hand, and on your left, and my Spirit shall be in your hearts, and mine angels round about you, to bear you up." (D&C 84:88). With such assurance, how could we imagine to turn away from our Book of Mormon studies, to persist in our wickedness, and to deceive ourselves by believing that we could fly solo, without the safety that is provided by His Atonement's parachute?

As we ponder The
Book of Mormon, we
would do well to organize
ourselves, and prepare every
needful thing as we establish a
house of prayer, fasting, faith,
learning, glory, and order; in
other words, as we seek to
establish a house of
God. (See D&C
88:119).

In the
Book of Mormon, we
learn that God in heaven is
the Grand Architect of a divine
design that establishes our familial
roots and confirms His fatherhood, that
we might enjoy a witness that it is in Him
alone that "we live, and move, and have
our being; as certain also of (our) own
poets have said. For we are also his
offspring." (Acts 17:28).

We will
not endure
for long if we
rely only upon the
light that is generated
by our casual connections
to our Father in Heaven. He'll
provide our external power source
with ample energy for as long as we
manifest a desire to become members
of His Second Mile Club, which is a
privileged group to which we have
been invited, in consequence
of our acceptance of the
Book of Mormon.

Our
physical
surroundings in
this lone and dreary
world have been designed,
harsh though they may seem,
to provide a hint of familiarity.
We are sensitive to the Spirit as we
read and study The Book of Mormon,
and we establish a celestial connection
as we commune with the heavens across
space and time, bursting the barriers
of our telestial habitation.

The Book of
Mormon frees us, not
only from the limitations
of our own ignorance, but also
from the constraints of mortality.
It is in the scriptures that we learn to
be at one with the majestic clockwork,
"like a bird that, pausing in her flight
a while on boughs to light, feels them
give way beneath her and yet sings,
knowing that she hath wings."
(Victor Hugo).

In Third Nephi, we
read about those who survived the
chaos in the land after the crucifixion
of the Lord. From the unseen world, "there
was a voice heard among all the inhabitants
of the earth, upon all the face" of the land. (3
Nephi 9:1). It was not the deafening voice of a
hundred decibels, but simply a quiet sound
that was heard by everyone regardless of
their temporal surroundings. It was a
voice quite unlike any sound that
had ever before been heard, for
it came from immortal lips
with an effect on heaven
and earth that was
profound.

When we stand before the
Judgment Bar of God, we will concede that
the covenants to which we had been introduced
within the pages of The Book of Mormon were neither
haphazard nor arbitrary. There were neither corollaries
and footnotes, nor addenda and exceptions to the rule. Our
obedience had demanded neither analytics nor explanation by
legal counsel, and its accounting required no interpretation by
an expensive C.P.A. The ordinances had been clearly established
and carefully clarified with purposeful precision so that there
could be no disputation concerning their accessibility
or validity. In every sense of the word, God is
no respecter of persons, and He dots every
'I' and crosses ever 'T'.

It is
in The Book
of Mormon where
we take our bearings
on eternity. We get a fix
on the stars in the heavens.
Within its pages, our telestial
tendencies are transformed into
celestial sureties with the spiritual
equivalents of compasses, protractors,
chronometers, sextants, chart dividers, and
rulers. This process is not one of maturation
but of generation, to the extent that we are
'born again' in a house of learning that
also serves as a delivery room for our
spirits. Thus, we will also need the
spiritual equivalents of forceps,
clamps, catheters, and
specula.

At the end of
our mortal journey,
we will remember that it
was the counsel of The Book
of Mormon that channeled us
past the doctrinal dead ends, as
well as through the conceptual cul
de sacs and telestial traffic jams, that
always threatened to detour us from the
strait and narrow way. We will be forever
grateful for the holy scriptures that exposed
us to direct experience with the perfect law of
liberty, and that permitted us to exchange
the uncertain course adopted by those
who were bound for the telestial
kingdom, for the reality of
celestial surety.

As we
look about
us, at a world
that seems to have
gone mad, The Book
of Mormon stands as
a light that has been set
on a hill. As an island in a
storm, it provides refuge from
the uncertainties of life and the
vagaries of men. It speaks in a
language of stability, purpose,
and direction to all those who
might be afraid, hesitant,
and uncertain during
a crisis of their
faith.

We see in The Book of Mormon indistinct hints of those who sought to harness the power of the priesthood, "to break mountains, to divide the seas, to dry up waters, to turn them out of their course; to put at defiance the armies of nations, to divide the earth, to break every band, to stand in the presence of God, to do all things according to his will, according to his command, subdue principalities and powers; and this by the will of the Son of God which was from before the foundation of the world. And (those with) this faith, coming up unto this order of God, were translated and taken up into heaven." (J.S.T. Genesis 14:30-32, see Alma Chapter 13).

For many of us, perhaps for most of us, it will only be during our journey to the veil that will have been accompanied by our study of The Book of Mormon, that we will comprehend how we might one day "flourish in immortal youth, unhurt amidst the war of elements, the wreck of matter, and the crash of worlds." (Joseph Addison).

Millions have discovered that
it has largely been within the pages
of The Book of Mormon that their souls
have been liberated to go forth from their
dwelling places. They have discarded
the poor lenses of the body, to peer
thru the telescope of truth into
the expansive reaches of
immortality.

Our
acceptance of
Alma's invitation to
enter into the waters of
baptism is life-sustaining
and life-generating, for just as
we are "born into the world by water,
and of blood, and the spirit" and have
become of dust living souls, even so, we
"must be born again into the kingdom of
heaven, of water, and of the Spirit, and
be cleansed by blood," even the blood of
Jesus our Redeemer, that we "might be
sanctified from all sin, and enjoy
the words of eternal life in this
world, and eternal life in the
world to come." (Moses
6:59-60).

Don't overlook the 50 answers, 200 observations, and familiar scriptures in Volume One.

As we engage the
Book of Mormon, we embark
upon an incredible journey through
thousands of years of history, as the pages
of a most profound text unfold before the panorama
of great civilizations. Within its pages lies the intrigue of
ancient Asia as warlords battle for supremacy and tension in
Jerusalem rises as empires of the Near East struggle for power. We
witness the thrill of those whose eyes were fixed on a Land of Promise
beyond the horizon of their vision, and we feel the exhilaration of
prophets of God who counseled all mankind. Those who truly
appreciate it, will feast upon the word of God and devour
the book as if it were literally the bread of life. They
will seek, and yearn, and strive, and wrestle
for their blessing.

The Book of Mormon makes the bold claim that
its pages contain the fulness of the gospel. (See D&C 42:12).
Even members of The Church of Jesus Christ of Latter-day Saints
sometimes misinterpret this. It does not mean that there will be found
on its pages detailed instruction regarding every doctrinal principle,
nor does it mean that the Nephites participated in every ordinance of
the gospel, as we know it. Today, we live in the Dispensation of the
Fulness of Times, when all that has been revealed throughout the
ages will be given. The members of the church in Book of
Mormon times were given knowledge sufficient for
their own salvation. More properly, this is the
context within which the definition 'the
fulness of the gospel' makes the
most sense.

There are many more answers in The Book of Mormon. The challenge, after we've posed the questions, is to find them through study and prayer.

There is unity within the church regarding the religious dogma that's embedded within The Book of Mormon. Every day all over the world, millions of Latter-day Saints open their translations of this scripture and explore identical doctrinal themes. Contrast this unity of the faith with the thousands of denominations who interpret with significant differences hundreds of variants of single biblical verses of scripture. It is far better for the church to proclaim that The Book of Mormon was translated by the gift and power of God through the Prophet Joseph Smith. This leaves little room for doctrinal interpretation either within or outside the church.

We left our heavenly home with assurances from our Father that, while on earth, we would have the Light of Christ and the influence of the Holy Ghost, and that heavenly power would help us to recognize the truth when we heard it. As Brigham Young declared: "Every gospel principle carries within it a witness that it is true."

# Topical Index
## to Subjects
(Referenced by Question Number)

The Book of Mormon is like a stethoscope that has the ability to measure our cardiac vital capacity. When our hearts have broken in contrition, we're able to detect a steady sinus rhythm confirming the congruence that must exist between ourselves and the greater light of heaven.

The Book of Mormon tenderly lifts us to higher ground, to our own Mount of Transfiguration. When we reach its spiritual plateau, our faces will shine and our raiment will radiate with a dazzling glow that could only have been kindled by one source, which is the glory of God's celestial fire.

Accountability – 46
Accountability – Age of – 62
Additional scripture – 7
Agency – 43
American Indians – origin of – 95
Americas – 56
Ancient scripture – 5
Another Testament of Jesus Christ – 7, 78
Apostasy – 17
Are Mormons Christians? – 1
Atonement – 31
Atonement and Resurrection – 34
Atonement – Necessity of – 32
Bad things / Good people – 63
Baptism – Covenant of – 59
Baptism – Necessity of – 58
Baptism of Children – 62
Baptism of Jesus – 60
Baptism – Renewal of covenant – 61
Bible – 6
Birth of Jesus – 56
Blessings from obedience – 8
Book of Mormon – Another Testament – 21 & 78
Book of Mormon errors – 19
Book of Mormon – Mention of in the Bible – 13
Born again – 16
Capabilities – 65
Chains of Hell – 30
Charity – 79
Children of God – 4
Children – Raising – 96
Christian nations – missionaries to – 76
Church of Jesus Christ of Latter-day Saints – 3
Conscience – 42
Covenants with God – 26
Creation – Purpose of – 40
Cross – Significance of – 90
Crucifixion of Jesus – 57
Death – A part of God's Plan – 40
Death – Where do the righteous go? – 53
Death – Where do the unrighteous go? – 54
Death – What happens next? – 51
Desire to believe – 22
Does God care about us? – 86

Earth – Purpose of its creation – 40
Enduring to the end – 48
Errors in The Book of Mormon – 19
Eternal life – 85
Existence – Purpose of – 41
Faith – 22
Father and Son, One – 25
First Resurrection – 35
Forgiveness – 37
Free will – 43
Garments – 91
God and Jesus – Separate Beings – 29
Godhead – 92
Gold plates – 11
Good and evil – 70
Gospel of Jesus Christ – 39
Grace – 50
Happiness and wickedness – 72
Heavenly Father and Jesus Christ – 24
Hell – 30
Hidden Scripture – 9
Holy Ghost – 92
Holy Ghost, Gift of – 93
House of Israel – 89
Image and Likeness of God – 27
Immortality – 84
Immortality and Eternal Life – 85
Improvement – 68
Indians – American – 95
Isaiah quoted in The Book of Mormon – 97
Jesus Christ born in Bethlehem – 56
Jesus Christ – Crucified – 57
Jesus Christ – Personal Savior – 99
Jesus Christ – Son of God – 1
Jesus Christ – What do we think of Him – 100
Jews – 89
Joseph Smith – Author – 12
Judgment Bar – 52
Justice and Mercy – 33
Knowledge – 83
Mary – Mother of Jesus – 98
Metal plates – 10
Missionaries – 75
Missionaries to Christian Nations – 76

Because The Book of Mormon is more than just history, and because it is another testament, or second witness, of Jesus Christ, it is used to great effect as a principal tool of conversion. The book was inspired to assist God as he continues to perform His work to bring to pass our immortality and eternal lives, by teaching the principles of faith, repentance, baptism, and the ordinances of the priesthood. There was method to his madness when Mormon abridged the records with which Ammaron had entrusted him.

One thing that is important to our comprehension of the monumental themes addressed in The Book of Mormon is familiarity with the underlying structure of the text. It is not too difficult to understand, as long as we remember that Mormon was the prophet who gathered all the records together, and who then abridged certain of these into the Plates of Mormon. This is the main reason why the text is called The Book of Mormon. In a larger sense, though, it is not really his book alone.

Moroni's promise – 15
Moroni statue – 20
Mysteries – 80, 83
Negative peer pressure – 73
No respecter of persons – 86
Oneness – 29
Opposition – 44
Opposition - Satanic – 71
Ordinances – 29
Other sheep – 55
Peer pressure – 73
Plan of Salvation – 38
Plates – 10
Personal revelation – 94
Prayer - About what? – 67
Prayer - To Whom? – 66
Prayer, How – 66
Prophets - Role of – 81
Protection of the righteous – 64
Respecter of persons – 86
Responsibility – 8
Restoration – 18
Resurrected bodies – 36
Resurrection – 34
Resurrection - First – 35
Revelation – 8

Revelation – 94
Right and Wrong – 42
Righteous - Protection of the – 64
Saints – 2
Satanic opposition – 71
Saving faith – 23
Scripture - Value of – 14
Seer - Definition of – 82
Service to God – 28
Shame – 77
Spirit Prison – 51
Spirit World – 53
Stewardship – 74
Stretching ourselves – 65
Testimony – 15
Testimony of Jesus Christ – 75
Thoughts, words, and deeds – 45
Underwear - Religious – 91
Warfare – 87
Weakness – 47
Wicked behavior – 69
Wickedness & happiness – 72
Wisdom – 83
Works – 50
Zion – 88

Mormon said that he couldn't write "the hundredth part of the things of (his) people." (Words of Mormon 1:5). Even though Joseph wrote in his history that the plates on the Hill Cumorah were deposited in the earth in a box fashioned out of stone, other sources indicate that there were many more plates at that site. Brigham Young said that there was a whole room, with plates stacked high against the walls. Together, he said that they would comprise several wagon-loads.

What we do have swells in significance with the realization that the fraction of the record that was included in the book is a condensation which comprises only the history that Mormon considered to be of most importance to those living in the last days.

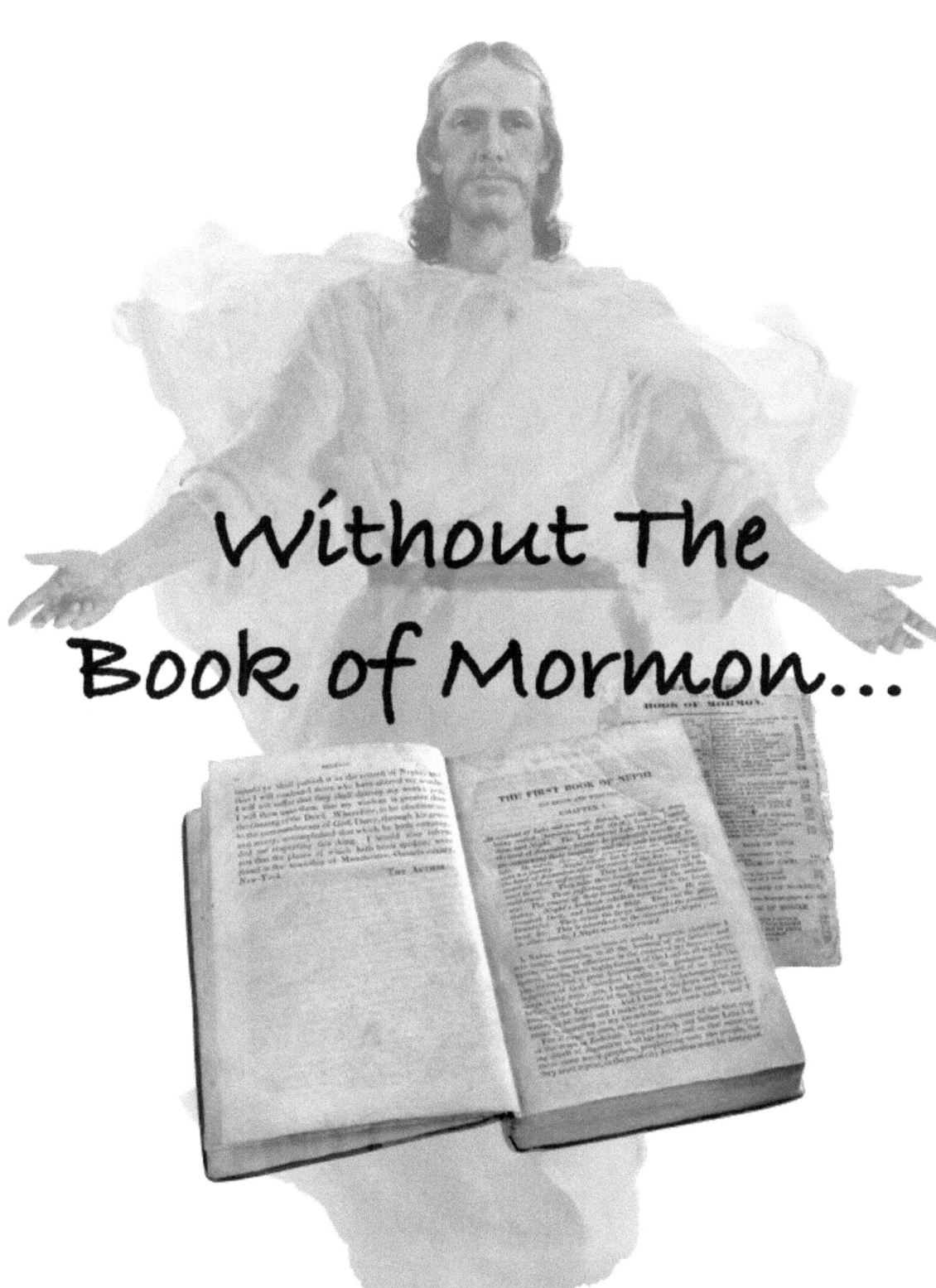

It is intriguing to ask ourselves: "What would the Restoration have looked like without The Book of Mormon?

The Book of Mormon is a blueprint for our survival in the Last Days. Without it, the construction of our eternal identities might have looked quite different.

Because of The Book of Mormon, those who have embraced the gospel stand out from those who have feathered their nests in Babylon.

Because of
The Book of Mormon,
we have mentors to guide us
as we embrace the mysteries of
the kingdom. These are the saving
principles and ordinances of
the gospel of Jesus
Christ.

The publication
of The Book of Mormon, on
March 26, 1830, permitted the
Restoration to move forward, and
the church to be organized,
on April 6, 1830.

Without The Book
of Mormon, we would know
nothing about the fulfilment
of the Savior's promise that He
would visit His other sheep.
(See John 10:16, & 3
Nephi 15:21).

It is in the pages of The Book of Mormon where we find the fulfilment, or a description of the realization, of many biblical prophecies. Without the clarification and illumination of its narrative, our understanding would be clouded by confusion, and we would see through a glass, darkly. (To name just a few examples, see 1 Nephi 13:12-15, 1 Nephi 13:16-19, 2 Nephi 2-27, Helaman 13-16, Genesis 49:22-26, Deuteronomy 33:13-16, Isaiah 29:1-2 & 18, Ezekiel 37:15-22, John 10:16, & 2 Corinthians 13:1).

Without The Book of Mormon, church members would stand out far less prominently, as Christians.

Without The Book of Mormon, the line in the sand would be far less clearly defined. (See Joshua 24:15).

Without The
Book of Mormon,
God's children would be
more heavily influenced by
darkness, and less by the
light of the gospel.

Without The Book
of Mormon, we would have
far less symmetry, balance,
stability, harmony, clarity,
focus, and purpose in
our lives.

Without The Book
of Mormon, we would have
fewer stories of inspiration that
touch us personally and
individually.

Without The
Book of Mormon, there
would be less truth
in the world.

Without The Book of
Mormon, we would have more
difficulty receiving the confirming
witness of the Spirit in order to become more
observant followers of righteousness, to possess
greater knowledge, to be the progenitors of
nations and ambassadors of peace, and
to receive instruction, and keep
the commandments.

Without The Book of
Mormon, we would lack
another testament, one that
is perhaps the most powerful
witness of all, that Jesus
is the Christ, the Son
of the living
God.

Without The Book of Mormon, we would have fewer stories, parables, and sermons that teach us how to rely on the Savior as the source of our inspiration.

Without The Book of Mormon, we would lose a standard by which we can interpret the Bible and other prophecies, that as stand-alone scriptures are difficult to understand. If we did not have The Book of Mormon, we would have to make do without the Bible's greatest friend.

Without The Book of Mormon, Alma's powerful premise that the pen is mightier than the sword would forever be lost. (See Alma 31:5).

Without The Book of Mormon, where could we turn, to so easily learn about the necessity of authority when administering the ordinances of the gospel?

Without The Book of Mormon, there would be confusion regarding the proper administration of the ordinance of baptism.

Without the firepower that is provided by The Book of Mormon, the soldiers in the army of Christ could not so easily teach with authority.

Without The
Book of Mormon, our
confidence when proclaiming the
principles of the restored gospel
would be diminished.

Without
The Book of Mormon, we
would know nothing of, and
consequently would fail to learn
from, the life experiences of many of
God's children, most of whom we
discover, were very much
like ourselves.

Without The Book of
Mormon, where would
we turn in our quest
to find scriptural
mentors?

Without The Book of Mormon, there would be a conspicuously empty space upon the bookshelf of time, instead of a prominently displayed chronicle of religious history that was written especially for our age.

Bereft of The Book of Mormon, we would have no other choice but to less comprehensively investigate the mysteries of God, which are the saving principles of the gospel.

Without the guidance that is provided by The Book of Mormon, we would know far less about the meaning and purpose of life.

Without the
clear and unambiguous
explanation of the principles and
doctrine that is found throughout The
Book of Mormon, the importance
of personal accountability
would receive far less
emphasis.

Were it not for
The Book of Mormon
teachings that relate to
the Atonement, it would
be easier for guilt to
hold our future
hostage.

Without The
Book of Mormon,
the sweet miracle of
forgiveness might
be less tenderly
treated.

Without The Book
of Mormon, we might be
less likely, in a violent world,
to find the inner peace of
the gospel of Jesus
Christ.

Without The
Book of Mormon, what
it means to be 'born again'
would be more difficult to
understand. (See John
Chapter 3).

Without The
Book of Mormon,
finding our way Home
through telestial traffic
would be much more
difficult.

Without The Book of Mormon, discovering God's Rest might be more elusive. (See Alma 13:12).

Without the key of knowledge that is provided by The Book of Mormon, it would be far more difficult to discern truth from error. (See Moroni 10:5).

Without The Book of Mormon, there would, arguably, be less faith in the world. (See D&C 1:21).

Without
The Book of Mormon,
there would be less hope
in the world. (See
Jacob 4:4).

Without The Book of
Mormon, there would
be less charity in
the world. (See
Moroni 7).

Without The Book of Mormon, our age would
continue to be insufferably and mind-numbingly
retrospective. It would build only upon the sepulchres of the
fathers. Without The Book of Mormon, we would have at our
disposal nothing but biographies, histories, and criticisms. The
ancients beheld the God of Abraham, Isaac, and Jacob face to face;
but we would only see Him through their eyes. "But why should
we not also enjoy an original relation to the universe? Why
should we not have a poetry and philosophy of insight
and not only of tradition, and a religion by
revelation to us, and not just the history
of theirs?" (Ralph Waldo Emerson).
Such is the power of The Book
of Mormon to deliver on
these promises.

Learning
the language
of The Book of Mormon
(and especially of 2 Nephi
Chapters 12-24) will bless us
with comprehension of a celestial
vernacular that is soothing to our
ears and calming to our souls. The
voice of the Spirit can be rhythmical
and melodious. As we hear it quietly
whisper: "You're a stranger here," it
is comforting for us to realize
that we "have wandered from
a more exalted sphere."
(Eliza R. Snow).

The
Book of Mormon
will help us to "believe
the gospel of Jesus Christ."
(Mormon 3:21). As Joseph Smith
declared: "I told the brethren that The
Book of Mormon was the most correct of
any book on earth, and the keystone of
our religion, and a man would get
nearer to God by abiding by
its precepts, than by
any other book."

The Book of Mormon was written so all the world might know that "every soul who belongs to the whole human family of Adam ... must stand to be judged of (his or her) works, whether they be good or evil." (Mormon 3:20). Everyone will be redeemed from spiritual death, to stand, at least briefly, in the presence of God at the Judgment Bar of Christ.

The Book of Mormon takes up its narrative in earnest in a land that was choice above all other lands, that was preserved so the children of God could flourish 'beyond the wall.'

It was
written and
preserved to come
forth in our day, so
that both the Jews and
and Gentiles might be
convinced that Jesus is
the Christ, the Son of
the Living God.

The Book of Mormon serves as another witness
to "the Jews, the covenant people of the Lord ... that
Jesus, whom they slew, was the very Christ and the very
God." (Mormon 3:21). As Nephi wrote, The Book of Mormon
will be given to the Jews in the Last Days "for the purpose of
convincing them of the true Messiah, who was rejected by
them; and unto the convincing of them that they need
not look forward any more for a Messiah to come ...
for there is save one Messiah spoken of by the
prophets, and that Messiah is he who
should be rejected of the Jews."
(2 Nephi 25:18).

Our Book of Mormon scholarship provides us with an attractive return on investment, and also with mad money that is sufficient for our immediate needs. But it also allows us, if we so choose, to substitute its legal tender for bundles of counterfeit currency with which late payments may be made with both interest and penalties tacked on for bad behavior. Without the Atonement, our lease on life would be threatened with cancellation for the nonpayment of the levies and the charges that accumulate as we conduct our lives within a speculative environment in an arena of agency and the circus of commerce.

Mormon saw our day and knew our needs. He understood that The Book of Mormon would help a world that did not know how to "repent, (to) prepare to stand before the judgment-seat of Christ. (Mormon 3:22).

# Observations

"Men are free according to the
flesh; and all things are given them
which are expedient unto man. And they
are free to choose liberty and eternal life,
through the great Mediator of all men, or
to choose captivity and death, according
to the captivity and power of the devil;
for he seeketh that all men might be
miserable like unto himself."
(2 Nephi 2:27).

"And upon these
I write the things of my soul,
and many of the scriptures which are
engraven upon the plates of brass. For my
soul delighteth in the scriptures, and my
heart pondereth them, and writeth them for
the learning and the profit of my children.
Behold, my soul delighteth in the things
of the Lord; and my heart pondereth
continually upon the things which
I have seen and heard."
(2 Nephi 4:15-16).

A Book of
Mormon requirement is
that we take calculated and
acceptable risks, in order to break
free from the comfort zones, safety
nets, and ports of refuge to which the
timid apprehensively retreat at the first
sign of danger, to squeak out their lives
as they scurry about from one shadowy
sanctuary to another, in a flight from
both freedom and faith.

It is
our faith that
points us in the
direction of doctrine,
so when we encounter
the principles of the Plan
in The Book of Mormon, we
will all experience religious
recognition, or a re-knowing
of things we have previously
been taught. We will respond
to the truth with action that
has the form and substance
of a godly walk that is a
bold testament of our
confidence in God's
power to save.

It took J.R.R.
Tolkien 17 years to write
"The Lord of The Rings". Margaret
Mitchell took nearly 10 years to complete
"Gone With The Wind". J.D. Salinger spent 10
years to complete "The Catcher in The Rye". It took
Victor Hugo 12 years to complete "Les Misérables".
Michael Crichton spent 8 years writing "Jurassic
Park". It took Joseph Smith roughly 3 months to
translate The Book of Mormon. How did he
do it so quickly? He simply said that
the task was accomplished "by
the gift and power
of God".

As we
lift the latch and
force the way, and we
learn more about the Plan
of God by studying The Book
of Mormon, we begin to discern a
distinct afterglow from the light of
our premortal lives, that establishes a
subtle but undeniable link between
the heavens and the earth that
remains undeniable.

The second
mile of faith that
is nurtured by the
Plan of God and by The
Book of Mormon asks us to
shun the telestial temptations
that are so cunningly peddled by
snake oil salesmen who have set up
shop within the great and spacious
buildings that dot the landscapes
of our lives, and that pop up in
the most unexpected places on
the side streets that border
the strait and narrow
way.

As we read and study The
Book of Mormon, we feel the word
enlarging our souls and enlightening
our understanding. As Brigham Young
said: "Every gospel principle carries within
it a witness that it is true." In the economy of
the gospel, "we often catch a spark from the
awakened memories of the immortal soul,
which lights up our whole being as with
the glory of our former home."
(Joseph F. Smith).

When we
feel the power of
The Book of Mormon
swelling within us, we
realize that it can lift us
to the zenith of experience,
until lines differentiating
mortality and eternity blur.
At that moment, when we see
ourselves in a condition that,
for the lack of better words,
can only be described as if
we were being born again,
we will be consumed in
fires of everlasting
burnings.

All of those
who have renounced
the world and have entered
into the Covenant "are born of
him." (Mosiah 5:7). Covenants are
binding contracts between ourselves
and God. Therefore, no person may enter
into such except upon the basis of revelation
from Him, and upon the exercise of priesthood
power by His appointed servants who have been
ordained to administer the ordinances of the
gospel. When these conditions have been
met, those in the embrace of fidelity
and fraternity with the Savior
are described as being
"born again."

Our temporal baggage is one of the obvious contraries with which we have to deal as we engage the grand themes of the Plan of Salvation. It creates imbalance leading to confusion, whereas the principles and doctrine of The Book of Mormon jar us out of our collective complacency by upsetting the stagnation of the status quo. They invite us to enjoy a settled conviction of the truth by getting our juices flowing, prodding us to constructively expend our energy, and putting our agency to work in the best tradition of opposition in all things.

As we study correct principles and make determined efforts to incorporate the teachings of The Book of Mormon into our lives, we are obliged to return to the real world, where we are resigned to be sent forth as sheep in the midst of wolves. However, the efforts we have made to internalize its principles and doctrines will create a shield of protection against the spatter of corrosive perspiration cast off by the destroyer, who is working overtime to damage our doctrinal defenses, diminish our charitable capacity, deplete our bountiful reservoirs of empathy, dampen our spiritual sensitivities, and destroy our devotions.

Whether we
are scions of society
or practiced panhandlers,
living in the fast or the slow
lane of life, whether we have rags
or riches, or are leaders or lepers, are
early prodigies or late bloomers, venture
capitalists or welfare recipients; no matter
what our circumstances may be, The Book of
Mormon is as a bridge over the troubled waters
of faltering faith. When we embark upon its
study, we move past the yellow brick road
that leads only to Oz, to find the strait
and narrow path that is cobbled with
gold and that will take us to
the gate of heaven itself.

When we are
introduced to The
Book of Mormon and our
souls have been illuminated
by the burning Spirit of God,
we can no longer remain passive.
The flickering fire of faith warms up
our souls as we begin to recognize the
upward reach within ourselves. We are
sensitized to truth and beauty, and to
a goodness above and beyond our
own attainment. We experience
the unmistakable stirrings
of the Spirit from deep
within our hearts.

Every one of the Book of Mormon prophets invites us to choose liberty and eternal life, rather than its contrary, which is captivity and spiritual death, and to live out our lives within the framework of the gospel and its laws. Without it, unbridled freedom would lead to tyranny. We are free to elect whether or not we wish to be governed by its principles and doctrines, but we cannot escape the consequences should we choose unwisely.

Those who share The Book of Mormon with others are faithful, and they endure, that they might obtain the prize of eternal life. They claim the promises of the Lord, Who said He would disperse the powers of darkness from before them, and would cause the heavens to shake for their good, as they go about the work of the ministry, bringing others into the fold.

Once we have embraced
The Book of Mormon, we speak
of principles with such incendiary
rhetoric that those who are of hesitant
and faltering faith are encouraged to
take their first tentative steps toward
commitment, while, simultaneously,
more spiritually mature disciples, as
they realize that present levels of
performance aren't acceptable,
are inspired to lengthen
their stride.

Paul knew
what it meant to go
the second mile. He labored
among the Corinthian Saints,
whom he was pleased to discover
had a working relationship with the
laws and ordinances of the gospel. He
characterized the revelatory gifts of God as
being written on 'tables of stone'. That is all
well and good, but he hinted that there exists yet
another order of mind. It is a connection that can
be ours if we will embrace The Book of Mormon.
"Ye are manifestly declared to be the epistle of
Christ ministered by us, written not with
ink, but with the Spirit of the living
God; not in tables of stone, but in
(the) fleshy tables of the heart."
(2 Corinthians 3:3).

We know that God is sensitive to our needs, because we have the evidence of our effectual and fervent prayers. We understand the laws of heaven that govern the acceptance by the world of The Book of Mormon. We draw virtue from the life force that is the Holy Ghost, and encourage those who find themselves lost in the press of the jostling crowd to reach out and touch the hem of the garment of the Savior. (See Matthew 9:21).

When our hearts have been touched by the Spirit, and we begin to grasp the nature of The Book of Mormon and how it was conceived, we learn more about how we fit in to God's divine design. We learn how faith can drive the law into our inward parts. When it does so, the articles of our faith become the particles of our faith.

We who have
experienced the power
of The Book of Mormon
will distain the amusement
parks of Babylon. Instead, we
will gratefully frequent the aid
stations that our Heavenly Father
has providentially positioned all
over Zion. We find our way by
avoiding telestial turf, and we
keep a sharp lookout for those
signposts that will lead us
to celestial boulevards
that are paved with
gold.

Those who have been
blessed with the capacity to
have wholeheartedly embraced
the principles and doctrines of The
Book of Mormon will find that they
have been endowed with an ability to
break free from "the influence of that
spirit which hath so strongly riveted
the creeds of the fathers, who have
inherited lies, upon the hearts of
the children, and filled the
world with confusion."
(D&C 123:7).

Those who have
so freely partaken of
the sustaining influence
of The Book of Mormon have
experienced God's power that
stems from love as opposed to
the Machiavellian influences
of lust and the unrighteous
desire for dominion that
dominate the agendas
of the worldly.

Is
it easier
to just throw
in the towel, and
harder to push on,
to continue the good
fight? Is it easy to settle
for average, and difficult
to be extraordinary? Those
who apprehend the philosophy
of The Book of Mormon accept
and will ultimately overcome
their challenges, not because
they are easy, but precisely
and pointedly because
they are hard.

The Book of
Mormon asks us to
emulate the protocols
of a criminal pathologist,
with one caveat. It seeks to
identify the fingerprints of
a master criminal, who is the
Prince of Darkness, which are
smeared all over a plethora of
penurious programs, parties,
politics, and policies that do
little else than to promote
personal and provincial
proclamations related
to plans that are, at
best, petty.

Too often,
the Nephites were
overzealous in their
outward observances. As
hypocrites, they pretended to
be pious, when, in fact, they were
simply professors of religion. They
crept into nameless graves, unwept,
unhonored, and unsung, while
now and then, a few of them
forgot themselves into
immortality.

The
Book
of Mormon
factors into our
success strategy,
because it lies at the
foundation of our hope
in Christ. Its assurance
of peace and the comfort of
our convictions will create a
momentum in our lives that
will propel us on a trajectory
that will streak across the
sky as it arches beneath
the heavens.

Without
baptism for
a remission of
sin that follows
on the heels of our
repentance and our
witness of the restored
gospel and of The Book of
Mormon, there is no way we
can reasonably expect to inherit
the glory of celestial realms. This
is particularly true when we have
aforetime been agreeable to abide
only by telestial or terrestrial
principles that inherently
put fewer demands on
our discipleship.

For over 2,000 years, Christians have looked forward to a God-centered earth that is "full of the knowledge of the Lord, as the waters cover the sea." (2 Nephi 30:15). In all that time, it has become clear that "no form of government, and no level of material well-being, will save us. We will be redeemed only when towers fall, and Jerusalem has triumphed over Babylon. Finally, what is at stake is not only intelligence, but also feeling. We have to change our hearts." (Abba Eban).

"Blessed are all the peacemakers, for they shall be called the children of God." (3 Nephi 12:9). They are the spiritually begotten sons and daughters of Christ, who go about promoting goodwill. They are the fashioners of amity who model the Savior, Who was the Prince of Peace. "Theirs is not the peace of this world, of ease, luxury, idleness, or the absence of turmoil and strife, but the peace born of a righteous life. It is the peace that lifts the soul, that day by day brings us closer to the home of Eternal Peace, the dwelling place of our Father." (J. Reuben Clark, Jr.).

Gluttony and
drunkenness prejudice
the judgment of the weak-willed.
Flirting with physical impairment will
blind them to the path of progress toward the
kingdom that is before their eyes. Of such, the
prophet Isaiah wrote: "They regard not the work of
the Lord, neither consider the operation of his hands."
(2 Nephi 15:12). They are held captive because their
character no longer harmonizes with holiness, and
they are past feeling, for their overindulgence
demands an ever-greater intensity of
validation for the same quality,
or even decreased levels, of
gratification.

When the lives
of both the Nephites and the
Lamanites conformed to the pattern
that had been established by the Savior,
scales of darkness fell away and the eyes of
their spiritual understanding were opened. (See 4
Nephi 1:2). Their ears increasingly comprehended
the otherwise inaudible whisperings of the Holy
Ghost as spiritual fluency was developed,
and their hearts were softened by
the pure love of Christ.

The Savior offers us
the gifts and powers by which we
may attain His stature, so that we might
enjoy not only what He has, but also what He is.
"If ye, by the grace of God, are perfect in Christ, and
deny not his powers, then are ye sanctified in Christ
by the grace of God, through the shedding of the
blood of Christ, that ye become holy, without
spot." (Moroni 10:33).

The blueprints of Babylon (see
1 Nephi 11:36) seem to have been drawn with
a stylus that is moved by the unsteady hands of
Beelzebub's architects of anarchy, those who fancy
themselves as creators of chaos and the masters of
mayhem, those who figure prominently in the
frightening stories that are found in the
narratives that fill too many of the
pages of The Book of Mormon.

Those who
refuse to repent have
forsaken their core values,
and yield to an obsession for
things that can never satisfy
their voracious appetites.
(See Moroni 9:3).

Lessons
from The Book of
Mormon can neutralize
the negative aspects of the
contraries that've been built
into the fabric of God's Plan.
They can harmonize the trials
we'll all face in our every-day
experience with the blessings
that have been preserved for
the repentant faithful who
will triumph over every
adversity to inhabit
mansions in the
kingdom of
God.

When the law has been
stitched into the sinews of our
souls as we read The Book of Mormon,
so that it becomes the tapestry of our lives
and is the pattern upon which we trace our
movement along the path of progress, our
"minds become single to God, and the
days will come that (we) shall
see him; for he will unveil
his face" unto us.
(D&C 88:68).

For the Plan
of God to succeed, The
Book of Mormon teaches us
that there needs to be opposition
in all things, both good and evil,
light and darkness, pleasure and
pain, and happiness and misery,
which makes baptism mandatory,
because, let's face it, most of us
lack the spiritual horsepower to
consistently choose the right,
much less to save ourselves
when things go horribly
wrong. We need God
every hour of our
lives.

Nephi clearly taught (1 Nephi 3:7) that when the Lord gives us a commandment, He also prepares the means to accomplish the task that is set before us. We see what might be best for ourselves and for the Kingdom of God, develop a testimony that it should be, and then work with all our capacity to make it happen, whatever the cost might be. Then, when we are so richly blessed far beyond the measure that we deserve, the price, once paid so painfully, is recalled in gladness. We receive full value, and all because of the boundless grace of God.

A life-changing comprehension of the doctrine that is found in The Book of Mormon often follows on the heels of obedience to the baptismal covenant. After their own baptisms, Joseph Smith and Oliver Cowdery reflected: "Our minds being now enlightened, we began to have the scriptures laid open to our understandings, and the true meaning and intention of their more mysterious passages revealed unto us in a manner which we never could attain to previously, nor ever before had thought of." (J.S.H. 1:74).

Hope is the unalterable
reward of our well-founded faith,
and it is the interest we've accrued on
the investment that has been made
with our undeviating trust in God,
in the Book of Mormon, and in
His promise of guidance to
save us from our own
follies.

The torrent
of filthy water that Lehi
beheld in his vision represented "an
awful gulf which separated the wicked
from the tree of life, and also from the saints
of God." (1 Nephi 12:16). The Plan of Salvation
requires that there always exists a barrier between
the spirits of the righteous and the unrighteous,
as both await the resurrection. That barrier is
nothing more than the justice of God "and
the brightness thereof (is) like unto the
brightness of a flaming fire, which
ascendeth up" unto the heavens,
the dwelling place of deity.
(1 Nephi 15:30).

The Book of Mormon teaches
us that we are God's chosen people,
and that for as long as we observe
to keep His commandments, we
will live within His embrace,
enjoying a security that
others cannot
know.

The Book of
Mormon leads us to enter
into covenant relationships with
the Lord. "I will give unto the children
of men line upon line, precept upon precept,
here a little and there a little; and blessed are
those who hearken unto my precepts, and lend
an ear unto my counsel, for they shall
learn wisdom; for unto him that
receiveth, I will give more."
(2 Nephi 28:30).

As the
battle rages on in the
hearts of men and women,
those who have accepted The
Book of Mormon live their lives
in crescendo. The deafening roar
of their righteousness commands the
attention of the angels in heaven who
wield the sword of Justice, and who
only wait upon God's command
before letting it fall upon an
unrepentant world.

Our purposeful study
of The Book of Mormon opens
up windows of opportunity, that we
may better understand the principles of
the gospel that are mysteries to those who
have not spiritually prepared themselves for
personal revelation from God. The Lord has
assured us that if we expend soul-sweat,
we "shall know of a surety that these
things are true, for from heaven
will (He) declare it" unto
us. (D&C 5:12).

The
Savior
employed
the metaphor
of the mote and
the beam (3 Nephi
14:3) to illustrate that
it seems to be our human
nature to point out the sins
of others, and to emphasize
their weaknesses, though it
is we who are frequently
guilty of more serious
transgressions.

Alma emphatically
taught his son Helaman
that faith is the first principle
of the gospel (see Alma 37:33) and
that profane temporal power will be a curse
to those who place their trust in its ephemeral
authority. For the support of the devil and his
angels will be a millstone around the necks of
the heart-hearted and stiff-necked at the last
day, when they will be abandoned and left
terrifyingly alone, as they are catapulted,
kicking and screaming, down into an
abyss of their own creation, that will
have the appearance of their very
own personalized and hand
crafted versions of hell.

As presents, and in commemoration of the occasion of being born again, every member of the church is given gifts by the Spirit of God. (See Alma 9:20-22). These gifts are positive, motivational, uplifting, and enduring. In the fiery crucible that is the learning laboratory of life, it is our spiritual gifts that provide us with repetitive opportunities to vividly role-play, with the Holy Ghost acting as our dialogue coach. For our life lessons to be meaningful, we must pre-play and re-play, and then practice over and over again until we get it right, so that we can even do it with our eyes closed.

When the Nephites were enveloped within the tender watch care of the Lord, they began to enjoy the glimmering facets of the light of the Spirit. With enhanced vision, they saw as clearly as had Hans Christian Anderson. They knew that every one of their lives could be "a fairy tale waiting to be written by the finger of God."

The gates of hell are symbolized by gaping jaws. (See D&C 122;7 & 2 Nephi 24:15). They are dripping with the sickening slurry of the saliva of Satan that has been saturated by sin. They menacingly portray the entrance to the forbidding spirit prison of the unjust. The way to avoid this awful portal is to offer the Lord the required sacrifice, as the Nephites often did, which is to be broken in our hearts with sorrow for sin, and in the spirit of contrition to approach the throne of God in an attitude of sincere repentance, hoping to obtain forgiveness through the tender mercies of His grace.

It was in the midst of conflict with the Lamanites that Captain Moroni surely must have remembered that "the mystic chords of memory, stretching from every battlefield and patriot grave to every living heart and hearthstone all over the broad land (of Zarahemla, would) yet again swell the chorus of (the Nephites') union, when again touched, (as he was sure they would be), by the better angels of (their) nature." (Abraham Lincoln).

The wicked Lamanites
found out by sad experience that
wickedness is the companion of frailty,
friability, and futility. It is the bedfellow of
desperation, despondency, and distress. Those
poor lost souls from the pages of The Book of
Mormon who abounded in iniquity had no
expectation of forgiveness, progression,
redemption, or salvation. Without
hope, they were in despair; for
spiritual death was the
wages of their sins.

A grasp
of truth is the first
critical step that must
be taken before we can hope to
reach a successful conclusion to
any intellectual or spiritual journey,
but this is especially so if our desire is to
obtain a testimony of The Book of Mormon.
Truth is deed, and our belief is the catalyzing
influence that motivates us to purposeful action.
The horizon of our knowledge extends only as far
as our action. This is why deeds are an important
companion to our vital, active faith, which, without
works has no life-generating or sustaining power,
because alone, it is vain; it is impotent. It is
ineffective, and is dead in the sense that
it is inadequate to the task at hand.
(See James 2:17).

When we
have determined
to walk in the light
of The Book of Mormon,
we will go out of our way,
as we embrace the principles of
God's great Plan of Salvation. We
will be filled with gratitude as we are
introduced to luxurious accommodations
that have been provided for our enjoyment
in the household of faith.

Our
faith allows
us to see beyond
our limited horizons,
and to be touched by The
Book of Mormon's vision of
the virtue of God's Great Plan
of Salvation. It stimulates us
to savor revealed truth with a
discriminating taste and to
discover for ourselves the
distinctive flavor of
eternal worlds.

If the octane rating of the fuel firing our faith in The Book of Mormon is too low, we may be able to just barely get by, but only for a time. As we limp along with our engines knocking badly, the raw fear of doubt will ultimately overpower our faith to believe in the merciful plan of our Father.

Joseph's coat of many colors was a gift from Jacob. In like manner, we receive the fabric of principles and doctrine from the prophet historians of The Book of Mormon. We are sure they have very carefully selected every bolt of cloth and have thoughtfully cut each one of them to accommodate the vibrant patterns that weave their way thru the divine design that God has so imaginatively created for each and every one of His children.

The Book
of Mormon
shows us how
to be unshackled
from sin, and to be
cleansed in the blood
of Jesus Christ; to stand
steadily upon gospel sod.
Our faith in that inspired
volume separates us from
those who precariously hop
about on the flotsam and
the jetsam that bobs up
and down, and tosses
to and fro, on the
capricious sea
of life.

Telestial EMTs are at
a total loss for diagnosis,
while the prophets of The Book
of Mormon provide a virtual war
chest of therapies for cold, stony,
and hard hearts. The gospel of
Jesus Christ is the remedy of
choice when the steady pulse
of faith has grown weak, or
if it doesn't seem to be
detectable at all.

In
the midst
of Babylon, we
recoil as we encounter
a sprawling wasteland of
worldliness reeking of a rotting
stench of sin. We must not allow
our faith in the divine direction that
is provided by The Book of Mormon to
be contaminated by the raw sewage that
has been unleashed upon an unsuspecting
world by Satan's servants, who frequently
are only thinly disguised as sanitation
workers. The Savior cautioned us to
be suspicious of such, who are no
more than wolves dressed
in sheep's clothing.

We
are lucky
if we are blessed
with the faith to be
perfect in Christ (see
Moroni 10:33) and to be
witnesses of His power. We
are sanctified in Him by the
grace of God, and through
the shedding of His blood,
which is in the covenant
of the Father leading to
remission of our sins.
The Plan consecrates
us to be holy, and
without spot.

The
Book of
Mormon will
definitely make
it easier to have backs
that have become sturdy
enough to brace us against
the fierce winds of adversity
and the wiles of the adversary,
and hearts that are the receptacles
of pure and virtuous principles that
can become reserves of strength
in our times of greatest
need.

Knowledge of
the gospel, that we have
acquired through our exercise
of faith in The Book of Mormon,
is the mortar that binds together the
building blocks of our testimony and
our conversion. Notwithstanding the
clarity of our faith in the principles of
the Plan, the prophets still implore us
to manifest the discipline to keep our
eyes fixed on a prize that may seem,
at times, to be elusive. And thus, we
persevere, and we extend ourselves
beyond our zones of comfort. We
know in our hearts that when
we do so, we will be able to
grasp the golden ring
on the carousel
of life.

Innumerable
mentors have guided
our lives with a profound
influence that's helped us to
nurture the tender feelings that
have shaped our faith to believe. With
The Book of Mormon, we can unleash a
vital power that becomes the underlying
component of a spectacular tapestry whose
design will be revealed to us in all its glory.
When our nature begins to correspond to the
harmony of heaven as we pay closer attention
to the counsel of the prophets in that inspired
text, our mortal clay will be molded and take
on the form and the substance of a perfect
frame. It will dawn on us that, all along,
there had been hiding just beneath our
rough exterior a vibrant coat of
many colors.

In virtually
every age, and not just
among the poor Zoramites in
Antionum, tender shoots of young
testimony spring up and germinate in
harmony with Alma's inspired counsel (see
Alma Chapter 32) without the ecclesiastical
embroidery that too frequently needlessly
complicates the simple sewing, as well as
the sowing, of the gospel messages that
reinforce our understanding of the
principles of the Plan of
Salvation.

The Book
of Mormon invites
us to experience the best of
both worlds; to live on earth,
but still enjoy a heavenly
peace that surpasses
understanding.

The
faithful
soon learn to
their delight that
darkness cannot be
carried into a lighted
room. They seize every
occasion to be enveloped
within the brilliance of The
Book of Mormon. They have
resolved to face the Son, so the
shadows will always be behind
them. Darkness will still exist,
but its companions that take
the identity of apprehension,
trepidation, uncertainty,
and fear, will be out
of sight and out
of mind.

If we
postpone our
quest for the holy
grail of saving faith
in the doctrine that is
illuminated by The Book
of Mormon, only to find that
we have become desensitized to
the Light of Christ, we'll become
subjected to the spirit of the devil.
When he captures our hearts, they
will mutate to become stony and
cold, and we'll lose the ability to
distinguish good from evil and
light from darkness. When we
exchange the sunshine that is
generated by the foundation
of faith for wintry weather
and worldliness, the Spirit
of the Lord will withdraw
to visit warmer climes,
allowing Satan's icy
breath to be sucked
into the vacuum
we've created
for him.

When
the Nephites and
Lamanites repented,
they were better able to
recognize that they were
beings of light and truth
who had been blessed by
God to enjoy mortal
experiences.

In the grand scheme
of the universe, it makes
no difference if we turn to the
right or to the left, in the sense that
the detractors of The Book of Mormon
will always be there, but will fall by the
wayside, as has always been the case. The
Book of Mormon, on the other hand, isn't
going away anytime in the near future.
When we lift our eyes to the heavens, the
Savior will be watching us from above.
No matter that we bear the weight of
sin or sorrow with downcast eyes;
He is always beneath us, to lift
us up and carry our burdens.
If we ask in faith, He will
bless us in kind, and
beyond measure.

In The Book of
Mormon, we're taught
to face the Son/Sun, that
we might feel the warmth of its
rays upon our cheeks, listen with
greater sensitivity to hear without
ambiguity the word of the Lord, and
see with a lucidity that encourages
us to be benevolently blind when
we witness the shortcomings
of others of our fellow
travelers.

Who will enjoy
God's rest? Those who
study The Book of Mormon.
Those who "walketh righteously,
and speaketh uprightly; (those) that
despiseth the gain of oppressions, that
shaketh (their) hands from (the) holding
of bribes, that stoppeth (their) ears from (the)
hearing of blood, and shutteth (their) eyes from
seeing evil. (They) shall dwell on high. (Their)
eyes shall behold the land that is very far
off" in a paradise that is the habitation
of the Gods. (Isaiah 34:14-17).

To appreciate
just how thoughtfully
the principle of repentance has
been conceived, The Book of Mormon
transports us back to the creative period
when matter was organized, the elements
were brought out of chaos into harmony,
and a Garden was nurtured eastward in
Eden. All was brought to a head when a
Savior was provided, with the power to
nullify the transgression of Adam
and Eve, through an Atonement
for their own sins, as well as
for those of the children
of God who would
follow in their
footsteps.

The gospel principles that
are illustrated in The Book of
Mormon can only be tested if we
have nurtured a companionship
with the Spirit, for when we
fall under its spell, we
are at-one with the
Savior of the
world.

Our excitement
when reading The Book
of Mormon is manifested by
celestial sparks that are struck
off the divine anvil of God. These
ignite our desire to repent and to be
baptized. The Book of Mormon defines
not only immortal love, but also eternal
life. The eventual death of the body is a
horizon that is nothing, save the limit
of our sight, and we perish only if
we no longer retain the vision
of our heavenly home.

The Book
of Mormon blesses
us to employ intrinsic
countermeasures to wicked
imaginations. Our behavior is
driven by altruism, self-denial,
self-discipline, self-restraint,
and self-sacrifice. These all
come as we listen with our
hearts to the promptings
of the Spirit that are as
the quiet whisper of a
gentle breeze that
caresses our
cheeks.

Only after we have tried
the virtue of the word of God, can
we know that he "doth grant unto (us)
whatsoever (we) ask that is right, in faith,
believing that (we) shall receive. O then, how
(we) ought to impart of the substance that (we)
have, one to another." (Mosiah 4:21). The church
offers myriad opportunities, that we might practice
an active, meaningful brotherhood. Institutional
welfare, on the other hand, usually tenders little
more than the charade of a disinterested and
disconnected paternalism, whose economic
baseline either trivializes or ignores
the intrinsic worth of souls.

Since there
needs be opposition
in all things, even as
there is faith, so must there
also be its worldly counterpart.
Today, the grip of fear paralyzes
many of God's children. More than
ever, we need The Book of Mormon,
and the assurance of peace, that our
lives are moving in the direction of
our dreams, and that it is with the
gospel that we are given the tools
we need to hitch our wagons to
the stars created by God, that
we might be pulled along
on a pathway leading
to heaven.

The word "Liahona" is
from the forgotten language of
the fathers, which had to be interpreted
as a "compass" for readers in our day. That
the Liahona is an object lesson is made evident by
Alma's dictum to his son "that these things are not
without a shadow, for as our fathers were slothful to
give heed to the compass they did not prosper; even
so, it is with things which are spiritual." (Alma
37:43). As it was for Alma and his family,
so it is for us. The Word of Christ is our
Liahona. If we follow that compass,
we will find that no wind can
blow except it fills our sails.
We will be homeward
bound.

The Lord confirms that because His Hand rules in the latter days, His people need not fear the vile threats and oaths of the wicked. "For," He promises, "I will make thy horn iron, and I will make thy hoofs brass. And thou shalt beat in pieces many people; and I will consecrate their gain unto the Lord, and their substance unto the Lord of the whole earth." (3 Nephi 20:19).

The Book of Mormon asks us to set our sights upon the pole-star of the Atonement that was designed by God to lead us to a higher plateau of progress. We must work, but our lunch is free. It has been provided by the Savior of the world.

The
authority
of the Word,
as it is found in
The Book of Mormon,
prompts us to remember
our 'happy place' in heaven.
In our hearts, we return to the
magical kingdom of our childhood
to re-discover that special place where
dreams really come true. We are carried
away beyond temporal, spatial, and even
spiritual limitations and dimensions, to
experience the enchanting influence
of the Holy Ghost, Who is our Best
Friend Forever.

The body of scripture
that is collectively known
as The Book of Mormon is "not
of men ..... but of me," said the Lord.
"For it is my voice which speaketh (these
words) unto you; for they are given by my
Spirit unto you, and by my power you can
read them one to another ... Wherefore, you
can testify that you have heard my
voice, and know my words."
(D&C 18:34-36).

As The Book of Mormon prophesied would surely happen in the Last Days, mortal combatants have rekindled the ideological war that, long ago, was fought in heaven. Once again, they have established themselves within factions that are diametrically opposed to each other. Champions of righteousness use the words of the Lord as weapons that are sharper than a two-edged sword, dividing truth from error, penetrating to the innermost parts, and separating the sheep from the goats, and the wheat from the tares. Emissaries of Satan use words as well, but only as fiery darts to deceive the children of men and to lead them astray.

The Book of Mormon illustrates the principles and the doctrines that are necessary for us to become sanctified, so that we may be worthy to live once again in a state of holiness in the presence of our Father in Heaven. The gospel shows us how to come unto Christ, to "lay hold upon every good gift, (and to be) perfected in Him." (Moroni 10:32). If we "continue in the supplication of his grace," kneel before Him at His mercy-seat with the sacrifice of a broken heart and a contrite spirit, and rely upon His Atonement to receive a remission of our sins, it will be our privilege to stand blameless before Him when we meet Him at His pleasing bar.
(Alma 7:3).

As The Book of Mormon so clearly illustrates, every principle of the gospel carries within itself its own independent witness that it is true. The Lord delights in clarity, and "he speaketh unto men according to their language, unto their understanding." (2 Nephi 31:3). Communication via the Spirit is universally understood by those who have paid the price to develop fluency in that celestial language. The miracle is that as our spiritual rapport with the heavens confirms our faith, scales of darkness will fall from our eyes, and vistas of eternal proportion will be opened up to our view.

"For what praise is it, when ye be buffeted for your faults, ye take it patiently? But when ye do well, and ye suffer wrong and take it patiently, then is there thanks to God. Hereunto verily were ye called." (William Tyndale). "Blessed are ye, when men shall revile you and persecute, and shall say all manner of evil against you falsely, for my sake, for ... so persecuted they the prophets who were before you." (3 Nephi 12:11-12). At the end of the day, "we can never be injured by any mortals, except ourselves." (Heber J. Grant).

The contraries that are
found in The Book of Mormon
can vitalize our understanding,
enabling us to utilize opposition as the
tool that it was intended to be, to open up a
portal to the Spirit, Who will then empower
us to do all things that are expedient in
His sight. At that point, we will have
an epiphany, as we find ourselves
at-one with the mind and will
of God, Who likewise faced
opposition from his son
in the Council.

As the Book of
Mormon has prophesied,
we are beginning to witness,
like a train wreck in slow motion,
the spectacle of Babylon crumbling
into dust, as Heavenly Father overthrows
her towers. The unrighteous and uninspired
application of force and compulsion have failed
miserably, once again, as they have attempted to
establish a utopian society. God's battle plan, on
the other hand, addresses the transformation
of individual souls, one by one, as they are
redeemed from sin and are inspired to
righteously exercise their agency, to
live in harmony with the Plan
of their Eternal God.

The Savior always
encouraged His disciples
to focus their attention on their less
fortunate brethren, and to lose themselves
in service. He knew that by doing so, they would
eventually be brought into complete harmony with
the attributes of their Heavenly Father. By conforming
their lives to divine character traits, their very nature
would be transformed as they assumed not only the
image, but also the likeness, of God. They would
be of one mind and purpose. "And ye shall
be even as I am," He explained, "and I
am even as the Father, and the
Father and I are one." (3
Nephi 28:10).

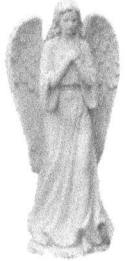

The Book
of Mormon
puts the day to
day elements of the
Plan in perspective, that
we might more clearly be
able to distinguish the grey
-toned obstacles scattered on
our path. These barriers to our
progression will then stand out
in sharp contrast against the
polychromatic backdrop of
the design that God has
created for each
one of us.

There are many of us who've
had times in our lives when the
gap between our secular knowledge
and sacred experiences has simply been
too wide to bridge with profane language.
We remember when Jesus Christ spoke to His
Father in the presence of the Nephite Saints,
"so great and marvelous were the words which
he prayed, that they cannot be written, neither
can they be uttered by man." (3 Nephi 19:34).
Nevertheless, the spiritual preparation of those
who had gathered at His feet allowed them to
receive these things in the spirit, and "they
did understand in their hearts the words
which He prayed." (3 Nephi 19:33).
Sometimes, we hear truth spoken
with freshness and clarity; it
speaks from within, in a
language heard only
with the soul.

If we scribe a line, having
set the stylus of our compass on
the process of purification, within the
circle that we have drawn we'll find Book
of Mormon doctrine that is in harmony
with ordinances that are driven by the
engine of the priesthood, that are, in
turn, given their vitality by the
only One with power that is
sufficient to light the
world.

Alma counseled Korihor that "all things that are upon the face of (the earth) do witness that there is a Supreme Creator." (Alma 30:44). In truth, "any man who hath seen any or the least of these hath seen God moving in His majesty and power." (D&C 88:48). As Ralph Waldo Emerson declared: "How does nature deify us with only a few and cheap elements! Give me health and a day, and I will make the pomp of emperors ridiculous."

Sometimes all too quickly, and at other times agonizingly slowly, those who have sold their souls to the Devil for a mess of pottage are dragged down to a hell on earth that is of their own construction. Their bad habits are the result of repetitively impulsive behaviors that, in a rising tide of wickedness, continually erode away at the foundations of free will. They are fettered by the chains of compulsions. They realize too late that unlimited freedom leads to tyranny. The Light of Christ, however, still has the power to guide them to The Book of Mormon, and to the path of safety that has been providentially provided by the gospel of Jesus Christ and that is illuminated by the Holy Ghost.

Mark E. Petersen declared that in the midst of the tribulations that will become commonplace in the Last Days, "God will send fire from heaven, if necessary, to destroy our enemies while we carry forward our work." The Master of the Universe would never permit Satan or his subordinates to thwart His purposes, no matter how hard they might try. As a matter of fact, those who've "perverted the right ways of the Lord ... shall tumble to the dust, and great shall be the fall" thereof. (1 Nephi 22:14).

It was an integral element of the Merciful Plan of the Great Creator, ratified in the grand Council in Heaven before the world was, that little children who died before the age of accountability would be saved in the Celestial Kingdom by the power of the Atonement. "If not so, God (would be) a partial God, and also a changeable God, and a respecter of persons; for how many little children have died without baptism!" (Moroni 8:12).

If we allow
ourselves to sink
into the quicksands
of prurience, ignoring
the teachings of The Book
of Mormon, and we lose the
wide-eyed innocence of youth,
our purity, and our holiness, we
will forfeit the happiness that can
only accompany untroubled souls.
The peace of which the Lord speaks is
not as the world gives; rather, it is the
product of an unafraid heart that
has been nurtured by the spirit
of reconciliation.

We are
comforted when we link
our testimonies with those of
faithful witnesses of old, who were
"inspired from heaven (and were) sent
forth, standing among the people
in all the land." (3 Nephi
6:20).

If we
examine it
closely, woven
within the fabric
of the material that
makes up the tapestry
of The Book of Mormon,
there will be "dark threads
that are as needful in the
Weaver's skillful hand as
the threads of gold and
silver, in the pattern
He has planned."
(B. Franklin).

To the
great relief of
grieving parents,
The Book of Mormon
affirms the innocence of
children. It was an integral
element of the Plan that was
ordained in a Council in Heaven
before the Creation, that little ones
who would pass away before they had
reached the age of accountability would
be saved in eternal glory by the power of
our Savior Jesus Christ. His influence will
extend to every corner of the earth, from the
beginning of the world to the very end of
time. It was with heavenly prescience
that He invited the little children
to come unto Him. (See
Mark 10:4).

The fulcrum
of our faith rests upon
Book of Mormon doctrine
that addresses the principles
of repentance, of forgiveness,
and the ordinance of baptism.
This trifecta just happens to
find itself to be the polar
opposite, or contrary,
of life without
light.

It is in this
life that we must
prepare for our reunion
with our Father in Heaven,
by striving to become pure and
holy. Our participation in Book of
Mormon study invites the Spirit. It
is the tangible expression of our appeal
to the Savior to come to our rescue, and
in particular of our desire to rely upon
His Atonement, that He might heal our
self-inflicted wounds that have been
caused by sin, that are the natural
consequences of the weaknesses
in the armor of our shields of
faith, and that God had
anticipated when He
conceived the
Plan.

In The Book of Mormon, in Alma Chapter 42, a loving father illustrated for Corianton how Jesus Christ used the bargaining chip of Mercy to negotiate with Justice and purchase our sins with the legally recognized currency of the Atonement. His sacrifice for our sins was flawlessly balanced and attuned to accomplish the task at hand, and it is augmented with our faith, repentance, baptism, the gift of the Holy Ghost, and finally, by the Sacrament, which focuses on the renewal of the covenant of baptism that we have made with our Heavenly Father.

It is the Holy Ghost who facilitates the process of bringing those who are investigating the claims of the church to a knowledge of the divine origin of The Book of Mormon, to their own independent testimony of the Savior, and to faith in His Atonement, just as He has done with those who are already members.

The infinite and
eternal Atonement of Jesus
Christ is the best addendum to a fire
insurance policy that could possibly
have been written, indemnifying all
against the prospect of being burned
as stubble at the last day. As long as
we pay our premiums, we will receive
our immortal bodies as benefits of
the resurrection, so that we might
dwell in celestial burnings and
yet avoid being consumed.
Such is the power of God's
Plan, that is described
in The Book of
Mormon.

Among the
earliest Hebrews, long
before Lehi had a dream and
took his family on a journey to their
own land of promise, were those "whose
tired eyes could see beyond the desert to the
invisible summit of the imagination, where cool
air existed and where the one true god, El Shaddai, he
of the mountain, lived. In later generations, El Shaddai
was destined to mature into that god whom much of the
world would worship. But of one thing these people were
sure. El Shaddai personally determined the destiny of
this group, for of all the people between the Euphrates
and the Nile, he had chosen this band of Hebrews
as his predilected people, and they lived within
his embrace, enjoying security that others
did not know." (James Michener,
"The Source").

It is the unblemished transparency, innocence, simplicity, purity, and virtue of little children who have prepared themselves to be baptized at the age of accountability that blesses us with the optimistic hope that the peace of God is within our own reach, as well. When we change our nature to be as they are, "submissive, meek, humble, patient, (and) full of love," the Holy Spirit invites us to put off the natural man and to become as little children, or as Saints (Mosiah 3:19), through the Atonement of Christ.

The Book of Mormon teaches us the only certifiable fire retardant that can be dumped on the raging inferno of sin is the Atonement. Because of the Savior's sacrifice, we'll receive the kinds of immortal bodies that we will need following the resurrection, since we will dwell in another kind of fire, in the divine fervor of God.

The Nephites'
failure to repent was
a form of rebellion against
the Plan of Redemption of our
Heavenly Father. As was the case
following Lucifer's insurgency,
there needed to be consequences,
even though they might have
seemed to be eternally
damaging in their
scope.

It takes just a few clicks on a
mouse to carry us "into enemy territory
without having to first go through passport
control." (Neal A. Maxwell). Knowledge can be
a dangerous thing if it is not accompanied by the
Spirit of God. "O that cunning plan of the evil one!
O the vainness, and the frailties, and the foolishness
of men! When they are learned they think they are
wise, and they hearken not unto the counsel of
God, for they set it aside, supposing they
know of themselves, wherefore, their
wisdom is foolishness, and it
profiteth them not."
(2 Nephi 9:29).

In The Book of Mormon, the prophets
who speak to us out of the dust teach that
only the Atonement can unshackle us from the
unpleasant consequences of Justice. Darkness is the
conjoined twin of misery, while it is the obedience of
faith that frees us to embrace the truth, to make
intelligent choices, to perform purposefully,
to carry on convincingly, and to progress
persistently; in short, to rise above the
cares of the world by becoming
at-one with Christ through
His sacrifice for our
sins.

The stellar
example of the Sons
of Mosiah illustrates that we
mustn't hold anything back. It
is necessary to invest everything we
have, including our confidence in the
power of the Atonement to deliver on the
almost incomprehensible promise from
our Lord that He can save us, and
even the most recalcitrant and
repugnant of our neighbors,
from our sins.

Our faith may as well be dormant, without the accompanying work of repentance that is given vitality by the Atonement and continually fortified as we partake of the Sacrament. Our faith notwithstanding, we do not possess the power to save ourselves from the unchangeable demands of Justice. The Book of Mormon teaches us that in order for Mercy to prevail, God created covenants that are linked by performance to each of the ordinances of the gospel.

Only if we exercise the moral discipline to incorporate into our lifestyles the steady and measured guidance of the Holy Ghost, will we be given the power to recognize, address, reverse, and erase with finality, the imbalance that plagues our lives. The imperative of Moroni's promise in Moroni 10:4 compels us to address two inevitable contraries: Will we, or will we not put it to the test? What will happen when we seek the guidance of the Spirit, and what will be the inescapable consequences if we don't?

The effects of sin are inevitable and inescapable, but for the intercession, by our faith, of the Atonement. The Book of Mormon tells us that the Maker and Fashioner of the universe must intervene by engaging laws that restore equilibrium, or all is lost. The Holy Ghost helps us to re-establish such a state of balance in our lives.

There is ample room and time in mortality for each of us to develop a capacity to see beyond our limited horizons all the way to the Atonement, that reaches, as illustrated in The Book of Mormon, to the best of us, the worst of us, and to the rest of us who lie somewhere in between those two extremes.

To some
degree, we find
ourselves susceptible
to the influences of the
Seven Deadly Sins. In every
case, however, the Savior stands
ready to rescue us. As we read The
Book of Mormon, our zest for life is
restored, enthusiasm is revived, and
divine fire is rekindled, as the celestial
compass residing within our beating
hearts is energized by a burning
feeling in our bosom.

Those
who "harden
their hearts, to
them is given the
lesser portion of the
word until they know
nothing concerning his
mysteries ..... Then they
are taken captive by the
devil, and led by his will
down to destruction. Now
this is what is meant by
the chains of hell."
(Alma 12:11).

If we allow
ourselves to become
assuaged to a sensitivity
to our surroundings, which
should be sweetly nurtured by
reading about and engaging the
lessons of The Book of Mormon, we
can become inured to our condition
in ways that leave us past feeling.
When that is so, the Atonement's
power is of no effect in our lives,
and the Savior suffered in the
Garden of Gethsemane and
died on the Cross for
naught.

A work
such as The
Book of Mormon
is hard for skeptics
to grasp because it was
conceived in heaven. It is
not of this world, and so if
they try to wrap their finite
minds around it, they will
fail in their efforts, for it
can only be spiritually
discerned.

Timid souls
of weak character
and faltering faith in
the life-changing lessons
found The Book of Mormon,
frequently think that they can
side-step both the requirements
of repentance and the demands
of discipleship. But it is because
they have never experienced the
freedom enjoyed by those who
move with willpower and grit
along the strait and narrow
path, due to the liberating
influence generated by
the covenants we make
and keep with our
Lord and Savior
Jesus Christ.

The symbolism
in the Lord's Last Supper
has been preserved in The Book of
Mormon (see 3 Nephi 18 & Moroni
4) and in accordance with revelation,
the ordinance of the Sacrament has been
restored in our day. (See D&C 20:75-79).
Broken bread represents the torn flesh of
the Savior, and the water represents
the blood that was shed during
His sacrifice, in the act
of Atonement for
our sins.

The Book of Mormon teaches that it was thru a supernal demonstration of His magnificent omniscience that our Savior Jesus Christ negotiated with Justice to execute the Law of Mercy. Our Heavenly Father had beforehand conceived the Atonement, in order to bring about our metamorphosis. The sacrifice of the Savior unchains us from condemnation to remain as fallen creations in a cruel twist of fate. We would instead be transformed by the power of heaven into beings of light.

Our salvation and exaltation have less to do with cherubim and flaming swords, and more to do with faith, repentance, baptism, forgiveness, mercy, Atonement, the Sacrament, and ultimately, redemption; principles that allow the Law of Mercy to trump the Law of Justice. All is made possible because of the sacrifice of Jesus Christ, and all is set forth and explained with clarity in the pages of The Book of Mormon.

Our greater understanding of God's great Plan that is revealed in The Book of Mormon blesses our lives in many ways. Its power creates the opportunity for dynamic change as wisdom flows along established channels. Additionally, our accountability, loyalty, and our commitment to obedience expand. A humble need to serve strengthens the bonds of brotherhood and sisterhood, and generates interdependency in a community of true believers in which any cultural differences are effectively expunged. We are no longer strangers or foreigners, but rather we become fellowcitizens with the Saints in the household of God.

Upon the altar of sacrifice, The Book of Mormon inspires us to consecrate to the Lord our time, our talents, our means, and all else with which He has providently blessed our lives.

The account of the Creation that was written by Moses provides us with the details that relate to the Fall of Adam and Eve, and to the Atonement of Christ, which is the doctrine that we must understand in order to have the faith to live abundantly and to become heirs of salvation. In the scriptures (see Moses 1:4 & 37) the Plan refers to worlds without number, but the application of its principles and doctrines, as we are led to understand them in The Book of Mormon, relates only to the sphere upon which we reside.

We are baptized because we have learned that the principles governing the Fall of Adam, as well as the Lord's Atonement, were "great and eternal purposes (that) were prepared from the foundation of the world." (Alma 42:26). Our baptism itself testifies that we understand the significant role of our Savior, and His sacrifice as our Redeemer.

On the routes that climbers
take to the summits of towering peaks, fixed
ropes are often placed to minimize the risks involved.
Mountaineers use jumars, or ascenders, that are attached
to the ropes, permitting the climbers to move upward without
ever having to let go of the rope. The Rod of Iron, as described in
The Book of Mormon, is similar to these fixed ropes, and church
organization is comparable to the jumar. The analogy, however,
breaks down in one significant way. Whereas mountaineers
follow ropes that have been placed in proximity to perilous
crevasses, the Rod of Iron plots a course that tries to be
a safe distance from disaster. It will not knowingly
lead us into peril. There will always be a zone of
safety between the clearly marked path of
righteousness and any treacherous
precipice of destruction.

The Book of Mormon
teaches us that the preparation for
our schooling in mortality began in
the pre-earth existence, and that now, our
rediscovery involves religious recognition, that
is, the re-cognition, or the recapturing, recollection,
reknowing, rekindling, revitalization, rejuvenation,
renewal, and restoration of the sum of our being. It is in
these many ways that each of us can be reconciled unto
Christ. If we deny or inhibit that instinctive response, we
are accountable, and to a degree, we condemn ourselves,
for we knew the Savior before this life, we have been
given the opportunity to become re-acquainted
with Him here on earth, and we will surely
recognize Him in the eternities.

In The Book of Mormon,
we are blessed with a description of
Jesus sweetly and tenderly attending to
each of the needs of the Nephite little ones,
and how he embraced them "one by one, and
blessed them, and prayed unto the Father for
them ... and they saw the heavens open, and
they saw angels descending out of heaven,
and they were encircled about with fire,
and the angels did minister unto
them." (3 Nephi 17:21-24).

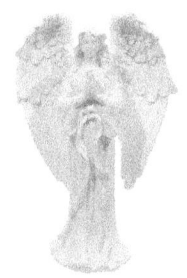

We
will all be
tested by trial
and temptation,
and we will make
mistakes. But we'll
rise above our failures
because of the love of the
Savior and His Atonement.
In next act of the Play, life's
mysteries will be solved, every
piece of the puzzle will be put in
its proper place, all the confusion
that often tormented us will be put
to rest, and all things will be made
right. For that to occur, we need to be
up and about, starting right now, by
making our way to, and through, The
Book of Mormon. As the White Rabbit
said to no-one in particular: "I'm late,
I'm late! For a very important date!
No time to say 'Hello!' Goodbye,
I'm late, I'm late, I'm late!"

In the arduous
process of repentance
that is illustrated so often
within The Book of Mormon, we
discover the strength we need thru
the infinite power of the Atonement.
As we determine to seek the Lord while
He may be found, a constant companion
will instruct us how we may become better
engaged in fashioning defensive weapons
in life's armory of thought. It is with these
tools that the Light of Christ will guide us
and direct our path. It will show us just
what we need to do in order to build up
our heavenly fortifications of love,
strength, service, compassion,
testimony, conversion,
peace, and joy.

Alma asked
the people of Zarahemla
if they had spiritually been born
of God, if they had received His image
in their countenances, and had experienced a
mighty change in their hearts. (See Alma 5:14).
And then, the more penetrating question, posed just a
few verses later: "And now, if you have experienced a
change of heart, and if you have felt to sing the
song of redeeming love, I would ask, can ye
feel so now?" (Alma 5:26).

In contrast to light that's provided by The Book of Mormon is a darkness that has the potential to cover the earth, and gross darkness the people. Without the influence of the Holy Ghost to intervene in our behalf by reintroducing us to the Atonement that was promised from before the foundation of the world, we would all forever be subject to the evil source of that darkness, to rise no more. The Holy Spirit confirms our faith to see all the way back to heaven's gate, and is quick to respond to our pleadings when we cry: "O God, where art thou, and where is the pavilion that covereth thy hiding place?" (D&C 121:1).

Immersing ourselves in the study of The Book of Mormon can bind us to the influences of heaven by creating pulsing streams of inspiration whose flow has no temporal boundary and no spatial limitation. We can be at one with eternity, with both the mind and will of our Father in Heaven.

As we
read The Book
of Mormon, and
as our testimonies of
the Savior swell in our
breasts, faith intensifies
our desire to repent, and the
effort we've made to maintain
our worthiness centers our lives,
bringing us into harmony with
true principles. As we endeavor to
be obedient, we find ourselves in a
constant state of improvement and
we begin to believe in ourselves, not
to mention God. Our hearts race as
we realize that He always honors
his promises, and that as long
as we are moving forward in
the right direction, we will
be reconciled unto
Him.

Because charity is a Christ-like
virtue, and is the embodiment of His love, "it
endureth forever, and whoso is found possessed of
it at the last day, it shall be well with him." (Moroni
7:4). Encouragement to Christian service prepares us to
be like Him. It has been bestowed upon us by the generosity
of His Spirit, that we might be better equipped for the day
when we will find ourselves on our knees before His
throne, and we are completely overwhelmed,
and even consumed, by His love.

Joseph Smith "has shown unto us the plates ... which have the appearance of gold; and as many of the leaves as ... Smith has translated we did handle with our hands; and we also saw the engravings thereon, all of which ha(d) the appearance of ancient work, and of curious workmanship." (Testimony of The Eight Witnesses).

We live in the world, but we make sure that our feet are firmly planted on gospel sod so that we might recognize sounding brass and tinkling cymbals for what they really are. The Book of Mormon catalyzes a mystical and metaphysical transformation wherein we have been figuratively born of God. With new eyes, we can see from here to eternity, and with new ears, we can hear the word of the Lord above so many other voices that are competing for our attention.

All who follow His star and come to worship the Babe of Bethlehem share a common bond. They are no longer Jehovah's Witnesses, Catholics, Mormons, Episcopalians, Quakers, or Evangelicals, but are 'Christians'. Those who bear His sacred name will "be found at the right hand of God, for (they all) shall know the name by which (they) are called, for (they) shall be called by the name of Christ." (Mosiah 5:9). As the Savior said: "My sheep hear my voice, and I know them, and they follow me." (John 10:27).

The object and design of our existence is that we might find happiness, peace, and rest; that we might obtain the blessings of the fathers, including the fruits of faith, which is baptism by immersion for the remission of our sins, thru forgiveness that is founded on the Atonement of Jesus Christ. The path leading to happiness is faith, virtue, holiness, uprightness, and keeping the commandments, said the Prophet Joseph Smith.

When we
resolve to walk in
the light of revealed truth
and we enter into life via the
teachings of The Book of Mormon,
we may be very pleasantly surprised
by the luxurious accommodations that
have been provided by God in the household
of faith. His forgiveness will remove the awful
stains of sin from the tapestries that have been
created with the threads of experience which He
has designed for the walls of our individual
accommodations in the Celestial Kingdom.
Even now, He awaits our arrival at a
check-in date that has largely
been pre-determined.

It is
within the
pages of The
Book of Mormon
where we learn that
"millions of candles
can be ignited by one
single flame without
shortening the life of
that first candle".
(Buddha).

For too long,
Israel has "drunk of the
dregs of the cup of trembling." (2
Nephi 8:23). However, in the Last Days,
she will put on her strength by exercising
the authority of the Holy Priesthood of God. As
Moroni exhorted: "Awake, and arise from the dust,
O Jerusalem ... and put on thy beautiful garments,
O daughter of Zion; and strengthen thy stakes, and
enlarge thy borders forever, that thou mayest no more
be confounded, that the covenants of the Eternal Father
which he hath made unto thee, O house of Israel, may be
fulfilled." (Moroni 10:31). Moroni summarized his own
mission statement: "Come unto Christ, and lay hold
upon every good gift ... and be perfected in him, and
deny yourselves of all ungodliness." If we do this,
"and love God with all (our) might, mind and
strength, then is his grace sufficient."
(Moroni 10:30-32).

We are
not ashamed to
"declare ((our Father's)
doing among the people."
Fearlessly and convincingly,
we will yoke ourselves with those
"who make mention that His name
is exalted." (2 Nephi 22:4). We link
arms with those who have also made
the decision to "stand as witnesses
of God at all times and in all
things, and in all places
..... even until death."
(Mosiah 18:9).

Even as we
make valiant efforts
to focus the powers of our
intellect on eternal elements,
because we are hedged in on all
sides by a crushing present reality,
if our hearts have not been softened to
relate to the things of the Spirit, we can't
expect to understand the creations of God,
except in the most academic, abstract, and
obtuse ways. Joseph Smith explained that we
need a change of heart if we are to comprehend
the Kingdom of God. The Book of Mormon is
a schoolmaster that turns our attention to
the Savior, and it mentors us, that our
hearts might be softened. And not
only that, to top it off, it is the
Bible's best friend. It truly
is a marvelous work
and a wonder.

As we approach
the conclusion of The
Book of Mormon, and by the
time we've encountered the promise
in Moroni 10:4, we are prepared to act.
We sense the expansion of God's powers,
as the glittering facets of the life of the
Spirit wash over us. Quiet stirrings
that penetrate to our very core propel
us to a greater appreciation of the
significance of the revelatory
content of the book.

A number
of the chapters in
the story of our lives have
already been set to type, and
we aren't really sure how many
remain to be written. But this we
know: The fairytale was created by
Heavenly Father, and we must honor
its declaration that we are His sons and
daughters. We cannot start over to write
a new beginning, but we can begin now
to create a new ending, with the help of
a talented and gifted Ghostwriter,
Whose nom du plume hints at
His power and authority as
the third member of the
Godhead.

In stark opposition to the
grace of God is a darkness that is so
pervasive that it has the potential to cover
the earth, and gross darkness the people. The
teachings found in The Book of Mormon help
God heal our blindness to the evil source of
that melancholy, that we might not be
left destitute, to hesitantly tap our
way through life, bereft of the
power to triumphantly rise
in the resurrection of
the just.

We must determine to drag
our broken and bleeding bodies
to church every Sabbath because it is
there that we will receive the transfusions
of a spiritual element. It can be a heavenly
dialysis center where worldly contaminants
may be removed from our systems, because
we are quite incapable of accomplishing
the task on our own. The resources that
are necessary can only be found in
the Atonement, in doctrine that
is unambiguously taught
by Book of Mormon
prophets.

As we read
The Book of Mormon,
our attention turns to the
downtrodden, the friendless,
the unappreciated, and those who
feel that they are hopelessly mired in
sin. We find that we are willing to bear
the burdens of others so "that they may be
light (and to) mourn with those that mourn;
yea, and (to) comfort those that stand in
need of comfort." (Mosiah 18:8-9).

We retain a hope "through the Atonement of Christ and the power of his resurrection to be raised up unto life eternal, and this because of (our abiding) faith in him according to the promise." (Moroni 7:41). Our hope isn't wishful thinking or misguided trust, nor is it a high-stakes gamble. It is the inevitable reward of well-founded faith, the product of our discipline to control our desires and emotions within the bounds the Lord has set, and then to act upon the principles of His gospel.

"Sound the great trumpet for our freedom. Raise the banner for gathering our exiles from the four corners of the earth into our own land." (Jewish Prayer). The gospel will be preached to the elect of God, who will then rally around its standard, ultimately to congregate with the Saints in the stakes of Zion. Then, the work will commence in earnest, and His people will be "gathered home to the land of their inheritance. And I will go before them, saith the Father." (3 Nephi 21:28-29).

The Book of Mormon is absolutely non-discriminatory as far as its audience is concerned. It was designed to be read by the world's heaviest person, who weighed in at 1,400 pounds, by the world's tallest person, who stood 8 feet 11 inches tall, by the world's wealthiest person, who boasts $230 billion in assets, by the world's smartest person whose I.Q. is 230, as well as by the other 8 billion of us who fall somewhere within these extremes.

Living water is so crucial to our well-being that our Father has provided the means for it to penetrate solid limestone, as it were, so that it might flow freely into our lives. The Book of Mormon is one of His tools that is powerful enough to creates a conduit that He has chiseled through our rough exterior and our stony nature. All that is required to activate in our behalf God's artesian well of gospel doctrine is faith, obedience, study, prayer, and good works.

The Book of
Mormon reacts rather
spectacularly to our needs.
With a clear vision, its warnings
give us the tools to detect storm clouds
even before they appear on our horizons,
and it proactively responds to each of the
described scenarios by issuing timely
weather bulletins that are applicable
to an infinite variety of
situations.

Our love
of the scriptures,
and in particular of
The Book of Mormon, was
nurtured within our spiritual
kindergarten, is heightened in
our mortal classrooms, and will
be established in eternity, when
angels will smile upon us and
we will be clothed in the robes
of a heavenly academia
that symbolizes our
acknowledgement
of the glory
of God.

If we engage in an examination of The Book of Mormon's merits, but then reject its inspiration, we're at serious risk of withering and dying, and becoming as empty shells, and structures of custom and convenience, illuminated only by the flickering candlelight of superstition and magic. We need the luminosity of the Lord to free us from our bondage to ignorance. The glow of the scriptures, the Light of Christ, and clearly, the illumination that's provided by the Holy Ghost, deliver all the photons we need to light our dark world. (See 2 Nephi 32:5, 3 Nephi 11:10, & Moroni 7:17).

In The Book of Mormon, we are taught that economic, physical, and intellectual health lack the power to save us, since what is at stake is feeling, and not knowledge or our temporal security. Only our spiritual well-being can come to our rescue. As we begin the long journey of discovery, our hearts and our nature will be changed as scales of darkness fall from our eyes. The path that lies before us will be best illuminated if we've nurtured the eye of faith, enabling us to see all the way from here to eternity.

When we finally put
down The Book of Mormon
after completing a first reading,
we are left heavy with anticipation
as we breathlessly look forward to the
last pages of the script in the production
that finds its expression in the theater of
life. It is in the third act of the Three Act
Play that, having prayed ourselves hot
and read ourselves full, we will let
ourselves go, to live happily ever
after in a magical kingdom
where dreams really do
come true.

Every faithful participant in
the Three Act Play of God's perfect Plan
will now and forever be independent in that
stage of development to which their decisions
have led them. Poised on the edge of forever,
they need little incentive other than the
promise given in Moroni 10:4 & 5 to
push themselves off onto a voyage
into the heavens toward the
unknown possibilities
of existence.

The path
to a witness of
The Book of Mormon
can follow a lonely road.
Still, as Robert Frost mused:
"I shall be telling this with a sigh
somewhere ages and ages hence: Two
roads diverged in a wood, and I, I took the
one less traveled by, and that has made all
the difference." In matters of faith, we will,
at times, need to take a few halting steps
into the darkness, on a road that is less
traveled by. Only then, will the way
ahead of us be illuminated. It is
that act of the courage of faith
that will make all the
difference.

There is no variability on
the path that leads to the gospel
of Jesus Christ. We simply trust the
Lord when He reassures us that if we will
come unto Him, we will enjoy eternal life.
(See 3 Nephi 9:14-15). Our submission to
the rigorous requirements of the Plan of
God requires our consistent exercise of
moral discipline, so that its eternal
principles might be clothed in a
more enduring substance that
renders them more easily
and conveniently
obeyed.

The Nephites who were living in Zarahemla received the image of God in their countenances, in response to Benjamin's, and later, to Alma's entreaties. (See Mosiah 5:2 & Alma 5:14). Their faces reflected the light of the Spirit, and because of the mighty change in their hearts, they became new creatures who'd been created to reach their potential in both the image and likeness of God their Father. Their testimonies became the foundation for a sustained, saving faith that gave them confidence, that they might one day stand in the presence of God and before angels and witnesses, to be judged according to their works.

The Plan of God that is described in The Book of Mormon provides us with instinct, insight, impulse, intuition, inspiration, and especially with commanding impressions that we feel as revelation, to streak beneath the heavens and find their way into our hearts. As we lift up our eyes to map their flaming trajectory across the cosmic ocean, these influences will trace a path that pulses with a luminosity whose trail leads all the way back until it has found its source, which is the abode of the Gods.

A striking and enduring image of the world's pride and vain imaginations is the great and spacious building seen by Lehi in vision. His description matches the appearance, from afar, of cities to the Bedouin of the desert. When surrounded by brick and mortar, those who made their homes in tents always felt uncomfortable, and were often made to feel inferior by the worldly inhabitants of more developed communities.

As
The Book
of Mormon
endows us with
faith in the power
of Christ to save us
from our sins, we will
be profoundly motivated
to live in compliance with
law, and the Holy Ghost will
hallow each of us with eternal
perspective. We will not only
believe in Christ, but we will
believe Christ, as the Spirit
whispers to us that we have
celestial potential. At the
end of the day, the Plan
teaches us that we are
the work of God's
hands.

It would
be interesting
to think of Joseph's
coat of many colors as
a metaphor for the fabric
of our faith, stitched together
by God. (See Alma 46:23). We
try to visualize the threads that
have been individually tailored to
represent the principles of the gospel.
The garment that we've been given to
wear is not a drab representation of
the monotone of the world, but is an
actual Technicolor DreamCoat that
signifies both the glories and the
riches of His divine design for
every precious member of
His family.

The Book of Mormon blesses us with
the desire to be born again; to be set free by
the perfect Law of Liberty, so we might reach our
potential that is described by the Plan of Salvation.
It visualizes each of us as the acorn of a mighty oak
that has been vitalized by our faith, and that basks
within God's nurturing influence to grow strong
"like a silver tree against the storm, that will
not bend with the wind or the change, but
stands to fight the world alone on its
last night, on Saturday."
(Doug Stewart).

Nephi correctly taught that "it is by grace that we are saved, after all we can do." (2 Nephi 25:23). Latter-day Saints, however, tend to emphasize works to the point that it may seem to others that the grace of God takes a back seat to their own efforts to earn salvation by good works. In spite of their focus on accountability, agency, industry, and labor, as they encourage each other to devotion, diligence, and duty, there is nothing we could do that would qualify us to enjoy eternal life. It is through the blood of Jesus Christ, and in His sacrifice, that we may be redeemed from our fallen state.

As we express ourselves through our positive and independent actions, The Book of Mormon introduces us to the exhilarating emotions and feelings of freedom from incarceration to sin that can only be experienced when we have subjugated our own will to that of a power that is greater than ourselves.

The Merciful Plan that is illustrated in Alma 42 describes a powerful financial instrument providing over-draft protection when, as participants in the theater of life, we make repetitive withdrawals. It is our guardian, and our personal asset manager as it were, to make sure that our checks that are co-signed by the Savior can later be cashed by a creditor whose name is Justice, when foolish debts become due and payable, and reckless investments have depleted our treasury.

A small stipend and an annuity are linked to our participation in the Plan of Salvation, but we are also presented with the tools of the trade, so that by the sweat of our brow we might earn enough to obtain our own lodgings, pay our bills on time, and indulge ourselves, occasionally, with a few of the finer things of life. After all, God's divine design is not Puritan in its nature, but rather is a magnanimous Plan of self-actualization. (See Alma 42:8).

The light of the gospel endows us with the capacity to love ourselves, as well as the Savior. As we embrace its principles, the Lord blesses us. Illumination dissipates the cobwebs of doubt, smooths out the rough edges of testimony, builds our self-confidence to tackle the tough questions, and provides the self-assuredness we require to exercise our agency wisely. Light bestows upon us the gifts of harmony, comfort, and a clear conscience. It illuminates the gospel as the ultimate measure of truth. Light exerts a liberating influence, as it releases us from apprehension, despair, doubt, fear, ignorance, hesitancy, unsteadiness, and worry, while empowering us to keep that which we hold near and dear insulated from those who scurry about in the shadows as they wait for opportunities to ransack our treasury. When our learning style embraces the Spirit, we discover a pattern that soon becomes our norm, and we draw closer and closer to the perfect light of day.

When reading The Book of Mormon, if you have heard the voice of the Lord speak to you, it will most assuredly have accomplished its purpose.

As we read The
Book of Mormon, we
sometimes have a moving
experience when light or truth
steadily distills upon our souls.
Just so, in the Sacred Grove, light
"descended gradually," entering the
quiet grove slowly enough that Joseph
was able to gauge its approach, until it
finally reached him and enveloped him
within dazzling brilliance. It was only
then that he "saw two Personages, whose
brightness and glory (were beyond all)
description," and who stood suspended
in the air within the encircling light.
(J.S.H. 1:17). We may not often see
beings from the eternal worlds, but
when we are the grateful recipients
of inspiration or revelation, we
can be sure, as was Joseph,
that we dwell in holy
precincts.

When we embrace both the doctrine and
the principles of The Book of Mormon, we will
find that we have been liberated to enjoy peace of
conscience, to receive the blessings of the priesthood,
to serve others in more powerful and meaningful
ways, to resolutely work toward our potential, to
commune with the Infinite, and to benefit
from every blessing that God wants to
give us, as we move forward in
faith in the direction of
enlightenment.

If the
collapse of
entire cultures
is imminent, as
was so often the case
in The Book of Mormon,
external restraints may be
imposed to influence behavior;
to maintain at least a semblance
of societal steadiness. Our escalating
dependence upon civil laws to define and
regulate moral discipline says something
about us, and about the critical need to have
faith in the ability of The Book of Mormon
to synchronize our righteous desires into
a single force for good with the power
to secure the spiritual blessings
of heaven and the temporal
blessings of earth.

The Book
of Mormon tells us
that only Jesus Christ
can unshackle us from the
unpleasant consequences of the
Law of Justice. While darkness is the
conjoined twin of misery, the obedience
of faith in the Great Plan of our God frees
us to embrace truth and to make intelligent
choices, to progress persistently, to carry on
convincingly, and to perform purposefully;
in short, to rise above every care of the world
because of an Atonement that anchors us
thru the Law of Mercy to the "Hope of
Israel". (Jeremiah 17:13).

All around us,
we see the fulfillment
of the prophecies that we are
now in the Last Days, when the
hearts of men shall fail them, as
their shields of faith begin to falter.
When that happens, the Devil has free
reign to toy with their minds and stir
them up, and to rant and rave against
The Book of Mormon's proven principles.
Others, he will pacify as he hypnotizes
them into a distorted sense of cardiac
security. In either case, the damage
has been done, and nothing short
of a spiritual heart transplant
that illustrates their faith in
Christ will be able to restore
a normal sinus rhythm
that is in harmony
with heaven.

When we are first
introduced to the wonder
of The Book of Mormon, we
press forward, but not with the
crowd who jostles for position in
the mosh pit of telestial trivialities,
but rather with the Saints, who seek
wisdom that they might understand
the mysteries of God. We take a fix
on the stars, but the real focus
of our attention runs more
deeply; it points to the
heavens.

Those who have become well-acquainted with The Book of Mormon have learned how to use it to turn stumbling blocks into solid stepping stones. Crises becomes opportunities, and victory is snatched from the jaws of defeat. They know that change will come to them "like a flash of lightning and a resounding clap of thunder. While others shrink in fear, they realize that it is only after the tempest, that flowers will bloom." ("The Chinese Book of Proverbs").

All of the prophet-historians from Nephi to Moroni needed the courage of faith as they effectively faced the demons that played a role in the opposition in all things that was built into their experiences. In the fight or flight scenario, faith became their launch pad for the anticipated adrenalin rush that carried them beyond the contraries that were manifested by their ever-present night terrors.

Because there needs to be opposition in all things, (see Alma Chapter 42) even as there is faith, so must there be its worldly contrary. In the latter days, the grip of fear paralyzes many of God's children. Today, more than ever we need a hope in Christ and an assurance of peace, that our lives are moving in the direction of our dreams, and that when we follow God's Plan, we are effectively hitching our wagons to the stars in heaven.

The divine optimism of Moroni's promise (see Moroni 10:4) waits for a moment "when we will be figuratively tapped on the shoulder and given the chance to do something very special that is unique to us and fitted to our circumstances. What a tragedy it would be, were that moment to find us unprepared or, worse yet, unqualified for what could have been our finest hour." (Sir Winston Churchill).

Some of those who
have embraced The Book
of Mormon and have enrolled
in the curriculum of the gospel, can
neither maintain a 100% attendance
record nor sustain saving faith. They set
their sights too low, and too easily reach
watered-down objectives. They no longer
stretch themselves, rarely venturing out
of the comfort zones to which they have
retreated. They have but little to show
for their consistently timid efforts
that deny the faith and sidestep
the inspired course of study
that has been created in
their behalf.

We follow the
yellow brick road
with our hearts, might,
mind, and strength, until
we have reached the Emerald
City of Oz. Our faith compels us
to trust The Book of Mormon instead
of the devilish doctrines that have been
concocted by the world's apologists. God's
unassuming Plan invites us to believe that
when we use our hearts, and our brains, and
have the courage of faith, our lives can become
wonderful "fairy tales that are just waiting
to be written" by His omnipotent hand.
(Hans Christian Anderson).

Wo unto those who will only casually accept an illumination of faith, that is a blessing of the study of The Book of Mormon, and that has been so freely given. Because of their misguided obsession with temporal trivia, they carelessly fritter away that gift, and waste the days of their probation by rooting thru telestial trash in a fruitless effort to find meaning in the barren dumpsters of their empty lives.

For our benefit, we are well-acquainted with evil as well as with good, with pain as well as with pleasure, with darkness as well as with light, and with error as well as with truth, while not forgetting punishment for the infraction of the eternal laws of God, as well as the blessings that follow our obedience. The Book of Mormon is our ace in the hole, and the Atonement is a royal flush and is an unbeatable hand, so that when we've concluded our mortal missions, we'll be able to abide the glory of heaven, to dwell with our Father.

The brother of Nephi addressed all those who gun their engines while waiting in telestial traffic jams, who become the hoarders of temporal trash, and who have a fascination with trivial pursuits, when he warned: "Wo unto him ... that wasteth the days of his probation, for awful is his state!" (2 Nephi 9:27). Particularly when individuals groan "under darkness and under the bondage of sin," they have lost hope and their lives have little meaning or stability. (D&C 84:49). They cannot begin to comprehend that fame is just a vapor, and popularity is an accident, and those who cheer you today may curse you tomorrow; and that, in the end, the only thing that endures, and the only thing that you can really count on, is your character. And that is something upon which a monetary price cannot be put.

"The harder is the conflict, the more glorious is the triumph. What we obtain too cheap, we esteem too lightly. 'Tis dearness only that gives everything its value. Heaven knows how to put a proper price upon its goods." (Tom Paine, "Common Sense"). It would be strange, indeed, if such a celestial article as a testimony of The Book of Mormon should not be so highly rated.

Joseph Smith taught: "It is contrary to the economy of God for any member of the church, or any one, to receive instructions for those in authority, higher than themselves. But if anyone have a vision or a visitation from a heavenly messenger, it may be for his own benefit and instruction." (H.C., 1:338). An example from the early days of the church in Utah illustrates the point. "A young man with a well-developed sense of humor managed the ward store. After preparing a special ink that could be read only after heat had been applied, he wrote scriptural messages on a certain brown hen's eggs. Soon, ward members gathered to see what the hen had to say about the latest gossip in town. When the young man's father, an apostle, returned from Salt Lake City and observed the situation, he called a special priesthood meeting. To the assembled men he explained that he had just visited President Brigham Young and had verified that God was still speaking to his prophet. The Lord, said the apostle, had not yet resorted to the hind end of a chicken to convey messages to his people." (Leonard J. Arrington, "The Mormon Experience").

"This shall be a law ... that ye receive not the teachings of any that shall come before you as revelations or commandments. And this I give unto you that you may not be deceived, that you may know they are not of me." (D&C 43:5-6). "At the moment that individuals look to any other source" than the leaders of the church, "they step outside of the pale of the Kingdom of God, and are on dangerous ground." (Joseph F. Smith, "Gospel Doctrine," p. 41-42). In Kirtland, there was a man named Hawley who condemned Joseph Smith "for allowing women to wear caps and men to sport pads on their coat sleeves. Brigham Young later recalled his own vigorous reaction to Hawley's claims: 'I put my pants and shoes on, took my cowhide, went out and, laying hold of him, jerked him around and assured him that if he did not stop his noise and let the people enjoy sleep without interruption, I would cowhide him on the spot, for we had the Lord's Prophet right here and we did not want the Devil's prophet yelling around the streets.'" (Leonard J. Arrington, "The Mormon Experience").

"The
Great Plan
of the Eternal God"
(Alma 34:9) is nothing
short of a divine design that
was conceived in heaven to test
the mettle of our convictions as we
dwell here on the earth. The Savior will
not cause us to misplace our trust, or our
confidence, in anything that can't deliver
on its promises. But we have no proof until
we act on the basis of faith. Then, comes
confirmation of the reality, as feelings
of self-assuredness grow and our
purposeful actions replace
tentative overtures.

When
we read The
Book of Mormon,
we adopt a culture of
faith that surrounds us
and helps insulate us from
worldly influences. It alerts us
to the misdirection of Satan, that
attempts to lead us from a brilliant,
dazzling white, through every shade
of grey, to a fathomless black which, by
subtraction, is as a void. It is the absence
of every uplifting thought, word, deed,
or sustaining principle.

The Book of Mormon
speaks to our spirits, for every gospel
principle carries within itself an independent
witness that it is true. Its language is universal,
and when the Holy Ghost illuminates our minds,
we enjoy fluency, an easy familiarity with the
doctrines, and a comfortable association with
the revealed word of God that opens up
vistas of eternal proportion
before our eyes.

The worth of the principles
that are taught by the prophets in The Book of
Mormon is validated through our personal experience
and our subsequent witness. Our desire to embrace them
becomes the outward expression of dedication to obedience.
Ordinances become the public manifestation of our desire
to have a private covenant relationship with God. They
represent the voluntary surrender of our agency to a
higher power, and the subjugation of our will to
His. Our testimonies reflect the promises
and covenants that we make
and keep with God.

In the ultimate
sense, our birth is not really a question
of development or of maturation, but rather of
generation. In a long list of emotional, miraculous,
and awe-inspiring experiences, becoming new creatures
in Christ (see Mosiah 27:26) becomes the quintessential
event of mortality. Just so, the process of kindling our
divine spark, of igniting the spirit lying dormant
within us, of awakening our divine potential,
and of nurturing the God in embryo
that is present within each of us,
is described as being
"born again".

The Book of Mormon is of such power
that it drives the law into our inward parts,
so that it is written upon our hearts. A mighty
change takes place as we experience the process of
sanctification. When we are born again, the
desired result of gospel-oriented teaching
has been achieved, and we have no
more disposition to do evil, but
to do good continually.
(See Mosiah 5:2).

# Introduction to The Isaiah Chapters
## 2 Nephi Chapters 12-24

"The version of Isaiah that is found in the Nephite scriptures hews an independent course for itself, as might be expected of a truly ancient and authentic record. It makes additions to the present text in certain places, omits material in others, transposes, makes grammatical changes, finds support at times for its unusual readings in the ancient Greek, Syriac, and Latin Versions, and at other times finds no support at all. In general, it presents phenomena of great interest to the student of Isaiah".
(Sydney B. Sperry).

"The text of Isaiah in The Book of Mormon is not word for word the same as that of the King James Translation. Of 433 verses of Isaiah in the Nephite record, Joseph Smith modified 234, or 53%. Some of the changes were slight, while others were radical. However, 199 verses are word for word the same as the K.J.T. We, therefore, freely admit that Joseph Smith may have used the K.J.T. when he came to the text of Isaiah on the plates. As long as the K.J.T. agreed substantially with the text on the plates, he let it pass; when it differed too radically, he translated the Nephite version and dictated the necessary changes."
(Sydney B. Sperry).

"The version of Isaiah in the Nephite scriptures hews an independent course for itself, as might be expected of a truly ancient and authentic record. It makes additions to the present text in certain places, omits material in others, transposes, makes grammatical changes, finds support at times for its unusual readings in the ancient Greek, Syriac, and Latin Versions, and at other times finds no support at all. In general, it presents phenomena of great interest to the student of Isaiah". (Sydney B. Sperry, "Book of Mormon Compendium," p. 512).

"The text of Isaiah in The Book of Mormon is not word for word the same as that of the King James Translation. Of 433 verses of Isaiah in the Nephite record, Joseph Smith modified 234, or 53%. Some of the changes were slight, while others were radical. However, 199 verses are word for word the same as the K.J.T. We, therefore, freely admit that Joseph Smith may have used the K.J.T. when he came to the text of Isaiah on the plates. As long as the K.J.T. agreed substantially with the text on the plates, he let it pass; when it differed too radically, he translated the Nephite version and dictated the necessary changes". (Sydney B. Sperry, "Book of Mormon Compendium," p. 507-508, see C.E.S. Manual, p. 90, & Commentary Reference to 2 Nephi 26:15).

As Hugh Nibley has pointed out: "Resemblances between the Bible and The Book of Mormon are not hard to explain. Far from being evidence of fraud, they are rather confirmation of authenticity. If The Book of Mormon is what it claims to be, we should expect to find a strong biblical influence in it. Its prophets sound like those of the Old Testament because they studied and consciously quoted the words of those prophets, and moreover, all prophets sound alike, being called for the same purpose under much the same conditions". ("Churches in The Wilderness").

Mark E. Petersen wrote: "When the King James translators began their work, they did so with fasting and prayer. For the most part they were pious men who sought the inspiration of the Lord in their work. We believe they received it. The preservation of the Bible thru the ages is itself a miracle. It was accomplished only thru the hand of God. Then why not its translation? The King James translators did everything they knew how to obtain divine inspiration for their task. Knowing the great value of that book to the Gentiles, as Nephi himself said, would God withhold the necessary inspiration?. Those humble translators were instruments in the hands of the Almighty to further His purpose among the Gentiles. ("Those Gold Plates!" p. 52 & 56).

Nephi himself revealed why a comprehension of Isaiah is difficult even for biblical scholars. He wrote: "Now I, Nephi, do speak somewhat concerning the words which I have written, which have been spoken by the mouth of Isaiah. For behold, Isaiah spake many things which were hard for many of my people to understand; for they know not concerning the manner of prophesying among the Jews". (2 Nephi 25:1). That is to say, the prophet Isaiah spoke in figures, using types and shadows to illustrate his points. Thus, the key to an understanding of his scriptural code requires some explanation.

Only Sam and Nephi and perhaps their wives had lived "at Jerusalem". Therefore, they alone had a first-hand understanding of their cultural heritage and the distinctive writing style of the Jews. On the one hand, it would be important that the people of Nephi be familiar with the contents of The Plates of Brass,

Early-on in The Book of Mormon, we discover a verse that explains why a comprehension of Isaiah is so difficult, even for biblical scholars. Nephi said: I "speak somewhat concerning the words which I have written, which have been spoken by the mouth of Isaiah. For behold, Isaiah spake many things which were hard for many of my people to understand; for they know not concerning the manner of prophesying among the Jews." (2 Nephi 25:1). That is to say, the prophet Isaiah spoke in figures, using types and shadows to illustrate his points. Thus, the key to an understanding of his scriptural code requires some elucidation.

Only Sam and Nephi, and perhaps their wives, had lived "at Jerusalem". Therefore, they alone had a first-hand understanding of their cultural heritage and the distinctive writing style of the Jews. On the one hand, it would be important that the people of Nephi be familiar with the contents of The Plates of Brass, because the teachings from that body of scripture included many important doctrinal truths. On the other hand, Nephi abhorred that part of the Jewish mindset which had been responsible for his family's persecution, its expulsion from their home, their trials in the wilderness, and the hardship of their lives on the sea and in the land of promise.

Because the teachings of that body of scripture contained many important doctrinal truths. On the other hand, Nephi abhorred that part of the Jewish mindset which had been responsible for the persecution of his family, its expulsion from their home, their trials in the wilderness, and the hardship of their lives in the promised land.

Nephi expressed his reluctance to teach his people many things concerning the manner of "the Jews," but at the same time, he wrote; "My soul delighteth in the words of Isaiah, for I came out from Jerusalem, and mine eyes hath beheld the things of the Jews, and I know that the Jews do understand the things of the prophets, and there is none other people that understand the things which were spoken unto the Jews like unto them, save it be that they are taught after the manner of the things of the Jews". (2 Nephi 25:6).

Indirectly, Nephi emphasized the importance of Book of Mormon scholarship and of studying his people, their culture, and their world. If we neglect to do that, we cannot understand the manner of prophesying of men like Nephi, Jacob, Abinadi, Alma, Helaman, Mormon, and Moroni, let alone Isaiah. They can be understood, but only if we are willing to first pay the price. Perspiration must precede inspiration, and there can be no revelation where there is no student.

Because Isaiah's writing style employed types and shadows, and because his prophecies were dualistic, meaning that they had application not only for ancient Israel, but also for Israel at the time of the mortal ministry of Christ, and for Latter-day and Millennial Israel as well, it is necessary in many cases to analyze nearly every word of a verse in order to comprehend its true meaning. It will also be necessary to study the chapters against the backdrop of the historical context in which they were written, in order to 'read between the lines' and better understand their meaning. At first, such an exercise might seem a bit cumbersome, but with a deeper understanding, Isaiah's writings will come alive with imagery and metaphor, and loom larger than life, because they were specifically written to transcend the ages.

The Lord declared: "Now behold, a marvelous work is about to come forth among the children of men." (D&C 4:1). "And if thou wilt inquire, thou shalt know mysteries which are great and marvelous." (D&C 6:11). "Now behold, I say unto you, that ye ought to search these things. Yea, a commandment I give unto you that ye search these things diligently; for great are the words of Isaiah." (3 Nephi 23:1).

Only when we have expended soul-sweat will the words of Isaiah flow easily and poetically to our minds. Scriptural fluency will come after practice that is manifested by memorization, recitation, individual and cooperative study, comparison with companion scriptures, and expansion of understanding by critical analysis of supportive commentaries, not to mention enduring faith and fervent prayer.

One final thought. The "Isaiah Chapters" may have been strategically placed, not in his first book, but within the Second Book of Nephi in order to give first-time readers of The Book of Mormon time to acquaint themselves with the "manner of the Jews" (2 Nephi 25:2) through a study of the 22 chapters of the First Book of Nephi, and the first 11 chapters of the Second Book of Nephi, so that they could, when they finally got to 2 Nephi Chapter 12, better appreciate the prophet Isaiah's style and subject matter. Rather than summarily skipping over these chapters, Nephi may have hoped that, with their purposeful placement, latter-day Israel would be in a better position to understand the prophet's messages, for both he and the resurrected Lord felt that the words of Isaiah were of great worth.

The "Isaiah Chapters" may have been strategically placed within the Second Book of Nephi in order to give first-time readers of The Book of Mormon time to acquaint themselves with the "manner of the Jews" (2 Nephi 25:2) through a study of the 22 chapters of the First Book of Nephi, and the first 11 chapters of the Second Book of Nephi, so that when they finally got to 2 Nephi Chapter 12, they could better appreciate the prophet's style and subject matter. Rather than summarily skipping over these chapters, Nephi may have hoped that, with their providential placement, latter-day Israel would be in a better position to understand the prophet's messages, for both he and the resurrected Lord felt that the words of Isaiah were of great worth.
(See 3 Nephi 23:1).

Only when we have expended soul-sweat, not only while studying 2 Nephi Chapters 12 to 24, but also while earning a familiarity with 1 Nephi Chapters 1-22, and 2 Nephi Chapters 1-11, will the words of Isaiah flow more easily and poetically to our minds. Scriptural fluency will come after practice that is manifested by memorization, recitation, individual and cooperative study, comparison with Isaiah's companion scriptures, and expansion of understanding by critical analysis of supportive commentaries, not to mention enduring faith, fervent prayer, and illumination by the Spirit.

"Ye ought to search these
things. Yea, a commandment
I give unto you, that ye search these
things diligently; for great are the words
of Isaiah. For surely he spake as touching
all things concerning my people which are
of the house of Israel; therefore, it must needs
be that he must speak also to the Gentiles.
And all things that he spake have been
and shall be, even according to
the words which he spake."
(3 Nephi 23:1-4).

"Wherefore, hearken, O my people, which
are of the house of Israel," wrote Nephi, "and give
ear unto my words; for because the words of Isaiah
are not plain unto you, nevertheless they are plain unto
all those that are filled with the spirit of prophecy ... Yea, and
my soul delighteth in the words of Isaiah, for I came out from
Jerusalem, and mine eyes hath beheld the things of the Jews,
and I know that the Jews do understand the things of the
prophets, and there is none other people that understand
the things which were spoken unto the Jews like unto
them, save it be that they are taught after the
manner of the things of the Jews."
(2 Nephi 25:4-6).

A Book of
Mormon requirement is
that we take calculated and
acceptable risks, in order to break
free from the comfort zones, safety
nets, and ports of refuge to which the
timid apprehensively retreat at the first
sign of danger, to squeak out their lives
as they scurry about from one shadowy
sanctuary to another, in a flight from
both freedom and faith.

It is
our faith that
points us in the
direction of doctrine,
so when we encounter
the principles of the Plan
in The Book of Mormon, we
will all experience religious
recognition, or a re-knowing
of things we have previously
been taught. We will respond
to the truth with action that
has the form and substance
of a godly walk that is a
bold testament of our
confidence in God's
power to save.

# "And it came to pass"
## In The Book of Mormon

Some have legitimately asked the question: Why is the phrase "and it came to pass" so frequently employed by the authors of The Book of Mormon? Mark Twain wondered this very thing, and famously joked that if the phrase were omitted from the text, the church could have instead published "The Pamphlet of Mormon". ("Roughing It," p. 33). As it turns out, however, the joke is on him. This much-maligned phrase actually provides powerful evidence of the authenticity of the record.

But why could it be that the phrase "and it came to pass" appears in The Book of Mormon so much more frequently, page for page, than it does in the Old Testament? The answer is twofold. First, the Book of Mormon contains much more narrative material, chapter for chapter, than does the Bible. Secondly, but equally important, the translators of the King James Version did not always render "wayehi" as "and it came to pass." Instead, they chose to draw from a multitude of similar expressions, such as "and it happened," "and it became," or "and it was."

Some have quite legitimately asked the question: Why was the phrase "and it came to pass" so frequently employed by the authors of The Book of Mormon? Mark Twain wondered this very thing, and famously joked that if the phrase were omitted from the text, the church could have instead published "The Pamphlet of Mormon." ("Roughing It," p. 33). As it turns out, however, the joke is on him. This much-maligned phrase actually provides strong evidence of the authenticity of the record.

Donald W. Parry, an instructor in biblical Hebrew at BYU, wrote in the "Ensign" (12/1992, p. 29): "The English translation of the Hebrew word wayehi (often used to connect two ideas or events), "and it came to pass," appears some 452 times in the King James Version of the Bible. The expression is rarely found in Hebrew poetic, literary, or prophetic writings. Most often, it appears in Old Testament narratives, such as the books by Moses that recounted the history of the children of Israel.

As in the Old Testament, the expression in The Book of Mormon (where it appears some 1,424 times) occurs only in the narrative selections, and is clearly missing in the more literary parts, such as the psalm of Nephi (see 2 Ne. 4:20-25); the direct speeches of King Benjamin, Abinadi, Alma, and Jesus Christ; and in the epistles.

But why does the phrase "and it came to pass" appear in the Book of Mormon so much more often, page for page, than it does in the Old Testament? The answer is twofold. First, the Book of Mormon contains much more narrative material, chapter for chapter, than does the Bible. Secondly, but equally important, the translators of the King James Version did not always render "wayehi" as "and it came to pass." Instead, they chose to draw from a multitude of similar expressions, such as "and it happened," "and it became," or "and it was."

The word "wayehi" is found about 1,204 times in the Hebrew Bible, but it was translated only 727 times as "and it came to pass" in the King James Version. Joseph Smith did not introduce that variety into the translation of The Book of Mormon. Rather, he retained the precision of "and it came to pass," which better performs the transitional function of the Hebrew word.

In all probability, the Prophet Joseph Smith likely would not have used the phrase at all in The Book of Mormon, or at least not consistently, had he created that record himself. Thus, the discriminating use of the Hebraic phrase "and it came to pass" in The Book of Mormon is further evidence that the record is what it says it is - a translation from reformed Egyptian with ties to the Hebrew language. (See Mormon 9:32-33).

As an afternote, there is also a New World connection to the phrase. Experts confirm that an element translated "and it came to pass" functioned in at least four ways in Mayan texts: (1) As a posterior date indicator in a text that meant "to count forward to the next date," and (2) as an anterior date indicator that signified "to count backward to the given date." Additionally, the phrase could also function (3) as a posterior or (4) anterior event indicator, meaning "counting forward or backward to a certain event."

There are instances of all four functions of "and it came to pass" in the Book of Mormon, as well as combined date and event indications in both posterior and anterior expressions. For example, "And it came to pass that the people began ..." is a posterior event indicator (3 Nephi 2:3), whereas "And it had come to pass ..." is an anterior event indicator. (3 Nephi 1:20)."

"The English translation of the Hebrew word *wayehi* (often used to link two ideas or events), "and it came to pass," appears some 727 times in the King James Version of the Old Testament. The expression is rarely found in Hebrew poetic, literary, or prophetic writings. Most often, it appears in Old Testament narratives, such as the books by Moses that recounted the history of the children of Israel. As in the Old Testament, the expression in The Book of Mormon (where it appears some 1,404 times) occurs only in the narrative selections, and is clearly missing in the more literary parts.

In all probability, Joseph Smith likely would not have employed the phrase at all in The Book of Mormon, or at least not consistently, had he created the record himself. Thus, the discriminating use of the Hebraic phrase "and it came to pass" in The Book of Mormon is further evidence that the record is what it says it is - a translation from reformed Egyptian with ties to the Hebrew language.
(See Mormon 9:32-33).

It was at the
very instant when their
unsatisfied craving for the praise
and the popularity of the world began to
sway their behavior, that the Nephites found
themselves in the uncomfortable position of
bending their character, when they thought
they were only taking a bow. It was chiefly
at this time that they needed the soothing
inspiration of the Holy Spirit, and the
healing guidance of their Lord and
Savior Jesus Christ, and finally
the nurturing encouragement
of their Father, Who looked
down upon them every
day of their lives,
from heaven
above.

It is the
gospel of Jesus Christ
as it is revealed in The Book
of Mormon that encourages us to
be enthusiastic. After all, it is the good
news that practically begs us to experience
the feeling of being possessed by a god, to
have supernatural inspiration, and enjoy
prophetic frenzy. The definition found
in the dictionary is unmistakable. If
we are suffused with enthusiasm,
our actions are no longer ours;
for it is God Who has taken
control of our destiny,
with kindness and
benevolence.

Baptism and the gift of the Holy Ghost, are the "fruit of the Spirit" (Galatians 5:22) that we enjoy when we have been taught the doctrine of Christ as it is found in The Book of Mormon. (See 2 Nephi 32:6).

'Father knows best', and has unbridled confidence in us, and in our divine potential to develop His nature. He commands us to repent, to be baptized, and to develop perfect faith. Because these are realistic goals that are within the reach of the weakest of His children, they become the basic requirements of those who put forth the effort to investigate the merits of The Book of Mormon and hope to one day triumphantly enter in thru the gates of His Celestial Kingdom.

# "And thus we see"
## In The Book of Mormon

The phrase
**"and thus we see"**
is unique to The Book
of Mormon; it is not found
in any other book of scripture.
Other related phrases that are also
unique to that ancient text include
"thus we see," "thus we may see," and
"we can see," as well as "and thus
we can plainly discern."

**"And thus we see"** has received attention
in the following presentations, to name a few: "And
Thus We See", "Ensign", August 2008, p. 40-43; Helaman
12. "And Thus We See," "Book of Mormon Seminary Student
Study Guide", p. 152-153; Henry B. Eyring, "And Thus We See:
Helping a Student in a Moment of Doubt," address to religious
educators, Temple Square Assembly Hall, Salt Lake City, 5
February 1993; and David A. Bednar, "Come unto
Christ," BYU - Idaho religion symposium
address, 29 January 2000.

"And thus we see"

- 1 Nephi 16:29
- 1 Nephi 17:3
- Alma 12:21-22 (twice)
- Alma 24:19 (twice)
- Alma 28:13-14 (three times)
- Alma 30:60 (twice)
- Alma 42:4, 7 & 14 (three times)
- Alma 50:19
- Helaman 6:34-36 & 40
- Helaman 12:3
- Ether 14:25

"Thus we see"

- Alma 24:27
- Alma 46:8

"Now we see"

- Alma 12:22

"We can also see"

- Alma 46:9

"And we may see"

- Helaman 12:3

"Thus we may see"

- Helaman 3:27

"We can behold"

- Alma 50:19
- Helaman 12:1
- Ether 2:9

"We can see"

- Helaman 12:1

"And thus we can plainly discern"

- Alma 24:3
- Alma 46:8)

"And now ye see"

- Alma 44:4

"And thus"

- Alma 42:26
- Alma 52:14

There are 2 other similar phrases in the Book of Mormon that are also found in other scriptures, but these phrases in the other scriptures don't convey the same significance as those in The Book of Mormon. The first is **"we see,"** found in Alma 9:14, 12:24, 19:23 & 36, 26:37, 29:8, 37:26, 42:3, & 50:21, in Helaman 3:29, as well as in the Old Testament in Psalms 36:9 & 74:9, Jeremiah 5:12, and in the New Testament in John 9:41, Romans 8:25, 1 Corinthians 13:12, and in Hebrews 2:8 & 3:19.

The second is **"we may see,"** that is found in 2 Nephi 15:9 and Helaman 12:2, and in the Bible in Isaiah 5:19, Mark 15:32 and in John 6:30. Other variations include **"we saw"** and **"we shall see."** A similar phrase that is unique to the Doctrine and Covenants is **"and thus we saw,"** found in D&C 76:89, 91, & 92.

"We see"

- Alma 9:14
- Alma 12:24
- Alma 19:23
- Alma 19:36
- Alma 26:37
- Alma 29:8
- Alma 37:26
- Alma 42:3
- Alma 50:21
- Helaman 3:29

"We may see"

- 2 Nephi 15:9
- Helaman 12:2

"And thus it is"

- Helaman 12:26

In total,
the phrase "and thus
we see" is used over fifty
times in The Book of Mormon,
(depending on how picky you get
about exact terminology) with the
record keeper Mormon using the
phrase or one of its variants in
nearly every one of those
instances.

| | |
|---|---|
| 1 Nephi 16:29 | Alma 42:14 |
| 1 Nephi 17:3 | Alma 42:26 |
| 2 Nephi 15:9 | Alma 44:4 (twice) |
| Alma 9:14 | Alma 46:8 |
| Alma 12:21 | Alma 46:9 |
| Alma 12:22 (twice) | Alma 50:19 (twice) |
| Alma 12:24 | Alma 50:21 |
| Alma 19:23 | Alma 52:14 |
| Alma 19:36 (3 times?) | Helaman 3:27 |
| Alma 24:19 (twice) | Helaman 3:28 |
| Alma 24:27 | Helaman 3:29 |
| Alma 24:30 | Helaman 6:34 |
| Alma 26:37 | Helaman 6:35 |
| 1Alma 28:13 | Helaman 6:36 |
| Alma 28:14 (twice) | Helaman 6:40 |
| Alma 29:8 | Helaman 12:1 (twice) |
| Alma 30:60 (twice) | Helaman 12:2 |
| Alma 37:26 | Helaman 12:3 |
| Alma 42:3 | Helaman 12:26 |
| Alma 42:4 | Ether 2:9 |
| Alma 42:7 (twice) | Ether 14:25 |

The events described by Mormon in his abridgements took shape over many centuries, while Nephi faithfully recorded his own impressions of personal experiences: "**And thus we see** that by small means the Lord can bring about great things." (1 Nephi 16:29).

"**And thus we see** that the commandments of God must be fulfilled." (1 Nephi 17:3).

"**Now we see** that the word of the Lord has been verified in this thing, and the Lamanites have been cut off from his presence, from the beginning of their transgressions in the land."
(Alma 9:14).

"What does the scripture mean, which saith that God placed cherubim and a flaming sword on the east of the garden of Eden, lest our first parents should enter and partake of the fruit of the tree of life, and live forever? **And thus we see** that there was no possible chance that they should live forever."
(Alma 12:21).

"**Now we see** that Adam did fall by the partaking of the forbidden fruit, according to the word of God; **and thus we see,** that by his fall, all mankind became a lost and fallen people."
(Alma 12:22).

"**And we see** that death comes upon mankind, yea, the death which has been spoken of by Amulek, which is the temporal death." (Alma 12:24).

"**Now we see** that Ammon could not be slain." (Alma 19:23).

"**And thus** the work of the Lord did commence among the Lamanites; **thus** the Lord did begin to pour out his Spirit upon them; and **we see** that his arm is extended to all people who will repent and believe on his name." (Alma 19:36).

"**And thus we see** that, when these Lamanites were brought to believe and to know the truth, they were firm, and would suffer even unto death rather than commit sin; **and thus we see** that ..... they buried the weapons of war, for peace."
(Alma 24:19).

"And there was not a wicked man slain among them; but there were more than a thousand brought to the knowledge of the truth; **thus we see** that the Lord worketh in many ways to the salvation of his people."
(Alma 24:27).

Mormon also employed a phrase found only one time in all of scripture: "**And thus we can plainly discern**, that after a people have been once enlightened by the Spirit of God, and have had great knowledge of things pertaining to righteousness, and then have fallen away into sin and transgression, they become more hardened, and thus their state becomes worse than though they had never known these things."
(Alma 24:30).

"Now my brethren, **we see** that God is mindful of every people, whatsoever land they may be in; yea, he numbereth his people, and his bowels of mercy are over all the earth."
(Alma 26:37).

"**And thus we see** how great the inequality of man is because of sin and transgression, and the power of the devil, which comes by the cunning plans which he hath devised to ensnare the hearts of men."
(Alma 28:13).

"**And thus we see** the great call of diligence of men to labor in the vineyards of the Lord; **and thus we see** the great reason of sorrow, and also of rejoicing – sorrow because of death and destruction among men, and joy because of the light of Christ unto life. (Alma 28:14).

"Therefore, **we see** that the Lord doth counsel in wisdom, according to that which is just and true." (Alma 29:8).

"**And thus we see** the end of him who perverteth the ways of the Lord; **and thus we see** that the devil will not support his children at the last day, but doth speedily drag them down to hell."

"Now, my son,
**we see** that they did
not repent; therefore they
have been destroyed."
(Alma 37:26).

"Now, **we see** that
the man had become as God,
knowing good and evil."
(Alma 42:3).

"**And thus we see** that there was a
time granted unto man to repent,
yea, a probationary time, a time
to repent and serve God."
(Alma 42:4).

"And now, **ye see** by this
that our first parents were cut off
both temporally and spiritually from the
presence of the Lord; **and thus we see**
they became subjects to follow
after their own will."
(Alma 42:7).

"**And thus we see** that all mankind
were fallen, and they were in the grasp of
justice; yea, the justice of God, which
consigned them forever to be cut
off from his presence."
(Alma 42:14).

"**And thus,**
God bringeth about his
great and eternal purposes,
which were prepared from the
foundation of the world."
(Alma 42:26).

"**Now ye see** that this is the true faith of God; yea, **ye see** that God will support, and keep, and preserve us, so long as we are faithful unto him, and unto our faith, and our religion."
(Alma 44:4).

"**Thus we see** how quick(ly) the children of men do forget the Lord their God, yea, how quick to do iniquity and to be led away by the evil one." (Alma 46:8).

"Yea, and **we also see** the great wickedness one very wicked man can cause to take place among the children of men."
(Alma 46:9).

"**<u>And thus we
see</u>** how merciful and
just are all the dealings of
the Lord, to the fulfilling of all
his words unto the children of
men; yea, **<u>we can behold</u>** that
his words are verified."
(Alma 50:19).

"And **<u>we see</u>** that these
promises have been verified
to the people of Nephi."
(Alma 50:21).

"**<u>And thus</u>** were the
Nephites in those dangerous
circumstances in the ending of the
twenty and sixth year of the reign of
the judges over the people of Nephi."
(Alma 52:14).

"**Thus we may see** that the Lord is merciful unto all who will, in the sincerity of their hearts, call upon his holy name." (Helaman 3:27).

"Yea, **thus we see** that the gate of heaven is open unto all, even to those who will believe on the name of Jesus Christ, who is the Son of God." (Helaman 3:28).

"Yea, **we see** that whosoever will, may lay hold upon the word of God, which is quick and powerful." (Helaman 3:29).

"**And thus we see** that the Nephites did begin to dwindle in unbelief, and grow in wickedness and abominations, while the Lamanites began to grow exceedingly in the knowledge of their God; yea, they did begin to keep his statutes and commandments, and to walk in truth and uprightness before him."
(Helaman 6:34).

"**And thus we see** that the Spirit of the Lord began to withdraw from the Nephites, because of the wickedness and the hardness of their hearts."
(Helaman 6:35).

"**And thus we see** that the Lord began to pour out his Spirit upon the Lamanites, because of their easiness and willingness to believe in his words."
(Helaman 6:36).

"**And thus we see** that they were in an awful state, and ripening for an everlasting destruction." (Helaman 6:40).

"**And thus we can behold** how false, and also the unsteadiness of the hearts of the children of men; yea, **we can see** that the Lord in his great infinite goodness doth bless and prosper those who put their trust in him." (Helaman 12:1).

"**And we may see** at the very time when he doth prosper his people ... then is the time that they do harden their hearts, and do forget the Lord their God, and do trample under their feet the Holy One." (Helaman 12:2).

"**And thus we see** that except the Lord doth chasten his people with many afflictions, yea, except he doth visit them with death and with terror, and with famine and with all manner of pestilence, they will not remember him."
(Helaman 12:3).

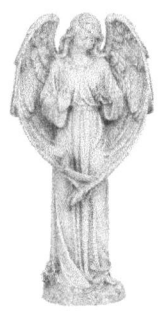

"They that have done good shall have everlasting life; and they that have done evil shall have everlasting damnation. **And thus it is**. Amen."
(Helaman 12:26).

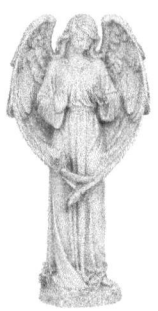

"**We can behold** the decrees of God concerning this land, that it is a land of promise; and whatsoever nation shall possess it shall serve God, or they shall be swept off when the fulness of his wrath shall come upon them."
(Ether 2:9).

"**And thus we see** that the Lord did visit them in the fulness of his wrath, and their wickedness and abominations had prepared a way for their everlasting destruction." (Ether 14:25).

Wise students of the scriptures will ponder carefully and consider personally applying any passage therein that is introduced by the words **"and thus we see."**

Modern-day prophets and apostles occasionally employ similar rhetorical phrasing in their sermons that signals emphasis, importance, or urgency. **"To all within the sound of my voice"** is one such phrase that is occasionally heard in general conferences. Whether it pertains to scripture or modern-day exhortation, let us be alert to the points of emphasis that are conveyed by the servants of God, and profit thereby.

A related phrase, and one that was equally designed to capture the attention of the reader, is **"that ye may learn..."** This can be found in Mosiah 2:17, Alma 32:12 & 38:9, and Mormon 9:31, and a broader application of the phrase **"that ye may..."** can be found in Mosiah 2:21, 18:9 & 24:14, Alma 13:13, 32:12, 34:17, 37:6 & 38:12, 3 Nephi 11:13, 12:45, & 30:2, Ether 2:23, Moroni 7:16 & 10:7, to name just a few. These verses are not just doctrinal thoughts, but are warnings that were designed to help us to understand how relevant they are to our own circumstances.

As we continue our spiritual education, The Book of Mormon will help us to expand our spiritual capacity, and to see as God sees, and to know and understand as He does. When we turn our attention to the interesting phrase "and thus we see", that is used by the prophets, and to its related variants, we open our minds to pearls of great price and hidden treasures of knowledge.

# "Behold"
## In The Book of Mormon

The word **"behold"** appears 1,669 times in the King James Translation of the Bible and 1,275 times in The Book of Mormon, so Another Testament of Jesus Christ has scored anther bulls-eye when it comes to being true to authentic ancient grammar usage, syntax, and gospel terminology.

The King James Translators encountered the Hebrew word "<u>hinneh</u>" in the Old Testament and the Greek word "<u>idou</u>" in the New Testament, and since no single word in English adequately conveyed its shades of meaning, they tended to leave the word as is, retaining the word **"behold"** because they could not find a suitable substitute. However, some modern English translations of the Bible have spurned the archaic phrasing in the King James Version in favor of more contemporary expressions.

The word "behold" appears 1,669 times in the King James Translation of the Bible, and 1,275 times in The Book of Mormon, so Another Testament of Jesus Christ has scored another bulls-eye when it comes to being true to authentic ancient grammar usage, syntax, and gospel terminology. Because it is a phrase that is encountered so often, though, the casual reader frequently passes right over it without thinking about what the word means and why it appears so often. The fact is that are good reasons why the word "behold" is used so many times, and these are linked to its different nuances, depending on the context.

The King James Translators encountered the Hebrew word "hinneh "in the Old Testament and the Greek word "idou" in the New Testament, and since no single word in English adequately conveyed its shades of meaning, they tended to leave the word as is, retaining the word "behold," because they could not find a suitable substitute. However, some modern English translations of the Bible have spurned the archaic phrasing in the King James Version in favor of more contemporary expressions.

Nevertheless, in a valiant attempt to retain the original meaning of the word "hinneh", the preface to the English Standard Version of the Bible explains: "Although 'Look!' and 'See!' and 'Listen!' would be workable in some contexts, in many others these words lack sufficient weight and dignity. Given the principles of 'essentially literal' translation, it is important not to leave "hinneh" and "idou" completely untranslated, for to do so would sacrifice the intended emphasis in the original languages. The older and more formal word 'behold' has usually been retained, therefore, as the best available option for conveying the original sense of meaning."

In the KJT, the word "behold" was translated from the Hebrew הִנֵּה, which translates into one of three meanings: First, the word is used to call attention to a person, object, principle, or doctrine. For example, Exodus 24:8 reads: "And Moses took the blood, and sprinkled it on the people, and said, Behold the blood of the covenant, which the Lord hath made with you concerning all these words."

Secondly, the word can be employed to introduce or reassert a principle, truth, or doctrine, as in Genesis 1:29, where God says to Adam and Eve, "Behold, I have given you every herb bearing seed, which is upon the face of all the earth, and every tree, in the which is the fruit of a tree yielding seed; to you it shall be for meat."

Thirdly, the word may dramatize a concept. Genesis 1:31 reads: "And God saw every thing that he had made, and, behold, it was very good."

Each of the three different variations of meaning of the word depends upon who is being addressed. "Behold" can be directed to persons in in the narrative, but in other cases, it reaches outside of time and space to draw the reader in, either to ensure that attention is given to a particular detail of the narrative, or to instill a sense of excitement within the reader.

But what about the cultural and literary milieu that surrounded the translation of The Book of Mormon? By the 1820s, these classical distinctions relating to the use of the word "behold" had become blurred. In the 1828 edition of Webster's Dictionary, the word "behold was defined as: "to fix the eyes upon; to see with attention; to observe with care". In other words, the 19th century definition focused only on directing one's attention to a particular event or person, and completely ignored the other definitions that had classically

But what about the cultural and literary milieu in which Joseph found himself during his translation of the plates? By the 1820s, these classical distinctions relating to the use of the word **"behold"** had become blurred. In the 1828 edition of Webster's Dictionary, "the word **"behold"** was defined as: "to fix the eyes upon; to see with attention; to observe with care". In other words, the 19th century definition focused only on directing one's attention to a particular event or person, while ignoring the other definitions that had been classically related to the introduction of new truth, and to dramatization. But, as one would expect from the inspired translation of an ancient text, the word **"behold"** in the Book of Mormon remains true to the pattern of the ancient Hebrew Bible, rather than to its contemporary 1828 definition.

Each of the different variations of meaning of the word depends upon who is being addressed. The word **"behold"** is incredibly nuanced, and can be directed to persons within the narrative, but in other cases, it reaches outside of time and space to draw the reader in, either to ensure that attention is given to a particular detail of the narrative, or to instill a sense of excitement in the mind of the reader.

been related to the introduction of new truth and to dramatization. But, as one would expect from the inspired translation of an ancient text, the word "behold" in the Book of Mormon remains true to the pattern of the Hebrew Bible, rather than to its contemporary 1828 definition.

Examples from The Book of Mormon illustrate how this literary feat is accomplished.

1). When "behold" is employed to instill enthusiasm:

"For behold, it came to pass that the Lord spake unto my father, yea, even in a dream, and said unto him…" (1 Nephi 2:1). In this instance, Nephi used the term "behold" to instill enthusiasm in the mind of his readers, relating to his father's dream. That he would do so is reasonable, because Nephi recognized the dream's beautiful symbolism and meaning that would resonate with readers throughout the rest of his narrative, and in fact, throughout the entire Book of Mormon.

"And now, because thou hast done this with such unwearyingness, behold, I will bless thee forever; and I will make thee mighty in word and in deed, in faith and in works; yea, even that all things shall be done unto thee according to thy word, for thou shalt not ask that which is contrary to my will. Behold, thou art Nephi, and I am God. Behold, I declare it unto thee in the presence of mine angels, that ye shall have power over this people, and shall smite the earth with famine, and with pestilence, and destruction, according to the wickedness of this people. Behold, I give unto you power, that whatsoever ye shall seal on earth shall be sealed in heaven; and whatsoever ye shall loose on earth shall be loosed in heaven; and thus shall ye have power among this people." (Helaman 10:5-7). With the term "behold" used 4 times in these verses, three new concepts are introduced with its use: 1) Nephi will be blessed forever, 2) God reasserts who Nephi is, and Who He is, in an interesting parallel statement, and 3) Nephi is given the sealing power.

2). When "behold" is used for added emphasis, to encourage the reader to "see" what is written, and as an introduction to newly discovered truth:

"And when Amulek saw the pains of the women and children who were consuming in the fire, he also was pained; and he said unto Alma: How can we witness this awful scene? Therefore, let us stretch forth our hands, and exercise the power of God which is in us, and save them from the flames. But Alma said unto him: The Spirit constraineth me that I must not stretch forth mine hand; for behold the Lord receiveth them up unto himself, in glory; and he doth suffer that they may do this thing, or that the people may do this thing unto them, according to the hardness of their hearts, that the judgments which he shall exercise upon them in his wrath may be just; and the blood of the innocent shall stand as a witness against them, yea, and cry mightily against them at the last day. Now Amulek said unto Alma: Behold, perhaps they will burn us also. And Alma said: Be it according to the will of the Lord. But behold, our work is not finished; therefore, they burn us not." (Alma 14:10-13).

3). When "behold" is used to introduce new truth:

"Behold, I speak unto you as if ye were present, and yet ye are not. But behold, Jesus Christ hath shown you unto me, and I know your doing." (Mormon 8:35

The word **behold**
is, at times, employed
to instill enthusiasm in
the mind of the reader. It is
also used for added emphasis, to
encourage the reader to 'see' what is
written, and finally, it is serves as
an introduction to newly
discovered truth.

At
the end of the
day, Joseph Smith
said that he translated
The Book of Mormon by the
gift and power of God, and he
let it go at that. And that's pretty
much all we can say about it. It
stands on its own merits and
that alone. But all things
considered, its quite
clear that he did
very well.

Behold, I speak unto you as though I spake from the dead; for I know that ye shall have my words." (Mormon 9:30).

These verses beautifully capture all three meanings of the word "behold," that calls attention to a principle, introduces a truth, and dramatizes a concept. Near the conclusion of the thousand-year history of the Nephites, Moroni reached out through time and space to lift our gaze, and as an experienced teacher, and with renewed energy, he redirected us to a startling truth. We are figuratively stopped in our tracks, lest we breeze past the final pages of the book without consciously recognizing the importance and intent of what we've read. It's a final plot twist that leaves us wanting more. As is the case many times in The Book of Mormon, new truth is adroitly emphasized and reasserted in such a way that the intent of the message cannot be overlooked.

The bottom line is that The Book of Mormon follows Hebraic patterns such as its faithfully accurate use of the word "behold." This is yet another example of the miraculous nature of the translation. Joseph Smith did not initiate his study of Hebrew until 1835, five years after the Book of Mormon was published, and due to his belated efforts, an independent translation of the Book of Mormon would have been impossible. As some antagonists purport, he could never have created such a neat, tidy, and entirely appropriate narrative as the product of his own wild imaginations.

In accordance with Occam's Razor, the most likely explanation is the simplest one: The Book of Mormon is what it says it is: "An abridgment of the record of the people of Nephi, and also of the Lamanites - Written to the Lamanites, who are a remnant of the house of Israel; and also to Jew and Gentile - Written by way of commandment, and also by the spirit of prophecy and of revelation - Written and sealed up, and hid up unto the Lord, that they might not be destroyed - To come forth by the gift and power of God unto the interpretation thereof - Sealed by the hand of Moroni, and hid up unto the Lord, to come forth in due time by way of the Gentile - The interpretation thereof by the gift of God." (Book of Mormon: "Introduction").

One could not do better than to employ the testimony of our Lord and Savior Jesus Christ: "And (Joseph Smith) translated the book, even that part which I have commanded him, and as your Lord and your God liveth, it is true." (D&C 17:6).

The prophets who wrote
in, or are quoted in, The Book
of Mormon point us to doctrine, and
so it is that when we encounter within its
pages vernacular that is so characteristic of
ancient Hebraic patterns, we respond to the
truth with actions that have both the form
and substance of a godly walk, and
that boldly testify of our faith
in the divine origin of the
text.

The truth freed
the Nephites from
sin, guilt, confusion,
skepticism, apprehension,
misgiving, uncertainty, and
ignorance. It liberated them to
make thoughtful choices, receive
priesthood ordinances, and to serve
others with more charity, influence,
and significance. As they more fully
enjoyed the blessings of the Plan of
Salvation, continuing obedience
to gospel principles moved them
steadily forward along the
path that leads back to
our heavenly home
and the warm
embrace of
God.

# "Wherefore" and "Therefore" in The Book of Mormon

Beginning with the abridgement by Mormon (that is loosely called The Plates of Mormon) there is an abrupt shift in the use of **"wherefore"** versus **"therefore"** in The Book of Mormon.

The Small Plates of Nephi overwhelming employ the use of the word **"wherefore"**, whereas the translation that is an abridgement by Mormon instead prefers the use of **"therefore"** (including the record that was written by Moroni, comprising chapters 8 and 9 of the Book of Mormon, and the Book of Moroni, excluding chapters 7-9 that were written by his father Mormon).

Beginning with the abridgement by Mormon (that is loosely called The Plates of Mormon) there is an abrupt shift in the use of "wherefore" versus "therefore" in The Book of Mormon. The Small Plates of Nephi overwhelming prefer the use of "wherefore", while the books that are an abridgement by Mormon prefer the use of "therefore" (including the record that was written by Moroni, comprising chapters 8 and 9 of the Book of Mormon, and the book of Moroni, excluding chapters 7-9 that were written by his father Mormon).

1 Nephi
Wherefore – 97 uses (88%)
Therefore – 13 uses (13%)

2 Nephi
Wherefore – 97 uses (88%)
Therefore – 13 uses (13%)

Jacob
Wherefore – 137 uses (83%)
Therefore – 28 uses (17%)

Enos
Wherefore – 6 uses (100%)
Therefore – 0 uses (0%)

Jarom
Wherefore – 3 uses (100%)
Therefore – 13 uses (0%)

Omni
Wherefore – 6 uses (100%)
Therefore – 9 uses (0%)

Words of Mormon
Wherefore – 4 uses (100%)
Therefore – 0 uses (0%)

Mosiah
Wherefore – 1 use (1%)
Therefore – 123 uses (00%)

Alma
Wherefore – 3 uses (1%)
Therefore – 291 uses (00%)

Helaman
Wherefore – 0 uses (0%)
Therefore – 63 uses (100%)

3 Nephi
Wherefore – 3 uses (0%)
Therefore – 97 uses (100%)

4 Nephi
Wherefore – 0 uses (0%)
Therefore – 5 uses (100%)

Mormon
Wherefore – -0 uses (0%)
Therefore – 22 uses (100%)

Ether
Wherefore – 63 uses (70%)
Therefore – 24 uses (30%)

Moroni
Wherefore – 0 uses (0%)
Therefore – 22 uses (100%)

The exception to this pattern
is found in the Book of Ether.
But this is where it gets interesting,
because Ether 4:17-18 is a message from
God, that is quoted by Moroni: "**Therefore**, when
ye shall receive this record ye may know that the
work of the Father has commenced upon all the face
of the land. **Therefore**, repent all ye ends of the earth,
and come unto me, and believe in my gospel, and
be baptized in my name; for he that believeth
and is baptized shall be saved; but he that
believeth not shall be damned; and
signs shall follow them that
believe in my name."

Prior to this commandment to be baptized,
almost twice as many instances of the word
"**therefore**" are found in the Book of Ether (13),
and only 7 instances of "**wherefore**." After the
commandment, however, a dramatic shift in
emphasis occurs. There are 11 instances
of "**therefore**." and 54 instances of
"**wherefore**." So, what may have
happened to precipitate
the shift?

The exception to this pattern is the Book of Ether. But this is where it gets interesting. Ether 4:17-18 is a message from God, that is quoted by Moroni from memory: "Therefore, when ye shall receive this record ye may know that the work of the Father has commenced upon all the face of the land. Therefore, repent all ye ends of the earth, and come unto me, and believe in my gospel, and be baptized in my name; for he that believeth and is baptized shall be saved; but he that believeth not shall be damned; and signs shall follow them that believe in my name."

It is a commandment that is directed to those in the last-days, that they must repent and be baptized. Unlike previous references to baptism in The Book of Mormon, where Lehi's descendants were repetitively commanded to be baptized, this time, the commandment is specifically pointed at those in the last days.

Prior to this commandment to be baptized, the Book of Ether contains 13 instances of the word "therefore" and 7 instances of "wherefore". After the commandment, Ether contains 11 instances of "therefore" and 54 instances of "wherefore". So, what may have happened to precipitate the shift?

Lucy Mack Smith stated in her history: "One morning ... they sat down to their usual work, when the first thing that presented itself to Joseph was a commandment from God that he and Oliver should repair to the water, and each of them be baptized." ("The Revised and Enhanced History of Joseph Smith By His Mother", Chapter 27). The only verse in The Book of Mormon that fits this description is Ether 4:18, and that fits the timeline of where Joseph would have been in the process of translation at the time of his baptism.

Now consider the impact Joseph says his baptism had on him. "Immediately on our coming up out of the water after we had been baptized, we experienced great and glorious blessings ... Our minds now enlightened, we began to have the scriptures laid open to our understandings, and the true meaning and intention of their more mysterious passages revealed unto us in a manner which we never could attain to previously, nor ever before had thought of." ("Joseph Smith History", 1:73-74).

For whatever reason, Joseph's baptism may have had a subtle, yet significant impact on the way he "viewed" the text of the plates from which he was translating the record, and if that is the case, he may have unconsciously modified his use of the words "therefore" and "wherefore".

One more observation is that the variation between "wherefore" and "therefore" cannot be discussed without considering larger questions of narrative structure, for example, those that address the use in The Book of Mormon of the words "whoso" and "whosoever", "oft" and "often', and "privily" and "secretly" to name a few.

The Book of Mormon is a marvelous work and a wonder, no less because of its consistent use of words that, at the very least, pique our interest and invite further inquiry. Most of us blow right past these words without considering their potential to provide significant evidence supporting Joseph's assertion that the book was translated by the gift and power of God.

For whatever reason,
it may be that Joseph's baptism
had a subtle, yet significant impact
on the way he "viewed" the text of the plates
from which he was then translating the record.
If that is the case, he might have unconsciously
modified his use of the words **"therefore"**
and **"wherefore"**.

The Book of Mormon
is a marvelous work and
a wonder, no less because of its
consistent use of words that, at the
very least, pique our interest to invite
further inquiry. Most of us blow right
past these words without considering
their potential to provide significant
evidence supporting Joseph's claim
that the book was translated
by the gift and power
of God.

# "The Appearance of Gold"

The Prophet Joseph recorded in his History that Moroni had told him that the book which was hidden in the Hill Cumorah was written upon gold plates. (See J.S.H. 1:34). However, the Book of Mormon record itself doesn't corroborate the Angel Moroni's characterization of the golden composition of the plates. In the church, however, it is commonly accepted that the records, other than the Plates of Brass, were 'gold plates'.

The Three Witnesses to The Book of Mormon wrote that they had "seen the plates which contain this record" without reference to the specific composition of the metal, although they went into great detail to describe the engravings themselves and their purpose to benefit humanity. Various Book of Mormon record-keepers referred to "plates of ore". "Plates of gold" are mentioned only twice, in Mosiah 8:9 and 28:11, where they specifically refer to the 24 Gold Plates of Ether. Mormon, who had access to all the records, and who abridged many of them, never referred in his writings to plates of gold.

Joseph Smith recorded in his History that Moroni told him that the book that was hidden in the Hill Cumorah was "written upon gold plates." (J.S.H. 1:34). But The Book of Mormon record itself does not corroborate Moroni's characterization of the gold composition of the plates. In the church, however, it is commonly accepted that the records, other than the Plates of Brass, were "gold plates." Gold has always denoted value, and at the very least, the precious gift of The Book of Mormon is equivalent to the gifts of gold, frankincense, and myrrh, bestowed by the Wise Men of the East upon the Christ child in Bethlehem.

The first plates that we actually encounter in The Book of Mormon are The Plates of Brass, (see 1 Nephi 3:12) which had "the records of the holy scriptures upon them," including "the genealogy of (Lehi's) forefathers." (Alma 37:3). These plates would yet fulfil prophecy, for they were to be "kept and preserved by the hand of the Lord until they should go forth unto every nation, kindred, tongue, and people, that they shall know of the mysteries contained thereon." (Alma 37:4, see Mosiah 2:9). By these mysteries, Alma meant history and doctrine discerned and understood only by the power of the Spirit.

The Three Witnesses to The Book of Mormon wrote only that they had "seen the plates which contain this record" without reference to the specific composition of the metal, although they went into great detail to describe the engravings themselves and their purpose to benefit humanity. Various Book of Mormon record-keepers referred to "plates of ore." (See 1 Nephi 19:1, Mosiah 21:27, and Mormon 8:5). When the prophets referred to a specific material, it was generally to "brass." (See 1 Nephi 3:3, 3:12, 3:24, 4:16, 4:24, 4:28, 5:10, 5:14, 5:18-19, 13:23, 19:21-22, 22:1, 22:30, 2 Nephi 4:2, 4:5, 5:12, Omni 1:14, Mosiah 1:3, 1:16, 10:16, 28:11, 28:20, Alma 37:3, & 3 Nephi 1:2 & 10:17). "Plates of gold" are mentioned only in Mosiah 8:9 and 28:11, where they specifically refer to the 24 Gold Plates of Ether, which had been found in "a land which was covered with bones of men, and of beasts, and (that) was also covered with ruins of buildings of every kind." (Mosiah 8:8). Mormon, who had access to all the records and who abridged many of them, never referred to plates of gold.

The verse that follows in Alma 37 is interesting because it may give us clues relating to the physical characteristics of the plates themselves. "And now behold, if they are kept, they must retain their brightness; yea, and they will retain their brightness; yea, and also shall all the plates which do contain that which is holy writ." (Alma 37:5, see 1 Nephi 5:19). This might suggest that the plates were subject to tarnishing (something that gold does not do), or the quality of "brightness" might refer to the substance of the messages inscribed on plates of various composition. In his abridgement, Mormon did not specify what Alma meant by "brightness."

We really do not know how many of the plates were actually made of gold. We do know, however, that the plates were heavy. The Eight Witnesses to The Book of Mormon testified that the plates they were shown and "hefted" had "the appearance of gold." The bound plates they handled are estimated to have weighed in the neighborhood of 36 kilograms (nearly 80 pounds). The plates from which Joseph translated The Book of Mormon may have been thin sheets of gold, (see "Testimony of Joseph Smith," J.S.H., 1:34) but the text itself suggests that, in general, the Nephite prophets engraved their records on a variety of metals.

Interestingly, not one of The Book of Mormon's authors describe the records upon which they engraved the history of their people as "gold plates," with the prominent exception, noted above, of the Plates of Ether, that were specifically characterized as being of "pure gold." (Mosiah 8:9). Nephi's record was engraven upon "plates of ore." (1 Nephi 19:1). It was the record upon these plates that was pleasing to Mormon and not the plates themselves. (The Words of Mormon, 1:4). As a matter of fact, when occasion arose, the various record keepers in The Book of Mormon almost pointedly described only the intrinsic quality of the plates entrusted to their care, while pointedly and characteristically ignoring the temporal value of the metal upon which the records were engraven.

We really do not know how many,
if any, of the plates were actually made of gold,
but we know they were heavy. The Eight Witnesses to
The Book of Mormon testified that the plates they were shown
and "hefted" had "the appearance of gold." The bound plates they
handled are estimated to have weighed in the neighborhood of 80
pounds. The plates from which Joseph translated The Book of
Mormon may have been thin sheets of gold, but the text
itself suggests that, in general, the Nephite
prophets engraved their records on
a variety of metals.

Because the element of gold itself seems
to have been plentiful in the lands of The Book of
Mormon, it many have not mattered to the Nephites of
what material the plates were crafted. Jacob reported that his
people, who still had an 'Old World' mindset, had "begun to
search for gold, and for silver, and for all manner of precious
ores, in the which, this land … doth abound most plentifully".
(Jacob 2:12). In the same vein, (no pun intended. Mormon
reported: "Both the Lamanites and the Nephites … did
have an exceeding plenty of gold, and of silver,
and of all manner of precious metals."
(Helaman 6:9).

In any case, when Alma told Helaman that the records would "retain their brightness" (see Alma 37:4, noted above), he might have intended a dual meaning. On the one hand, if the plates were to be easily inscribed upon, they might be less tarnish resistant. In the Old Testament, "the word 'nechosheth' is sometimes improperly translated (as) 'brass'. In most places, the correct translation would be 'copper,' although it may sometimes possibly mean 'bronze', which is a compound of copper and tin." ("Smith's Bible Dictionary," p. 97). Oxidation easily clouds the luster of these metals. On the other hand, the clearly understood messages of the records would be preserved for future generations who would be dazzled by the brightness of their simplicity.

Because gold itself was plentiful in the Lands of The Book of Mormon, it many have not mattered to them of what material the plates were crafted. Jacob reported that his people, who still had an "Old World" mindset, had "begun to search for gold, and for silver, and for all manner of precious ores." Note that Jacob qualified as "precious" the ore his people sought. "In the which," or in these precious materials, he continued, "this land ... doth abound most plentifully." (Jacob 2:12). In the same vein, Mormon reported: "Both the Lamanites and the Nephites ... did have an exceeding plenty of gold, and of silver, and of all manner of precious metals." (Helaman 6:9). As had Jacob before him, Mormon characterized the hoarded materials as "precious metals." For context, it is estimated that between 1500 and 1650 A.D., the Spanish alone exported 181 tons of gold, (+/- nine billion dollars worth) and 16,000 tons of silver from the New World.

Mormon's son Moroni twice referred to the plates, but only in reference to hiding them in the earth. (See Ether 15:11, & Mormon 8:4). Likewise, "Ammaron, being constrained by the Holy Ghost, did hide up the records which were sacred, yea, even all the sacred records which had been handed down from generation to generation, which were sacred." (4 Nephi 1:48-49). It may simply be that the custodians of the record were more focused on the message than on the material.

Mormon's son twice referred to the plates, but only in reference to hiding them in the earth. (See Ether 15:11, & Mormon 8:4). Likewise, "Ammaron, being constrained by the Holy Ghost, did hide up the records which were sacred, yea, even all the sacred records which had been handed down from generation to generation, which were sacred." (4 Nephi 1:48-49).

It may simply be that the custodians of the records were more focused on their messages than they were on the materials upon which they had been engraved.

# The Use of the Name of Christ
## in The Book of Mormon

The first recorded use of the name of Christ in The Book of Mormon only occurs in 2 Nephi 10:3, 32 chapters into the book. It reads: "Wherefore, as I said unto you, it must needs be expedient that Christ - for in the last night the angel spake unto me that this should be his name - should come among the Jews."

This begs an interesting question: Since Christ is the central figure in The Book of Mormon, why wasn't His name used until its 78th page? The obvious answer is that it wasn't until then that the angel revealed His name to Jacob. But that simplistic explanation, that is supported by scripture (2 Nephi 10:3), begs another question: Why, then, didn't the angel reveal His name earlier in the narrative, to Lehi, Nephi, and/or Jacob? The answer may seem surprising, at first, but it lends credence to the assertion that the book is authentic ancient scripture.

The first use of the name of Christ in The Book of Mormon occurs in 2 Nephi 10:3, that reads: "Wherefore, as I said unto you, it must needs be expedient that Christ - for in the last night the angel spake unto me that this should be his name - should come among the Jews."

This begs the question: Since Christ is the central figure in The Book of Mormon, why wasn't the name "Christ" used until its 78th page? The obvious answer is that it wasn't until then that an angel revealed His name to Jacob. But that simplistic explanation begs another question: Why, then, didn't the angel reveal His name earlier in the narrative, to Lehi, Nephi, and/or Jacob? The answer may seem surprising, at first, but it lends credence to the assertion that the book is authentic ancient scripture.

The word "Christ" is Greek. The same term in Hebrew is "Messiah" which Nephi used 28 times prior to 2 Nephi 10:13 (excluding quotations from Isaiah). Neither he nor his family knew Greek, coming as they did, from a culture that spoke Hebrew. Instead, they used a name that was familiar to them and that was drawn from their own language and culture. Consistent with this explanation, Nephi used the term "Messiah" until Jacob received revelation about the name Christ. After that time, "Messiah" fell out of favor. Nephi used it only 10 times subsequent to Jacob's revelation, and "Christ" became the primary term that thereafter was used to identify the Savior.

Between 2 Nephi 10:3 and 2 Nephi 33:15, Nephi used the term "Messiah" only 10 more times, and Jacob never used it. After Nephi's death, "Messiah" was used only 3 times in the remainder of The Book of Mormon. Looking at it another way, before Jacob's revelation, the term "Christ" was never used, but afterwards, it was used nearly 400 times, with the highest percentage attributed to Jacob, Mormon, and Moroni.

This suggests that Nephi had the humility to listen to his younger brother, and to learn from him. He wasn't blinded by his own position, authority, influence, experience, or even his access to revelation, and by characteristically and consistently using the title of Christ as Jacob had received it by revelation, he provided provocative evidence that The Book of Mormon is ancient scripture.

The word "Christ" is Greek and the same term in Hebrew is "Messiah", which Nephi used 28 times prior to 2 Nephi 10:13 (excluding quotations from Isaiah). Neither he nor his family knew Greek, coming as they had, from a culture that spoke Hebrew. Instead, they used a name that was familiar to them and that was drawn from their own language and society. Consistent with this explanation, Nephi used the term 'Messiah' until Jacob received revelation about the name 'Christ'. After that time, 'Messiah' fell out of favor. Nephi used it only 10 times subsequent to Jacob's revelation, and 'Christ' became the primary term that was used thereafter to identify the Savior.

Our takeaway lesson here is that Nephi had the humility to listen to his younger brother, and to learn from him. He wasn't blinded by his own position, authority, influence, experience, or even by his access to revelation, and by characteristically and consistently using the title of Christ as Jacob had just received it by revelation, Nephi unconsciously provides us with provocative evidence that The Book of Mormon is ancient scripture.

# Pragmatism
## in The Book of Mormon

Pragmatism views language as a tool for prediction, problem solving, and action, rather than for describing, representing, or mirroring reality. Pragmatists contend that most philosophical topics, such as the nature of knowledge, language, concepts, meaning, belief, and science, are all best viewed in terms of their practical uses and successes. A person who is pragmatic is concerned more with matters of fact, result, and consequence, rather than with what could or should be. They evaluate beliefs in terms of the success of their practical application. Their emphasis is on actionable knowledge, a recognition of the relationships between experience, knowing, and acting, and inquiry as an experiential process. Although it could certainly be argued that The Book of Mormon is not a pragmatic text, (but is a religious text), there are within its pages examples of pragmatism. They include the following verses:

"And it came to pass that I was desirous that Laman and Lemuel should come and partake of the fruit also; wherefore, I cast mine eyes towards the head of the river, **that perhaps** I might see them."
(1 Nephi 8:17).

"For he truly spake many great things unto them, which were hard to be understood, save a man should inquire of the Lord; and they, being hard in their hearts, therefore, they did not look unto the Lord as they ought."
(1 Nephi 15:3).

And I, Nephi,
have written these things unto my
people, **that perhaps** I might persuade
them that they would remember
the Lord their Redeemer."
(1 Nephi 19:18).

"I pray the Father in the name of
Christ **that many of us, if not all**,
may be saved in his kingdom
at that great and last day."
(2 Nephi 33:12).

"Let us prune
it, and dig about it, and
nourish it a little longer, **that
perhaps** it may bring forth
good fruit unto thee."
(Jacob 5:27).

If "the Lord God would preserve a record of my people ... it might be brought forth at some future day unto the Lamanites, **that, perhaps**, they might be brought unto salvation."
(Enos 1:13).

"May God grant that he may survive them, that he may write somewhat concerning them, and somewhat concerning Christ, **that perhaps** some day it may profit them."
(Words of Mormon 1:2).

"**Perhaps**, they will give us a knowledge of a remnant of the people who have been destroyed, from whence these records came; or, **perhaps**, they will give us a knowledge of this very people who have been destroyed."
(Mosiah 8:12).

"The sons of Mosiah (desired to) go up to the land of Nephi that they might preach the things which they had heard, and that they might impart the word of God to their brethren, the Lamanites, **that perhaps** they might bring them to the knowledge of the Lord their God, and convince them of the iniquity of their fathers; and **that perhaps** they might cure them of their hatred towards the Nephites."
(Mosiah 28:1-2).

"I desire to dwell among this people for a time; yea, and **perhaps** until the day I die."
(Alma 17:23).

"If thou shouldst slay thy son, he being an innocent man, his blood would cry from the ground to the Lord his God, for vengeance to come upon thee; and **perhaps** thou wouldst lose thy soul."
(Alma 20:18).

"Let us retain our swords that they be not stained with the blood of our brethren; **for perhaps**, if we should stain our swords again they can no more be washed bright through the blood of the Son of our great God."
(Alma 24:13).

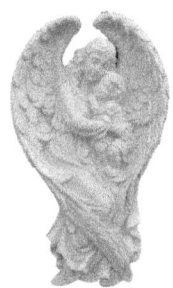

"We came into the wilderness not with the intent to destroy our brethren, but with the intent **that perhaps** we might save some **few** of their souls."
(Alma 26:26).

"This is my glory, **that perhaps** I may be an instrument in the hands of God to bring **some** soul to repentance."
(Alma 29:9).

"O my brethren,
if ye could be healed by
merely casting about your eyes"
rather than by heeding the counsel
of the servants of the Lord, "would ye not
behold quickly, or would ye rather harden
your hearts in unbelief, and be slothful,
that ye would not cast about your
eyes, that ye might perish?"
(Alma 33:21).

"Let there be a famine in the land,
to stir them up in remembrance of the
Lord their God, **and perhaps** they will
repent and turn unto thee."
(Helaman 11:4).

"Yea, he sent
a proclamation
among all the people,
that they should gather
together their women, and
their children, their flocks and
their herds, and all their substance,
**save it were their land**, unto one
place." (3 Nephi 3:13).

"And thus did the thirty and eighth year pass away, and also the thirty and ninth, and forty and first, and the forty and second, yea, even until forty and nine years had passed away, and also the fifty and first, and the fifty and second; yea, and even until fifty and nine years had passed away."
(4 Nephi 1:6).

"Turn ye unto the Lord; cry mightily unto the Father in the name of Jesus, **that perhaps** ye may be found spotless, pure, fair, and white, having been cleansed by the blood of the Lamb, at that last and great day." (Mormon 9:6).

# Dry Humor

## in The Book of Mormon

"I, Nephi, being exceedingly young, nevertheless being large in stature, (whatever that has got to do with what he is about to say) and also having great desires to know of the mysteries of God, wherefore, I did cry unto the Lord."
(1 Nephi 2:16).

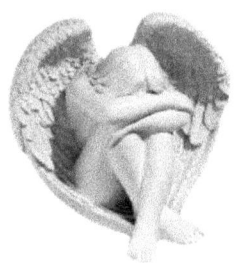

"The course of the Lord is one eternal round" (of golf)? (1 Nephi 10:19). This reminds us of the reference to tennis in the Book of Genesis, where we learn that Joseph served in Pharaoh's court.

"Now I, Chemish, write what few things I write, in the same book with my brother; for behold, I saw the last which he wrote, that he wrote it with his own hand; and he wrote it in the day that he delivered them unto me." (Omni 1:9). In other words, don't expect much, here.

"And it came to pass that after the space of two years that Abinadi came among them in disguise, that they knew him not, and began to prophesy among them," thereby, immediately blowing his cover. (Mosiah 12:1).

Zeezrom, who was "expert in the devices of the devil" when it came to trickery, debated Amulek on the most important question in the history of the universe: The existence of God. As his opening salvo, the lawyer asks: "Will ye answer the questions which I shall put unto you?" To which Amulek responds: "Yea". Then, of all the questions he could draw from his formidable arsenal, Zeezrom basically dropped the following bombshell (which, as it turned out, was a dud): "I will pay you if you deny the existence of God." Couldn't he possibly have done better than that? (Alma 11:21-22).

"And it came to pass that king Lamoni inquired of his servants, saying: Where is this man that has such great power? And they said unto him: Behold, he is feeding thy horses" (Alma 18:8-9) and probably mucking the stalls, as well.

This one speaks for itself: "Go in and see my husband, for he has been laid upon his bed for the space of two days and two nights; and some say that he is not dead, but others say that he is dead and that he stinketh, and that he ought to be placed in the sepulchre; but as for myself, to me he doth not stink."
(Alma 19:5)

"Now the joy of Ammon was so great even that he was full; yea, he was swallowed up in the joy of his God, even to the exhausting of his strength ... Now the joy of Alma in meeting his brethren was truly great, and also the joy of Aaron, of Omner, and Himni; but behold their joy was not that to exceed their strength." (Alma 27:17 & 19). It was great, but not nearly on a par with Ammon's joy.

"As he went forth among the people, yea, among a people who had separated themselves from the Nephites and called themselves Zoramites, being led by a man whose name was Zoram - and as he went forth amongst them, behold, he was run upon and trodden down, even until he was dead." (Alma 30:59). It sounds like the driver backed up his horse and cart over him a few times, just to make sure the deed was done.

"If ye could be healed by merely casting about your eyes that ye might be healed, would ye not behold quickly, or would ye rather harden your hearts in unbelief, and be slothful, that ye would not cast about your eyes, that ye might perish?"
(Alma 33:21).

"Whomsoever of the Amalickiahites that would not enter into a covenant to support the cause of freedom, that they might maintain a free government, he caused to be put to death; and there were but few who denied the covenant of freedom."
Duh! (Alma 46:35).

"They were thus cautious that no poison should be administered among them; for if their wine would poison a Lamanite it would also poison a Nephite." (Alma 55:32). Sounds about right.

"And it came to pass that when Coriantumr had leaned upon his sword, that he rested a little, he smote off the head of Shiz. And it came to pass that after he had smitten off the head of Shiz, that Shiz raised up on his hands and fell; and after that he had struggled for breath, he died." (Ether 15:30-31). The moral of this story is that it's hard to breathe after your head has been chopped off.

"A merry heart doeth good, like a medicine." (Proverbs 17:22). Humor can ease tension, relieve uncomfortable or embarrassing situations, change attitudes, generate love and understanding, and add sparkle to life. A properly developed sense of humor is sensitive to others' feelings and is flavored with kindness and understanding.

# A Book of Mormon Timeline

## A brief overview of the early days of the Restoration

(Adapted from the ChurchofJesusChrist.org website).

When we depart from
this life, wouldn't it be wonderful
if one of the first things we did after we
passed thru the veil was to warmly embrace,
not only our own loved ones, but also the Prophet
Joseph Smith. On one occasion, anticipating his
own family reunion, he declared: "I will tell you
what I want. If tomorrow I shall be called to
lie in yonder tomb, in the morning
of the resurrection, let me strike
hands with my father."
(H.C., 5:361).

The Three Pillars of Testimony in The
Church of Jesus Christ of Latter-day Saints
are the Lord Jesus Christ, The Book of Mormon,
and the Prophet Joseph Smith. So, if beyond the veil, we
should meet Brother Joseph, what will be our reaction, after we
have struck hands with him? B.H. Roberts, born 13 years after the
martyrdom, was once asked a question on the life and teachings of
the Prophet. "As he answered, the elders saw their beginning curiosity
expand to vast proportions. As they nodded in grateful admiration, all of
a sudden, he looked up, raised his hands, and exclaimed: "Brother Joseph,
I have fought for you, I have defended you, I have loved you!." ("Defender
of The Faith," p. 388). I hope, when we have our veil experience, we will
have a strong testimony of the Prophet, because no man or woman
in this dispensation will enter into the Celestial Kingdom of
God without the consent of Joseph Smith." (Brigham
Young, J.D., 7:289-290).

**December 23, 1805 - Joseph Smith is born in Sharon, Vermont.**

**April 1815 - Mount Tambora, in Indonesia, explodes**, ejecting so much sulphur dioxide, ash, and dust into the atmosphere that, the following Spring, it caused "the year without a summer" around the world. Temperatures in New England persisted in the 40s throughout July and August, and there were killing frosts. The Smiths lost their farm in Norwich, Vermont, settled their accounts, and moved to the western New York frontier in search of new opportunities. They settled in a town called Palmyra, over 300 miles away, in fertile, wheat-growing country.

**Early Spring, 1820 – At the age of 14, Joseph experiences the First Vision in the nearby Sacred Grove.** When he walked out of the grove of trees that beautiful spring morning in 1820, he would never be the same again. He knew the Father and the Son lived, and he would testify of this truth throughout his life. It was three years, however, after he experienced his vision of God before Joseph received further instructions concerning the important work to which he had been called.

During this period, Joseph passed through his mid-teens, a time when sympathetic teachers and a congenial community could have strengthened him. But his testimony instead aroused hostility. Even trusted friends turned against him; however, Joseph continually had the unconditional support of his family.

He acknowledged that during this period he "frequently fell into many foolish errors, and displayed the weakness of youth" (Joseph Smith History 1:28). His native cheery temperament was one reason he gave for sometimes associating with jovial company and being guilty of levity, which he considered inconsistent with the character of one called of God. (See JSH 1:28). He was not, however, guilty of any "great or malignant sins". (See JSH 1:28). During this time, he labored with his father on the family farm, working in the fields, clearing trees, or tapping sugar maples. Occasionally, he had an odd job, such as digging a building foundation or working in the corn fields for Martin Harris. This three-year interval gave young Joseph the time to grow, mature, gain experience, and receive further nurturing.

**The First Appearance of Moroni: September 21-22, 1823** – This is the first of at least 22 documented appearances of Moroni to Joseph Smith. (See H. Donl Peterson, "Moroni—Joseph Smith's Tutor", "Ensign", 1/1992, p. 22-29).

In 1822, Joseph had begun helping his older brother Alvin build a new frame house for the family. By September of 1823, it was two stories high but without a roof, and so, the family continued to live in their small log cabin just down the road.

It was in this log cabin, late in the evening of Sunday, September 21, 1823, that seventeen-year-old Joseph retired for the night. Concerned about his standing before the Lord, he earnestly prayed for forgiveness of his sins. Suddenly, his room began to fill with light, until a heavenly messenger stood by his bedside in partial fulfillment of the great prophecy of John the Apostle. (See Revelation 14:6-7).

In his history, Joseph later described this resurrected being: "He had on a loose robe of most exquisite whiteness. It was a whiteness beyond anything earthly I had ever seen; nor do I believe that any earthly

You "may profit
by noticing the first intimation
of the spirit of revelation; for instance,
when you feel pure intelligence flowing into
you, it may give you sudden strokes of ideas
... and thus by learning the Spirit of God
and understanding it, you may grow
into the principle of revelation."
(Joseph Smith, "Teachings",
p. 151).

If we were to rely only upon the biased
media that is so characteristic of the last days
to learn about Joseph Smith, we would be confronted
by doubt, skepticism, cynicism, ridicule, contempt, hostility,
derision, suspicion, disparagement, and scorn. But there is another
side to the Prophet. On one occasion, he said: "I can taste the principles of
eternal life, and so can you. They are given to me by the revelations of
Jesus Christ; and I know that when I tell you these words of eternal life
as they are given to me, you taste them, and I know that you believe
them. You say honey is sweet, and so do I. I can also taste the spirit
of eternal life. I know that it is good; and when I tell you of
these things which were given me by inspiration of
the Holy Spirit, you are bound to receive
them as sweet, and rejoice."
(H.C., 6:304).

thing could be made to appear so exceedingly white and brilliant. His hands were naked, and his arms also, a little above the wrist; so, also, were his feet naked, as were his legs, a little above the ankles. His head and neck were also bare. I could discover that he had no other clothing on but this robe, as it was open, so that I could see into his bosom.

Not only was his robe exceedingly white, but his whole person was glorious beyond description, and his countenance truly like lightning. The room was exceedingly light, but not so very bright as immediately around his person. When I first looked upon him, I was afraid; but the fear soon left me". (JSH 1:31-32).

The messenger introduced himself as Moroni, a prophet who had lived on the American continent. As holder of the keys of the "stick of Ephraim" (see D&C 27:5) the purpose of Moroni's visit was to reveal the existence of a record written on metal plates which had lain hidden in the ground for fourteen centuries. It was "an account of the former inhabitants of this continent. ... He also said that the fulness of the everlasting gospel was contained in it, as delivered by the Savior to the ancient inhabitants". (JSH 1:34).

Joseph recounted: "While he was conversing with me about the plates, the vision was opened to my mind that I could see the place where the plates were deposited, and that so clearly and distinctly that I knew the place again when I visited it."

"This messenger (Moroni) proclaimed himself to be an angel of God, sent to bring the joyful tidings that the covenant which God made with ancient Israel was at hand to be fulfilled, that the preparatory work for the second coming of the Messiah was speedily to commence; that the time was at hand for the gospel in all its fullness to be preached in power, unto all nations, that a people might be prepared for the millennial reign. I was informed that I was chosen to be an instrument in the hands of God to bring about some of His purposes in this glorious dispensation" ("History of the Church", 4:536-37).

Joseph was to translate the record and publish it, and because of this, his name would be known for good and evil among all people. (See JSH 1:33). Moroni cited several passages from the Bible quoting prophets such as Malachi, Isaiah, Joel, and Peter concerning the preparations to be made in the last days for the millennial reign of Christ. Thus commenced the gospel tutorship of Joseph Smith by Moroni, in September 1823, three years after his First Vision in what came to be known as the Sacred Grove, near his home.

"After this communication, I saw the light in the room begin to gather immediately around the person of him who had been speaking to me, and it continued to do so until the room was again left dark, except just around him; when, instantly I saw, as it were, a conduit open right up into heaven, and he ascended till he entirely disappeared, and the room was left as it had been before this heavenly light had made its appearance."

So important was Moroni's message and the need to impress it on the mind of the young boy that Moroni returned twice more that night, and once the following morning, to repeat the same instructions, adding additional information each time. On the first occasion, Joseph saw in vision the location of the plates. (See JSH 1:42). They were buried in a hillside about three miles from his home. During the second visit, Joseph was told of judgments which were coming upon the earth. (See JSH 1:45). Near the conclusion of the third visit, Moroni warned Joseph that Satan would try to wrest the plates from his possession, for their temporal value. The angel directed seventeen-year-old Joseph that there was to be one purpose only for obtaining the

Moroni cautioned Joseph: "Wherever the sound (of the work) shall go, it shall cause the ears of men to tingle, and wherever it shall be proclaimed, the pure in heart shall rejoice, while those who draw near to God with their mouths, and honor him with their lips, while their hearts are far from him, will seek its overthrow, and the destruction of those by whose hands it is carried. Therefore, marvel not if your name is made a derision and had as a by-word among such, if you are the instrument in bringing it, by the gift of God, to the knowledge of the people." (Reported in "The Messenger and Advocate").

The Prophet Joseph Smith has been described as a prism of the Lord Jesus Christ. In other words, "he reduced his teachings to the capacity of every man, woman and child, making them as plain as a well-defined pathway." (Brigham Young). Mercy Fielding Thompson, whose husband served as a clerk to Joseph Smith, said: "I have listened to his clear and masterly explanations of deep and difficult questions. To him, all things seemed simple and easy to be understood, and thus, he could make them plain to others as no other man could that I ever heard."

plates, and that was to glorify God. Only one motive should influence him, and that was to build up God's kingdom. (See JSH 1:46). Joseph's interviews with Moroni occupied most of the night, for at the end of the third visit he heard a rooster crow. Indeed, a new day of spiritual light was about to dawn. Isaiah had spoken of this day as a time when a "marvellous work and a wonder" would come forth. (Isaiah 29:14).

One is reminded of the description by Job, relating to his receipt of heavenly instruction. "For God speaketh once, yea twice, yet man perceiveth it not. In a dream, in a vision of the night, when deep sleep falleth upon men, in slumberings upon the bed; Then he openeth the ears of men, and sealeth their instruction." (Job 33:14-16).

**Continued Instruction From the Angel Moroni. Moroni instructs Joseph about restoring the gospel of Jesus Christ and teaches him from scripture.** John Taylor explained: "Joseph Smith was set apart by the Almighty according to the councils of the Gods in the eternal worlds, to introduce the principles of life among the people ... The principles which he had, placed him in communication with ... Abraham, Isaac, Jacob, Noah, Adam, Seth, Enoch, Jesus and the Father, and the apostles that lived on this continent as well as those who lived on the Asiatic continent ... Why? Because he had to introduce a dispensation which was called the dispensation of the fulness of times, and it was known as such by the ancient servants of God" ("Deseret News", 6/9/1880, p. 280).

Joseph also learned about the ancient inhabitants of the Americas, "who they were, and from whence they came; a brief sketch of their origin, progress, civilization, laws, governments, of their righteousness and iniquity, and the blessings of God being finally withdrawn from them as a people" (History of the Church, 4:537).

**Joseph Smith's first sees the Plates (but is not allowed to handle them). – His first visit to Cumorah.** After Moroni departed, Joseph related, "I ... went to the place where the messenger had told me the plates were deposited; and owing to the distinctness of the vision which I had had concerning it, I knew the place the instant that I arrived there". (JSH 1:50). Near the top of the hill Joseph found a large stone, "thick and rounding in the middle on the upper side, and thinner towards the edges". (JSH 1:51). It was the lid of a stone box. We can only imagine his excitement as he opened the box. There were the plates, the Urim and Thummim, and the breastplate, just as Moroni had explained.

"The box in which they lay was formed by laying stones together in some kind of cement. In the bottom of the box were laid two stones crossways of the box, and on these stones lay the plates and the other things with them". (JSH 1:52).

As Joseph had approached the Hill Cumorah, he had thoughts about his family's poverty, and the possibility that the plates or the popularity of the translation would produce enough wealth to "raise him above a level with the common earthly fortunes of his fellow men, and relieve his family from want." (Related by Oliver Cowdery, in "Messenger and Advocate", October 1835, p. 198).

As he harbored these thoughts, he reached down to handle the plates, but received a shock and was thus prevented from taking them out of the box. Twice more he tried, and was thrown back. In frustration, he cried out, "Why can I not obtain this book?" Moroni appeared, and told him it was because he had not kept

After experiencing our own
General Conference addresses via satellite,
it's hard to imagine how significant must have
been the communication challenges faced by the early
Saints, as they made extraordinary efforts to listen to the
counsel of their leaders. A contemporary named Amos Potter
described a sermon that Joseph gave in Nauvoo. As the Prophet
began his address, he said: "I have three requests to make of the
congregation: The first is, that all who have faith will exercise it
and pray that the Lord will calm the wind; for as it blows now,
I cannot speak long without seriously injuring my health;
the next is that I may have your prayers, that the Lord
will strengthen my lungs, so that I may be able to
make you all hear; and the third is, that you
will pray for the Holy Ghost to rest upon
me, so as to enable me to declare
those things that are true."

Those who took the time to
know the Prophet spoke of his honesty.
Eliza R. Snow declared: "His integrity was
as firm as the pillars of heaven." John Bernhisel,
who boarded in Joseph and Emma's home in Nauvoo,
recalled: "He is naturally a man of strong mental powers,
and he is possessed of much energy and decision of character,
great penetration, and a profound knowledge of human nature.
He is a man of calm judgment, enlarged views, and is eminently
notable by his love of justice. He is kind and obliging, generous
and benevolent, sociable and cheerful, and is possessed of a
mind of a contemplative and reflective character. He
is honest, frank, fearless and independent,
and as free from (false pretenses)
as any man to be found."

the commandments, but had yielded to the temptations of Satan to obtain the plates for riches instead of having his eye single to the glory of God as he had been commanded. ("History of Joseph Smith", p. 81)

Repentant, Joseph humbly sought the Lord in prayer and was filled with the Spirit. A vision was opened to him, and the "glory of the Lord shone round about and rested upon him. ... He beheld the prince of darkness, (and) the heavenly messenger (Moroni) said, 'All this is shown, the good and the evil, the holy and impure, the glory of God and the power of darkness, that you may know hereafter the two powers and never be influenced or overcome by that wicked one ... You now see why you could not obtain this record; that the commandment was strict, and that if ever these sacred things are obtained, (it) must be by prayer and faithfulness in obeying the Lord. They are not deposited here for the sake of accumulating gain and wealth for the glory of this world: they were sealed by the prayer of faith, and because of the knowledge which they contain, they are of no worth among the children of men, only for their knowledge." (See H.C., 4:537; George Q. Cannon, in "Journal of Discourses", 13:47; John Taylor, in "Journal of Discourses", 17:374 & 21:94).

Moroni concluded by warning Joseph that he would not be allowed to obtain the plates "until he had learned to keep the commandments of God - not only till he was willing, but able to do it. "The ensuing evening, when the family were all together, Joseph made known to them all that he had communicated to his father in the field, and also of his finding the record, as well as what passed between him and the angel while he was at the place where the plates were deposited." ("History of Joseph Smith", p. 83).

**Every September for four years, from 1823 to 1827, Joseph returns to the Hill Cumorah to view the plates, and to be taught by Moroni.** Joseph was 17 when he first saw the plates, but he wasn't allowed to remove them from the hill until 4 more years had passed. The monumental work of bringing forth the Book of Mormon had been foretold by ancient prophets. (See Isaiah 29, Ezekiel 37:15-20, & Moses 7:62). A work of this magnitude required careful preparation, necessitating four more years of tutoring. During that time, Joseph met annually with Moroni at the Hill Cumorah to receive instructions in preparation for receiving the plates. Other Nephite prophets who had a vital interest in the coming forth of The Book of Mormon also played a significant role in Joseph's preparation. Nephi, Alma, the twelve disciples chosen by the Savior in America, and Mormon all instructed Joseph. (See "History of Joseph Smith", p. 87). His religious education was intense during this period. (See Buddy Youngreen, "Reflections of Emma, Joseph Smith's Wife", p. 4).

**Interim Events.** Between Moroni's first appearance, and when Joseph received the plates, several significant events occurred in his life. In November of 1823, tragedy struck the Smith home, when Alvin, Joseph's oldest brother, became ill. On his deathbed, he counseled Joseph: "I want you to be a good boy, and do everything that lies in your power to obtain the record. Be faithful in receiving instruction, and in keeping every commandment that is given you." (H.C., 3:29). Years later, Joseph learned by revelation that Alvin was an heir to the Celestial Kingdom. (See D&C 137:1-6).

**October 1825 - Joseph works for Josiah Stowell, and meets Emma Hale.** Following Alvin's death, Joseph and his brothers hired out as day-laborers, performing whatever work was available. Treasure hunting, or "money-digging" as it was then called, was a craze in the western United States at this time. Josiah Stowell, a farmer, lumber mill owner, and deacon in the Presbyterian church,

Although the Prophet Joseph Smith was well-acquainted with sadness, his contemporaries spoke of his cheerful disposition. Parley P. Pratt described him as "mild, affable, beaming with intelligence, mingled with a look of interest and an unconscious smile, or cheerfulness, and his benevolence unbounded as the ocean." Joseph recognized that "happiness is the object and design of our existence, and will be the end thereof if we pursue the path that leads to it, and this path is virtue, uprightness, faithfulness, holiness, and keeping all the commandments of God." ("Teachings," p. 255).

Those who knew him recognized the clarity and power of his message. Lorenzo Snow said: "The people loved to hear him, because he was full of revelation." Mary Ann Stearns Winters, a stepdaughter of Elder Parley P. Pratt, remembered: "The Holy Spirit lighted up his countenance until it glowed like a halo around him, and his words penetrated the hearts of all who heard him." Orson Spencer declared: "At his touch, the ancient prophets sprang into life, and the beauty and power of their revelations were made to commend themselves with thrilling interest to all that heard." Edward Stevenson recalled: "The Prophet testified with great power concerning the visitation of the Father and the Son, and the conversation he had with them. Never before did I feel such power."

came to ask Joseph to assist him in the search for a legendary lost silver mine that was thought to have been opened by Spaniards in northern Pennsylvania. Stowell had heard that Joseph was able to discern invisible things and desired his assistance in the project. The impressionable boy was reluctant, but Stowell persisted, and since Joseph's family was in need, he and his father, together with other neighbors, agreed to help. It was a decision that would have a significant impact on Joseph's life, and on the future of the church.

In preparation for the venture, Joseph and his associates boarded with Isaac Hale in Harmony township, in Pennsylvania, not far from the supposed mine site. While boarding with the Hales, Joseph and Isaac's daughter Emma were attracted to each other, although she was Joseph's senior by a year and a half. The budding romance, however, was frowned upon by Emma's father, who disliked money digging and disdained Joseph's lack of education. His cultured daughter was a schoolteacher, and he thought she could do better. Meanwhile, the search for the silver mine proved to be unproductive. After nearly a month's work, Joseph was able to persuade Josiah Stowell that his efforts were in vain, and the pursuit of the mine in Harmony was abandoned.

Emma Hale was the seventh of nine children, and "a tall, attractive young woman with comely features. Dark-complexioned, with brown eyes and black hair, she possessed a singular, regal beauty of form and of character." ("History of Joseph Smith", pp. 100-101).

Ever since this episode in Joseph's young life, his detractors have used what they have described as "money digging" to question his motives, and to disparage the church he later organized. However, the circumstances are best understood in the context of their time and place. In New England and western New York, such activities were not frowned upon the way they would be many decades later. In his History, Joseph candidly acknowledged his participation in the venture, but characterized it as "insignificant". (See "History of Joseph Smith", p. 108).

While working in the borderlands of New York and Pennsylvania, Joseph made another contact that became important to him and to the early church in New York. Joseph Knight, Sr., a friend of Josiah Stowell, was a humble farmer and miller who lived in Colesville, Broome County, New York. Joseph Smith also worked for him for a time, and in the process developed close friendships with him and his sons, Joseph, Jr., and Newel. They accepted the testimony of the young Prophet, as he recounted his sacred experiences to them.

**January 18, 1827 - Joseph marries Emma Hale.** Between working for Josiah Stowell, Joseph Knight, Sr., and visiting his own family in Manchester, Joseph continued to court Emma Hale. Because of her father's strong opposition to the marriage, Joseph and Emma eloped. They were married by a justice of the peace in South Bainbridge, New York, on January 18, 1827. Immediately afterward, Joseph moved his new bride to the family home in Manchester, where he spent the succeeding summer farming with his father. Emma was well received by Joseph's family, and a close relationship developed between Emma and Joseph's mother, Lucy Mack Smith.

**On September 22, 1827, the Prophet finally receives the plates from the angel Moroni.** Little is known of Joseph's visits with Moroni between 1824 and 1827, but sometime before the fall of 1827, Joseph returned home one evening, later than usual. His family was concerned, but he told them he had been delayed because he had just received a severe chastisement from Moroni. He said that as he passed by the Hill Cumorah, "The angel met me, and said that I had not been engaged enough in the work of the Lord;

There are specific things we can do to treasure up the words of the Prophet Joseph Smith, and to live by his teachings. Brigham Young recalled: "From the first time I saw the Prophet Joseph … I hearkened to (his words), and treasured them up in my heart, laid them away, asking my Father in the name of his Son Jesus to bring them to my mind when needed. I treasured up the things of God, and this is the key that I hold today. I was anxious to learn, not only from Joseph, but also from the Spirit of God." (Logan Conference, 5/25/1877).

The following scripture relates specifically to ourselves, and to the mission of Joseph Smith: "Thou shalt give heed unto all his words and commandments which he shall give … you as he receiveth them, walking in all holiness before me; For his word ye shall receive, as if from mine own mouth, in all patience and faith. For by doing these things the gates of hell shall not prevail against you; yea, and the Lord God will disperse the powers of darkness from before you, and cause the heavens to shake for your good, and his name's glory." (D&C 21:4-6, a revelation received on the occasion of the organization of the church, on April 6, 1830).

that the time had come for the record to be brought forth; and that I must be up and doing and set myself about the things which God had commanded me to do." (See "History of Joseph Smith", p. 114; "Joseph Smith 1832 History", "Joseph Smith Letterbook", cited in Dean C. Jessee, "The Personal Writings of Joseph Smith" P. 7-8).

Much had transpired during Joseph's four years of preparation. He passed through his teens largely uninfluenced by the precepts of men. He enjoyed the emotional support of his family, and he took on the responsibilities associated with marriage. Angels prepared him to translate a divinely inspired record and taught him the necessity of self-discipline, repentance, patience, and obedience. He was undoubtedly anxious to begin translating The Book of Mormon.

**September 22, 1827 - Joseph is entrusted by Moroni with the records.** The work of translation of the plates began.. During the process, his scribes includde Martin Harris, Oliver Cowdery, Emma Smith, and John Whitmer.

Before sunrise on September 22, 1827, Joseph and his wife hitched Joseph Knight's horse to Josiah Stowell's spring wagon and drove three miles to the Hill Cumorah. Leaving Emma at its base, Joseph climbed the hill for another interview with Moroni. Moroni gave him the plates, the Urim and Thummim, and the breastplate. He also gave Joseph a specific warning and promise concerning his responsibilities. Joseph now had possession of these sacred objects, and if he were careless or negligent and lost them, he would be cut off. On the other hand, if he used all his efforts to preserve them until Moroni returned for them, he was assured that they would be protected. (See J.S.H 1:59).

For the first time in over fourteen hundred years, the records were entrusted to a mortal. In what might seem to some to be a surprising move, Joseph carefully hid the plates in a hollow log near his home. The Prophet's friends were not the only ones who eagerly anticipated his receipt of the plates. Others in the neighborhood had heard that Joseph was going to bring home valuable metal plates. Some of them may have also been involved in searching for the silver mine, and now felt that they should have a share in any treasure that had been found.

Joseph soon learned why Moroni had strictly charged him to protect the plates. "Every stratagem that could be invented" was used to get them from him. (See J.S.H. 1:60). For example, Willard Chase, a neighboring farmer, along with other treasure seekers, sent for a sorcerer to come and find the place where the plates had been hidden. When the Smiths learned of the plot, they sent Emma to get Joseph, who was working in Macedon a few miles west of Palmyra. He returned immediately and retrieved the plates. Wrapping them in a linen frock, he started through the woods, thinking that route might be safer than the well-traveled road. But just as he jumped over a log, he was struck from behind with a gun. Joseph, however, was able to knock his assailant down and flee. Half a mile later, he was again assaulted, but managed to escape once more, and before he arrived home, he was accosted a third time. His mother said that when he reached home he was "altogether speechless from fright and the fatigue of running." (See Stanley B. Kimball, "I Cannot Read a Sealed Book," "Improvement Era", 2/1957).

"The only safety
that we enjoy as members
of this church is to do exactly what
the Lord said to the church on that day
when the church was organized. There will
be some things that take patience and faith.
You may not like what comes from the authority
of the church. It may contradict your political views.
It may contradict your social views. It may interfere
with some of your social life. But if you listen to these
things, as if from the mouth of the Lord himself, with
patience and faith, the promise is that 'the gates
of hell shall not prevail against you."
(Harold B. Lee, C.R., 10/1970).

Mary Lambert, who lived in
Nauvoo, recalled: "Saints and sinners
alike recognized a power and influence
that he carried with him." Howard Coray
remembered: "As I sat and listened to his
preaching, I was completely carried away
with his eloquence and power of expression,
speaking as I have never heard any other
man." Wilford Woodruff testified: "In
his public and private career, he carried
with him the Spirit of the Almighty,
and he manifested a greatness of
soul which I had never
(before) seen."

Efforts to steal the plates only intensified, but Moroni's promise of protection was also fulfilled. Joseph often moved the plates from their hiding places just minutes before the treasure seekers arrived. Once, he hid them under the hearthstone of the fireplace of his home, and later he hid them under the wooden floor of the cooper shop on the Smith farm, before moving them to the loft.

**The Prophecy of Isaiah is Fulfilled.** During this period, Joseph's life was in danger, so he decided to take Emma back to Harmony, where he hoped to begin the translation of the record in peace. Before they left, Martin Harris, a citizen of Palmyra who would later play a role in the Restoration, stepped forward and offered to help. He was a prosperous farmer who had met the Smiths when they had first settled in Palmyra, and over the years, he had hired various family members to work for him. Now, he provided money so Joseph and Emma could liquidate their debts, and he also gave them fifty dollars to finance their trip to Harmony. With the plates hidden in a barrel of beans in the back of the wagon, they left town in December of 1827, headed for Harmony. Prior arrangements had been made to board temporarily with Emma's parents.

Except for Joseph Smith, no man played a more varied role in the coming forth of The Book of Mormon than Martin Harris. He served as a scribe, became a witness of the coming forth of The Book of Mormon, financially assisted in its publication, and testified of the truthfulness of the book throughout his life.

Following a brief stay with the Hales, the couple purchased a house from Emma's eldest brother, Jesse. It was a small two-story home on a thirteen-acre farm bordering the Susquehanna River. For the first time in weeks, Joseph was able to work in relative peace. Between December 1827 and February 1828, he copied many of the characters from the plates and translated some of them by using the Urim and Thummim. In the early stages of the work, Joseph spent considerable time and effort becoming familiar with the language of the plates and learning how to translate.

According to previous arrangements, Martin Harris visited Joseph in Harmony sometime in February of 1828, it having been revealed to him that the Lord had a work for him to do. In 1827, several personal manifestations had convinced Harris that Joseph Smith was a prophet, and that he should assist him in publishing The Book of Mormon. Therefore, he went to Harmony to obtain a copy of some of the characters from the plates to show several noted linguists of the time, thereby unintentionally fulfilling the prophecy of Isaiah 29:11-12, to help convince an unbelieving world. (See H.C., 1:20). This ancient prophecy of Isaiah continues to mystify Bible scholars, but Martin Harris and Joseph Smith linked it to The Book of Mormon. This has been verified by an expanded version of Isaiah's prophecy that appears in 2 Nephi Chapter 27.

**February 1828 - Martin Harris visits Charles Anthon in New York City.** Martin visited Professor Charles Anthon, affiliated with Columbia College in New York City, who was among the leading classical scholars of his day. At the time of Harris's visit, Anthon was adjunct professor of Greek and Latin. He spoke French, German, Greek, and Latin, and was familiar with the latest discoveries pertaining to the Egyptian language, including the early work of Champollion. (See "History of Joseph Smith", p. 116-17, § 122).

According to Harris, Professor Anthon examined the characters and their translation and willingly gave him a certificate stating that the writings were authentic. Anthon further told Harris that the characters resembled Egyptian, Chaldean, Assyrian, and Arabic, and expressed his opinion that the translation was

As we study his life, and our testimony of his mission becomes more powerfully entrenched in our hearts, we will be drawn to the conclusion that, when he receives his exaltation in the Celestial Kingdom of God, Joseph Smith "will be seated on the right hand of Christ." (Bruce R. McConkie, C.R., 10/1949). One of his greatest contributions "was his knowledge of what is to come after death. He clarified our understanding of heaven while making it seem worth working for." ("My Religion & Me" course manual). Every time we think of him and his mission, we are motivated to rededicate ourselves to honoring the principles of heaven for which he gave his life.

Our Savior Jesus Christ taught that, in the Last Days, there would be many false prophets who would arise, who would deceive many. (See Matthew 24:11). He didn't say that there would be no prophets, but instead implied that there would be confusion because the messages of false prophets would conflict with those of true prophets, suggesting that uninspired leadership is often clothed in gaudy paraphernalia that attracts the curious but that requires no commitment. It may draw moths to the fire, but only in a deadly dance with death, as the curious who desire nothing more than theological titillation flirt with the flickering flames.

correct. Martin put the certificate in his pocket and was about to leave when Anthon called him back, and asked how Joseph Smith had found the plates in the hill. Martin explained that an angel of God had revealed the location to Joseph, whereupon Anthon asked for the certificate, which Martin gave to him. "He took it and tore it to pieces, saying, that there was no such thing as ministering of angels, and that if I (Martin) would bring the plates to him, he would translate them. I informed him that part of the plates were sealed, and that I was forbidden to bring them. He replied, 'I cannot read a sealed book.'" ("History of Joseph Smith", pp. 128-29).

Martin Harris's experience with Anthon was significant for several reasons. First, it demonstrated a scholarly interest in the characters, and that there were academicians who were willing to give them serious consideration, as long as an angel was not part of the story. Secondly, it was, in the view of Harris and Joseph, the direct fulfillment of prophecy that related to The Book of Mormon. Thirdly, it demonstrated that translating the record would require the assistance of God; intellect alone would be insufficient. (See Isaiah 29:11-12 & 2 Nephi 27:15-20). Finally, it solidified Harris's own faith. He returned home, confident that he now had evidence to convince his neighbors of Joseph Smith's work. He was now ready to wholeheartedly commit himself and his worldly treasure to the publication of The Book of Mormon.

**February – June 1828 - The first 116 pages of the record are translated from the Large Plates of Nephi**, which was Mormon's translation of the Book of Lehi, but the manuscript copy is lost. Consequently, Joseph loses the gift of translation, and the plates and the Urim and Thummim are taken from him.

Martin's wife, Lucy, had been suspicious of Joseph Smith. She had questioned him about the plates and had demanded to see them. He had told her she could not, "for he was not permitted to exhibit them to any one except those whom the Lord should appoint to testify of them."

Lucy was angry that her husband had been spending so much time away from her, and she wondered if the Smiths might be trying to defraud him. She insisted on going to Harmony again, to meet with Joseph. This time, she announced that she was not going to leave until she saw the plates. She ransacked the entire house looking for them, but did not find them. From that day on, she claimed that her husband had been duped by "a grand imposter." After two weeks, Martin took her home. Despite her attempts to dissuade him, he returned to Harmony. In Martin's absence, Lucy continued her vocal criticism in Palmyra. (See "History of Joseph Smith", p. 135).

In Harmony, Joseph and Martin labored together on the translation until June 14, 1828. By that time, the translation filled 116 roughly legal-size pages, and Martin asked if he could take this manuscript home to show his wife and friends. He hoped this would convince Lucy that the work was legitimate, and that it would put an end to her opposition. Through the Urim and Thummim, Joseph inquired of the Lord regarding what he should do. The answer was no, do not release the 116 pages to the care of Martin Harris. Not satisfied, Harris persisted until Joseph once again asked the Lord. Still, the answer was no. Martin's pleadings and solicitations continued unabatedly. Joseph wanted to satisfy his benefactor; he was young and inexperienced, and he relied upon the age and maturity of Harris. Moreover, Harris was the only one Joseph knew who was willing to both work as scribe and finance the publication of the book. These considerations moved him to ask one more time. Finally, the Lord granted a conditional permission. Harris agreed in writing to show the manuscript to only four or five people, including his wife; his brother, his father, his mother, and Lucy's sister. Harris then left for Palmyra with the only copy of the manuscript.

The Savior warned against "false prophets," and said they would come "in sheep's clothing, but inwardly they are ravening wolves." (Matthew 7:15). Some have used this scripture to attack the church, claiming that it speaks of its prophet. This is quite a claim, coming as it does from a people "who never had faith enough to call down one scrap of revelation from heaven, and for all they have now are indebted to the faith of another people who lived hundreds and thousands of years before them. Does it remain for them to say how much God has spoken and how much he has not spoken?" (Joseph Smith, H.C., 2:17-18).

Joseph Smith was given "power from on high, by the means which were before prepared, to translate the Book of Mormon; which contains a record of a fallen people, and the fulness of the gospel of Jesus Christ to the Gentiles and to the Jews also; which was given by inspiration and is confirmed to others by the ministering of angels, and is declared unto the world by them — Proving to the world that the holy scriptures are true, and that God does inspire men and call them to his holy work in this age and generation, as well as in generations of old; Thereby showing that he is the same God yesterday, today, and forever." (D&C 20:8-12).

Shortly after his departure, Emma Smith bore a son who died the day he was born. Emma nearly died herself, and for two weeks, Joseph was constantly at her bedside. When she improved, his attention turned to the manuscript. By this time, Harris had been gone for three weeks, and they had heard nothing from him. Harris had not been totally irresponsible during this time. He had spent time with his wife, taken care of business in Palmyra, and served on a jury.

Emma encouraged Joseph to take a stage to Palmyra, to check on the matter. After walking the last twenty miles during the night, Joseph finally arrived at his parents' home in Manchester. He immediately sent for Harris, who usually came quickly, so breakfast was prepared for him and the Smiths. Several hours passed before Harris finally plodded up the walk with head hung down. He climbed on the fence and sat there with his hat down over his eyes. Finally, he came in and sat down at the breakfast table, but he could not eat. Lucy Mack Smith, Joseph's mother, recorded: "He took up his knife and fork as if he were going to use them, but immediately dropped them. Hyrum, observing this, said 'Martin, why do you not eat; are you sick?' Upon which Harris pressed his hands upon his temples, and cried out in a tone of deep anguish, 'Oh, I have lost my soul! I have lost my soul!'

"Joseph who had not expressed his fears till now, sprang from the table, exclaiming, 'Martin, have you lost that manuscript? Have you broken your oath, and brought down condemnation upon my head as well as your own?' 'Yes; it is gone,' replied Harris, 'and I know not where.'"

Joseph exclaimed, "'All is lost! all is lost! What shall I do? I have sinned. it is I who tempted the wrath of God. I should have been satisfied with the first answer which I received from the Lord; for he told me that it was not safe to let the writing go out of my possession.' He wept and groaned, and walked the floor continually.

"At length he told Harris to go back and search again. "'No", said Harris, 'it is all in vain; for I have ripped open beds and pillows looking for the manuscript; and I know it is not there.' "'Then must I,' said Joseph, 'return with such a tale as this? I dare not do it. And how shall I appear before the Lord? Of what rebuke am I not worthy from the angel of the Most High?' ... "The next morning, he set out for home. We parted with heavy hearts, for it now appeared that all which we had so fondly anticipated, and which had been the source of so much secret gratification, had in a moment fled, and fled forever." ("History of the Church", 5:423).

**September 1828 - Joseph regains possession of the plates and the Urim and Thummim. The gift of translation is restored, and the translation of the plates recommences.** Upon returning to Harmony without the 116 pages of manuscript, Joseph immediately began to pray for the Lord to forgive him for acting contrary to his will. Moroni appeared to Joseph and required him to return the plates and the Urim and Thummim, but promised that he could receive them back if he were humble and penitent. Some time later, he received a revelation which chastised him for negligence and for "setting at naught the counsels of God" but it also comforted him that he was still chosen to perform the work of translation if he repented. (See D&C 3:4-10). Joseph did repent, and again received the plates and the Urim and Thummim, along with a promise that the Lord would send a scribe to assist him in the translation. There was a special message: "The angel seemed pleased with me ... and he told me that the Lord loved me, for my faithfulness and humility." ("H.C., 2:170.)

With his divine gift restored, Joseph learned by revelation that wicked men intended to entrap him. They had altered the words of the manuscript, and if he translated the same material again and published it,

Something wonderful surrounds our testimonies of the living Prophet, Seer, and Revelator of The Church of Jesus Christ of Latter-day Saints. Not long after the Restoration of the gospel, John Greenleaf Whittier said of these modern prophets: "I discovered, as I think, the great secret of their success in making converts. They speak to a common feeling; they minister to a universal want. They speak a language of hope and promise to the weak, weary hearts, tossed and troubled, who have wandered from sect to sect, seeking in vain for the primal manifestations of the divine power." ("A Mormon Conventicle", p. 461).

The Savior said of His chosen prophets: "By their fruits ye shall know them." (Matthew 7:20). Do they speak in the name of the Lord and bless the lives of the people? Is their doctrine edifying and uplifting? Do they encourage a religion that promotes chastity, morality, and fidelity to family values? Do they hold dear the sanctity of life and the rights of the unborn? Do they believe that free will is an eternal principle vital to the successful completion of our probation on the earth? Do they believe in obeying, honoring, and sustaining the law of the land? Do they believe in being honest, true, chaste, benevolent, virtuous, and in doing good to all men? Do they believe all things, hope all things, have they endured many things, and do they hope to be able to endure all things? If there is anything virtuous, lovely, or of good report or praiseworthy, do they seek after these things? It is vital that those who seek the church of Christ recognize the fruits of faith, because "not every one that saith unto me, Lord, Lord, shall enter into the kingdom of heaven; but he that doeth the will of my Father who is in heaven." (Matthew 7:21).

they would say he was unable to do it the same way twice, and therefore, the work must not be inspired. (See D&C 10). God, however, had anticipated this scenario. The lost document was the Book of Lehi taken from Mormon's abridgment of the Large Plates of Nephi. But Mormon had been inspired to attach the Small Plates of Nephi to his record for "a wise purpose," which at the time he did not understand. (See Words of Mormon 1:3-7). These small plates contained an account similar to that in the Book of Lehi. Joseph was instructed not to retranslate, but to continue on and at the appropriate time to include the material from the Small Plates of Nephi. These records were the account of Nephi which the Lord said was "more particular concerning the things which, in my wisdom, I would bring to the knowledge of the people". (D&C 10:40).

**The Prophet's Preparation.** The five and one-half years between September 1823 and April 1829 had been important in Joseph Smith's preparation for translating The Book of Mormon and leading the church in the dispensation of the fulness of times. In 1829, he was now twenty-three years old. He was tall and strong; he worked on the farm, in the fields, and at odd jobs. Although he had had little formal schooling, Joseph had a hungry and curious mind. He liked to discover things for himself and to seek his answers from the scriptures. (See JSH 1:11-12). This thirst for knowledge, especially spiritual knowledge, never left him.

Twenty years later, in June of 1843, Joseph told the Saints: "I am a rough stone. The sound of the hammer and chisel were never heard on me until the Lord took me in hand. I desire the learning and wisdom of heaven alone." (H.C. 5:423). Courage, optimism, and faith were hallmarks of his personality. He had shown great courage at an early age, when he had endured a painful leg operation. He later faced moblike neighbors who were trying to get the plates from him. Despite his poverty and lack of education, he was optimistic about himself and life. Rebuked by the Lord and corrected by Moroni, he was always submissive, repentant, and energetic. He despaired when the 116 pages had been lost, but from that experience he learned obedience, and was later able to say, "I made this my rule: When the Lord commands, do it." (History of the Church, 2:170). He also learned valuable lessons about controlling his motives and purposes and was, therefore, able to keep his "eye single to the glory of God" (D&C 4:5) and channel his energies and thoughts toward building the kingdom.

By this time, Joseph Smith had gained considerable experience with various means of revelation. He had communed with God and his Son and with angelic messengers. He had seen visions, felt the promptings of the Spirit, and become skilled using the Urim and Thummim. But, we should not conclude that revelation came easy to him, for another lesson he learned during this time was the price in faith, diligence, persistence, worthiness, and obedience he had to pay to receive communication from God.

**April 7, 1829 - Oliver Cowdery begins his service as scribe to Joseph Smith.** He continued to serve until the translation of the Book of Mormon is completed, in June 1829.

**May 15, 1829 - While Joseph translates passages of the Book of Mormon about the necessity of baptism, he and Oliver Cowdery ask the Lord who has authority to baptize in His name.** They knelt in a secluded spot near Joseph's home in Harmony, Pennsylvania, when "the voice of the Redeemer spake peace to us," Oliver later wrote, and a heavenly messenger, John the Baptist, "came down clothed with glory." He conferred upon the two men the Aaronic Priesthood, which holds the priesthood keys "of the gospel of repentance, and of baptism by immersion for the remission of sins." Subsequent to their ordination, and on that same day, Joseph baptized Oliver, and Oliver baptized Joseph.

The prophets champion faith and promote its fruits, recognizing that there is no more power in faith that does not include works than there is strength in food that is not eaten, or warmth in clothes that are not worn. The teachings on faith and works by Luther and the other Reformers who founded Protestantism conform to the teachings of James. "By faith, Luther meant no merely intellectual assent to a proposition, but vital, personal self-committal to a practical belief. He heartily approved of our good works; what he denied was their efficacy for salvation. 'Good works,' he said, 'do not make a good man. But a good man does good works.' And what makes a man good? Faith in God, and Christ." (Wil Durant, The Story of Civilization, "The Reformation", p. 374-375). This is consistent with the doctrine that we are saved by grace after all that we can do. (See 2 Nephi 25:23, Acts 15:11, & Ephesians 2:5).

Spencer W. Kimball once observed: "Looking for the spectacular, we often miss the constant flow of revealed communication that comes." Because this is true of society as well as of Saints, the Lord's prophet, who has been commissioned to preach the saving principles of the gospel, frequently has a difficult time finding an audience. In contrast to the messages of Madison Avenue that are pleasing to those with itching ears and carnal desires, his strike more sensitive and selective chords. In this context, we read with poignancy Alma's remark to the poor Zoramites: "O my brethren, if ye could be healed by merely casting about your eyes" rather than by heeding the counsel of the Lord's servants, "would ye not behold quickly, or would ye rather harden your hearts in unbelief, and be slothful, that ye would not cast about your eyes, that ye might perish?" (Alma 33:21).

**June 1, 1829 – Joseph and Oliver move to Fayette, to continue the work of translation.**

**June 1829 (?) - The Melchizedek Priesthood is restored, and Joseph Smith and Oliver Cowdery are ordained under the hands of Peter, James, and John,** although there remains a question about the actual month and year of their ordination (See BYU Studies, 35:4, "Priesthood Restoration Documents" Brian Q. Cannon).

It is impossible to precisely date this heavenly manifestation from existing sources. The only firsthand account from Joseph that provides details about the circumstances of the vision is an 1842 letter (now canonized as Doctrine and Covenants 128) in which he testified he heard "the voice of Peter, James, and John in the wilderness between Harmony, Susquehanna County, and Colesville, Broome County; on the Susquehanna river, declaring themselves as possessing the keys of the kingdom."

In a blessing that Joseph Smith gave to Oliver Cowdery, recorded in October 1835, he spoke of Oliver's receiving "the holy priesthood under the hands of they who had been held in reserve for a long season, even those who received it under the hand of the Messiah." ("Blessing to Oliver Cowdery, 10/2/1835," in Patriarchal Blessing Book 1, 12, josephsmithpapers.org).

**How long did it take to translate the Book of Mormon?** The work of translation proceeded haltingly through 1828. Joseph's wife, Emma, and others served as scribes until the spring of 1829, when Oliver Cowdery took over, recording the bulk of the 275,000-word text from Joseph's dictation, concluding near the end of June 1829, during a period of about 60 to 90 days.

**What was the language of the ancient plates?** According to Moroni, the record was written in "reformed Egyptian." He further explained that if the "plates had been sufficiently large we should have written in Hebrew; but the Hebrew hath been altered by us also; and if we could have written in Hebrew, behold, ye would have had no imperfection in our record. But the Lord knoweth the things which we have written, and also that none other people knoweth our language ... therefore he hath prepared means for the interpretation thereof" (Mormon 9:32–34).

**June 1829 - The sacred records are shown to the Three Witnesses,** (Oliver Cowdery, David Whitmer, and Martin Harris) who declare that an angel of God appeared to them and showed them The Book of Mormon plates and that they heard the voice of the Lord declare that Joseph Smith's translation had been accomplished "by the gift and power of God." This takes place in June 1829, near the home of Peter Whitmer Sr. in Fayette, New York.

**June 28, 1829 - The sacred records are shown to the Eight Witnesses.** Subsequently, on June 28, 1829, near the Whitmer farm, the Three Witnesses have their own experience. Thereafter, the Smith and Whitmer families travel to the Joseph Smith, Sr. home in Palmyra, New York. On July 2, 1829, near the Smith home, the Eight Witnesses say that they had seen and handled the plates.

**March 26, 1830 - The Book of Mormon is published under the direction of printer Egbert B. Grandin, and goes on sale in Palmyra, New York.** The printing cost was $.60 per copy, but many were given away. Joseph was 24 years of age. The typesetting, printing, and calf-leather binding of 5,000 copies, consisting of nearly 3 million total pages, had begun in August 1829, at a cost of $3,000, paid for through the sale of

"I wrote, with my own pen, the entire Book of Mormon (save a few pages) as it fell from the lips of the Prophet Joseph Smith, as he translated it by the gift and power of God, by the means of the Urim and Thummim, or, as it is called by that book, 'holy Interpreters.' I beheld with my eyes and handled with my hands the gold plates from which it was translated. I also saw with my eyes and handled with my hands the 'holy interpreters.' That book is true ... It contains ... the everlasting gospel and came in fulfillment of the revelations of John where he says he saw an angel come with the everlasting gospel to preach to every nation, kindred, tongue, and people" ("Testimony of Oliver Cowdery," "Millennial Star", 8/20 1859, p. 544).

"There is one thing that we should have exceedingly clear in our minds," said Joseph Fielding Smith, Jr. "Neither the President of the church, nor the First Presidency, nor the united voice of the First Presidency and the Council of the Twelve will ever lead the Saints astray or send forth counsel to the world that is contrary to the mind and will of the Lord. An individual may fall by the wayside, or have views, or give counsel which falls short of what the Lord intends. But the voice of the First Presidency and the united voice of those others who hold with them the keys of the kingdom shall always guide the Saints and the world in those paths where the Lord wants them to be. I testify that if we shall look to the First Presidency and follow their counsel and direction, no power on earth can stay or change our course as a church, and as individuals we shall gain peace in this life and be inheritors of eternal glory in the world to come."
(C.R., 4/1972).

part of Martin Harris's farm. It is estimated that around 700 copies of that first edition have survived to the present day. Their value has increased significantly.

**April 6, 1830 – The Church of Jesus Christ of Latter-day Saints is formally organized, in Fayette, New York.** Initially, and in accordance with the laws of New York State, there are 6 members. Although about thirty people are present, only those six – Joseph Smith, Jr., Oliver Cowdery, Hyrum Smith, Peter Whitmer, Jr., Samuel H. Smith, and David Whitmer - become the first legal members of the church.

**April 6, 1830 - The first elders of the church are ordained.** Joseph and Oliver ordain each other. During the first few years after the church is organized, Joseph Smith and other early members of the church do not use the terms 'Aaronic Priesthood' or 'Melchizedek Priesthood' to describe the authority they had received. Their understanding of priesthood only develops over time and with the aid of continuing revelation.

**April 6, 1830 - The Sacrament is first administered for the first time in the church,** on the day it is organized, on Tuesday, April 6, 1830, when the thirty men and women referenced above gather "to partake of bread and wine in the remembrance of the Lord Jesus" (D&C 20:75).

**April 3, 1836 – Priesthood keys are restored in the Kirtland Temple,** with the keys of authority being given to Joseph Smith and Oliver Cowdery. First comes Moses to restore the keys of the gathering of Israel. Then comes an Elias from Abraham's day to restore the sealing power of the priesthood. Then comes Elijah, with the keys by which all gospel ordinances are sealed. When the sealing power of the priesthood is restored, it is on the second day of the Passover Feast, when many Jews throughout the world symbolically open their doors to invite the prophet in to their homes and their lives.

**Testimony of Emma Smith, Wife of the Prophet Joseph Smith.** "Joseph Smith could neither write nor dictate a coherent and well-worded letter; let alone dictate a book like The Book of Mormon. And, though I was an active participant in the scenes that transpired, and was present during the translation of the plates, and had cognizance of things as they transpired, it is marvelous to me, 'a marvel and a wonder,' as much so as to any one else" ("Last Testimony of Sister Emma," "Saints' Herald", 10/1/1879, p. 290).

**June 27, 1844 – After leading the church for just over 14 years, Joseph Smith is martyred at Carthage Jail, Illinois.** He was 38 years old.

Book of
Mormon study
helps us to break
away from limiting
beliefs. As we brush up
against the stars, we are
awakened to a new vision
that is, at first, blinding; but
as our eyes adjust to the light,
we might be surprised to see,
not just the world as it
really is, but the
eternities, as
well.

With The Book of Mormon,
our Heavenly Father has provided
a way for us to return to the secret garden
of our childhood, where we might fully mature.
As Wordsworth wrote: "Heaven lies about us in our
infancy. Shades of the prison house begin to close
upon the growing boy, but he beholds the light and
whence it flows. He sees it in his joy. The youth, who
daily farther from the (garden) must travel, still
is nature's priest, and by the vision splendid,
is on his way attended. At length, the man
perceives it die away and fade into the
light of common day.

# Commentary and Compendium Index

## Commentary Volume One
### Born in The Wilderness

- 1 Nephi
- 2 Nephi
- Jacob
- Enos
- Jarom
- Omni
- Words of Mormon
- Observations
- Author's Note
- Addendum – A Sampling of Scriptures

## Commentary Volume Two
### Voices From The Dust

- Mosiah
- Alma
- Observations
- Author's Note
- Addendum – A Sampling of Scriptures

## Commentary Volume Three
### Journey to Cumorah

- Helaman
- 3 Nephi
- 4 Nephi
- Mormon
- Ether
- Moroni
- Observations
- Author's Note
- Addendum – A Sampling of Scriptures

## Compendium
### Volume One

- Introduction
- Questions Answered by The Book of Mormon
- Topical Index
- Observations
- A few of my favorite things
- Familiar Scriptures
- Commentary & Compendium Index

## Compendium
### Volume Two

- Introduction
- Questions Answered by The Book of Mormon
- Topical Index
- Without The Book of Mormon
- Observations
- Introduction to the Isaiah Chapters
- "And it came to pass in The Book of Mormon
- "Ad thus we see" in The Book of Mormon
- "Behold" in The Book of Mormon
- "Wherefore" and "Therefore in The Book of Mormon
- The Appearance of Gold
- The Use of The Name of Christ
- Pragmatism in The Book of Mormon
- Dry Humor in The Book of Mormon
- A Book of Mormon Timeline\
- Commentary and Compendium Index

## Compendium
### Volume Three

- Essays That Relate to Teachings in The Book of Mormon
- Observations
- Commentary & Compendium Index

## Compendium
### Volume Four

- Essays That Relate to Teachings in The Book of Mormon
- Observations

## Compendium
### Volume Five

- Commentary & Compendium Index
- Essays That Relate to Teachings in The Book of Mormon
- Observations
- Commentary & Compendium Index

## Compendium
### Volume Six

- Essays That Relate to Teachings in The Book of Mormon
- Observations
- Commentary & Compendium Index

## Compendium
### Volume Seven

- Essays That Relate to Teachings in The Book of Mormon
- Observations
- Commentary & Compendium Index

## Compendium
### Volume Eight

- Introduction
- Hebrew Poetry in The Book of Mormon
- Synonymous Parallelism
- Antithetical Parallelism
- Synthetic Parallelism
- Climactic Parallelism
- Chiasmus
- Book of Mormon Scriptures Illustrating Hebrew Poetry
- Cognates in The Book of Mormon
- Observations
- Commentary & Compendium Index

# A Book of Mormon Commentary
## Volumes One - Three

# Compendia
## Volumes One - Eight

# Observations
## Volumes One - Four

www.ingramcontent.com/pod-product-compliance
Lightning Source LLC
Chambersburg PA
CBHW061400010526
44107CB00012B/1005